As the Walls of Academia are Tumbling Down

As the Walls
of Academia
are Tumbling Down

Edited by

Werner Z. Hirsch
and
Luc E. Weber

ᘓ ECONOMICA

London • Paris • Genève

*To Chang-Lin Tien
—Respected scholar, scientist and teacher,
distinguished university chancellor,
creative academic leader,
lifelong role model of the highest ideals in education—*

*his colleagues dedicate this book
with appreciation and admiration.*

CONTENTS

PREFACE

The Glion Colloquium, founded in 1997, assembles a group of higher education leaders from the United States and Western Europe, some still in office and some recently retired, whose shared endeavors in the Colloquium are without personal consideration of any kind. The objective is to define, advance, and disseminate knowledge about major issues facing research universities in the United States and in Western Europe. The Glion Colloquium is unique in its composition and in its exceptional depth of experience and broad knowledge of these issues.

At its first meeting in 1998, members of the Glion Colloquium identified some major challenges facing universities in the age of the information technology and communication revolution. One of these challenges is to set up new intellectual alliances within the university and new partnerships outside it. The third Colloquium, which took place from May 30 to June 3, 2001 in Glion, Switzerland, had as its topic *As the Walls of Academia Are Tumbling Down*.

The Colloquium observed that increasing external permeability of the university is both complemented by and made more complex by increasing internal permeability. More research and teaching cross the boundaries of conventional disciplines, while creating and imparting knowledge at their intersection. Contributions examined the various ways in which universities, especially research universities, cooperate with industry and the commercial sector generally, including but not limited to sponsored research, intellectual property, and new technologies as they affect traditional and new types of learners.

The papers in this volume are an output of the Colloquium. They have been supplemented by commissioned papers, prepared by Peter Lorange, Frank H. T. Rhodes, J. William Schopf and Werner Z. Hirsch, Ulrich W. Suter and Matthias Erzinger, Leslie Wagner, Harold M. Williams and Mary L. Walshok.

The book has four parts. An *Overview—Universities and the Global Village*—is followed by Part I, comprising five papers that examine *The New 21st Century Environment and its Implications for Universities*. In Part II, two papers address the *Lowering of Walls Inside the University*. In Part III, five papers investigate *The Lowering of External Walls of Universities*. Finally, Part IV explores *The Future of University Partnerships*.

We thank, in the USA, the William and Flora Hewlett Foundation and, in Europe, the Swiss Federal Agency for Education and Science in Bern, The Avina Foundation in Basel, The Foundation San Paolo Di Torino in Italy, The Leenaards Foundation in Lausanne and the research universities in the French-speaking part of Switzerland for their generous financial support.

Finally, we are particularly pleased to thank warmly Mrs. Mary O'Mahony, former Deputy Secretary General of the late Association of European Universities, who provided advice and editorial assistance.

Werner Z. Hirsch   *Luc E. Weber*
University of California, Los Angeles   *University of Geneva*

CONTRIBUTORS

James J. Duderstadt is President Emeritus and university Professor of Science and Engineering at the University of Michigan. His teaching and research interests span a number of areas in science, engineering, and public policy, including nuclear energy, information technology, higher education, and science policy. He has held a number of senior posts in higher education (dean, provost, and president of the University of Michigan), government (chair of the National Science Board and the Nuclear Energy Research Advisory Committee), and the National Academies (executive board, policy committees). He currently chairs several national advisory committees in areas such as nuclear energy, the federal R&D budget, and the impact of information technology on society.

Matthias Erzinger works since 1999 as communications manager with the office of the vice-president for research and business relations and ETH transfer at the Swiss Federal Institute of Technology (ETHZ). He studied chemistry and scientific photography at ETHZ. From 1980 to 1987, he worked for the late Swissair as Scientific and Aerial Photographer. From 1987 to 1997, he worked as a journalist, graphic designer, editor, publisher and marketing coordinator for different newspapers. In 1997 and 1998, he worked as a freelance communications consultant.

Sharon E. R. Franks earned her Ph.D. in oceanography from Oregon State University in 1992. Her scientific publications concern the biogeochemical fate of particles emanating from sea-floor hydrothermal vents. During the past eight years, she has focused on outreach and education, writing about the earth, ocean and atmospheric sciences for non-scientific audiences.

Werner Z. Hirsch is Professor of Economics at the University of California, Los Angeles, after having been at UC Berkeley, Washington University, Harvard University and Cambridge University. He has been the founding director of two public policy institutes, served on numerous boards, committees and councils and in an advisory capacity to Federal, State, and local governments in the United States, including the Executive Offices of the President of the United States, and international agencies and the RAND Corporation. He has chaired academic senate committees of the University of California System and of UCLA. He received his BS in 1947 and Ph.D. in 1949 from UC Berkeley, is a member of Phi Beta Kappa and Sigma Xi and was awarded citations by the Senate of the State of California and City of Los Angeles, and named by Japan's Zaisei-Gaku o Kaizuito Hitobito "Scholar Who Helped Build the Field of Public Finance". He is also the co-founder of the Glion Colloquium.

Charles F. Kennel has been director of the Scripps Institution of Oceanography since 1998. Prior to that, he served as executive vice-chancellor of UCLA, as associate administrator at NASA (1994-1996), and as professor of physics at UCLA (1967-1993). Prof. Kennel received his A.B. from Harvard University in 1959 and his Ph.D. from Princeton University in 1964. He is a member of the National Academy of Sciences, the International Academy of Astronautics, the American Academy of Arts and Sciences and has been awarded the NASA Distinguished Service Medal, the Aurelio Peccei Prize, the James Clerk Maxwell Prize and the Hannes Alfven Prize.

Peter Lorange has been the President of IMD since 1993. He is Professor of Strategy and holds the Nestlé Chair. He was formerly President of the Norwegian School of Management in Oslo. His areas of special interest are global strategic management, strategic planning and entrepreneurship for growth. In management education, Dr. Lorange was affiliated with the Wharton School, University of Pennsylvania, for more than a decade, in various assignments, including director of the Joseph H. Lauder Institute of Management and International Studies, and The William H. Wurster Center for International Management Studies, as well as being The William H. Wurster Professor of Multinational Management. He has also taught at the Sloan School of Management (M.I.T.). He serves on the board of directors of several corporations.

Jakob Nüesch is former president of the Federal Institute of Technology in Zurich (1990-1997) and a current member of the International Committee of the Red Cross (ICRC). He was formerly the head of pharma research at Ciba Geigy in Basel, Switzerland, and an associate professor at the University of Basel, where he taught microbiology. He has done extensive research in applied microbiology and biotechnology, and has some 120 publications in these fields and in microbial biochemistry, molecular biology, and genetic engineering. Professor Nüesch has served as president of the Swiss Society of Microbiology and as secretary general of the Federation of European Microbiological Societies (FEMS). He received his Ph. D. in microbiology and phytopathology from the Federal Institute of Technology (ETH) in Zurich in 1961 and became a research scientist at Ciba AG in Basel in 1961. Dr. Nüesch has conducted extended research in biochemistry and molecular biology in Canada, the United States and Germany.

Peter Preuss received his undergraduate degree form the Technical University of Hanover, Germany, in 1964. He was completing his doctorate in mathematics at the University of California, San Diego, when he founded one of the earliest software companies, specializing in the newly emerging field of computer graphics. He ran his company, Integrated Software Systems Corporation (ISSCO), for 17 years. It ultimately had over 500 employees, with 32 offices worldwide, and was traded on the NASDAQ. In 1985, Mr. Preuss founded the Preuss Foundation for Brain Tumor Research, specializing in facilitating communication among researchers. Since 1985, he has organized and run 28 highly specialized conferences for researchers in this field. Mr. Preuss was co-founder of the National Computer Graphics Association. He served a term on the Advisory Committee to the director of the National Institutes of Health and is a director of numerous for-profit and not-for-profit organizations. He is also a member of the California Council for Science and Technology and is currently serving a 12-year term on the Board of Regents of the University of California.

Frank H. T. Rhodes was president of Cornell University for eighteen years before retiring in 1995, having previously served as vice president for academic affairs at the University of Michigan. A geologist by training, Rhodes was a member of President Bush's Education Policy Advisory Committee. He has also served as chairman of the National Science Board and chairman of the boards of the American Council on Education, the American Association of Universities, and the Carnegie Foundation for the Advancement of Teaching. He was chairman of the American Council on Education's task force on minority education, which produced the report "One-Third of a Nation", for which former presidents Jimmy Carter and Gerald Ford served as honorary co-chairs. He is currently president of the American Philosophical Society.

Henry Rosovsky is the Lewis P. and Linda L. Geyser University Professor Emeritus at Harvard University. His fields of interest and publications concern economic history, Japanese economic growth, and higher education. Prof. Rosovsky served as Dean of the Faculty of Arts and Sciences at Harvard from 1973 to 1984 and from 1990 to 1991. From 1985 to 1997 he also served as a member of the Harvard Corporation, the executive Governing Board of the University. Most recently, he co-chaired the Task Force on Higher Education and Society sponsored by UNESCO and the World Bank that produced *Higher Education in Developing Countries: Peril and Promise* (2000).

J. William Schopf. Director of UCLA's Center for the Study of Evolution and the Origin of Life and a member of the Department of Earth and Space Sciences, J. William Schopf received his undergraduate training in geology at Oberlin College, Ohio, and in 1968 his Ph.D. degree, in biology, from Harvard University. A former Dean of UCLA's Division of Honors, College of Letters and Sciences, he has been honoured as a Distinguished Teacher, a faculty-elected Research Lecturer, and as recipient of the university-wide Gold Shield Prize for Academic Excellence. Author of *Cradle of Life*, awarded Phi Beta Kappa's 2000 national science book prize, and editor of two prize-winning monographs on the origin and early evolution of life on Earth, Professor Schopf is a member of the National Academy of Sciences and the American Philosophical Society, and a fellow of the American Academy of Arts and Sciences. He has received medals awarded by the National Academy of Sciences, the National Science Board, and the International Society for the Study of the Origin of Life; twice he has been awarded Guggenheim Fellowships.

Lucy Smith is a professor of law and a former rector of the University of Oslo. She has been leader of the Norwegian University Council and is presently vice-president of the European University Association and board-member of the Danish University of Education. Her research interests and publications include law of contracts, securities law, child law, human rights and higher education. She is chairperson of the board of the Norwegian Institute of Human Rights, chair of the Advisory Council of Dagbladet, a major Norwegian paper, member of the board of the Norwegian National Theatre and of the International Jury of the UNESCO Prize for Peace Education. In addition, she has held positions in Norwegian industry and various humanitarian organisations.

Ulrich W. Suter has been Professor of Macromolecular Chemistry at the Institute of Polymers of the Federal Institute of Technology Zurich (ETHZ) since 1988. In 2001, he was elected vice-president for research and business relations. Ulrich Suter was awarded his doctoral degree in the Department of Chemistry at ETHZ in 1973. He then spent two years as a postdoctoral researcher at Stanford University. From 1976 to 1981, he was a senior assistant in the Department of Chemistry, ETHZ, after which he transferred to the IBM Almaden Research Centre in San Jose, California, where he was visiting scientist for one year. In 1982, Suter took a position as professor in the Department of Chemical Engineering at MIT, until 1990. His research interests lie in the areas of macromolecular chemistry and physical chemistry of polymers, particularly structure-property relationships; polymeric materials, especially the predictability of properties; atomistic and molecular modelling; and the application of computers in education and research. Prof. Suter is co-editor of a number of international scientific journals, active on many scientific panels, and a member of many professional organisations. He was awarded the silver medal of the ETHZ, the Kern prize in 1974, and he has been a fellow of the American Physical Society since 1994.

Leslie Wagner, CBE. Professor Leslie Wagner is the Vice-Chancellor of Leeds Metropolitan University, having previously been the Vice-Chancellor and Chief Executive of the University of North London from 1987-1993. He currently chairs the University Vocational Awards Council in addition to the Widening Participation and Lifelong Learning Group of Universities UK and also the Advisory Group of Leeds Common Purpose. He is a member of the Council for Industry and Higher Education and is also a Director of Leeds Business Services Ltd. He has written or edited four books on economics and the planning of education and is a regular contributor on higher education in the media. He was awarded the CBE in June 2000 for services to higher education and the Jewish community.

Mary L. Walshok is Associate Vice Chancellor for Public Programs and Dean, University Extension at the University of California, San Diego, where she is responsible for a large and diverse portfolio of academic programs supporting regional economic development, civic engagement, executive and continuing education. A professor of Sociology at UC San Diego and a Visiting Professor at The Stockholm School of Economics, she has published extensively on the world of work, the challenges of the new economy and in her 1995 book *"Knowledge without Boundaries"* on the changing role of research universities in society. Over the years, Mary L. Walshok has been a member of a variety of regional and national boards and commissions. She is currently Board Chair of the San Diego Community Foundation and Vice-Chair of the California Council for the Humanities.

Luc E. Weber. Educated in the fields of economics and political science, Luc Weber is professor of Public Economics at the University of Geneva since

1975. As an economist, he serves as an adviser to the federal as well as to cantonal governments and he has been a member of the "Swiss Council of Economic Advisers" for three years. Since 1982, Prof. Weber is strongly involved in university management and Higher Education policy in the capacity of vice-rector, then of rector of the University of Geneva, as well as Chairman and, later on, Consul for international affairs of the Swiss Rectors' Conference. Presently, he is vice-president of the International Association of Universities and a member of the board of the European University Association, as well as of the Steering Committee for Higher Education and Research of the Council of Europe. He is also the co-founder of the Glion Colloquium.

Harold M. Williams is President Emeritus of the J. Paul Getty Trust, having served as President and Chief Executive Officer from 1981 to 1998. Trained as a lawyer, his career included fifteen years in industry, culminating as chairman of the board of a New York Stock Exchange listed company, seven years as Dean of the Graduate School of Management, UCLA and four years as Chair of the United Sates Securities and Exchange Commission. He served twelve years as a Regent, University of California. He is Co-Chair of the California Citizens Commission on Higher Education, member of the National Centre for Public Policy and Higher Education, was a member of President Clinton's Committee on the Arts and Humanities, and was a member of the Association of Governing Board's Committee on the Academic Presidency.

CHAPTER 1

Universities and the Global Village: An Introductory Overview

Werner Z. Hirsch

> *Progress in Science [and Education]*
> *thrives on cross-pollination across borders*
>
> Joseph E. Persico

INTRODUCTION

The first universities were founded in the 12th century in Paris and Bologna. They had different origins—the University of Paris having been founded by scholars, the University of Bologna by students. Yet they shared certain common features, which survived for a long time (Powicke & Emden, 1958). Both were challenged by the church, and faculty and members in both had a cloistered existence and often were intellectually isolated. Disciplinary walls were erected which, in combination with the tenure system, led in many cases to serious intellectual isolation and structural rigidity. Change came only slowly. It was brought about by the founding of new, more adventurous universities and the competition that they introduced into higher education.

Today's universities, especially research universities in the Western world, are operating in an altogether different environment. The far-reaching information and communication revolution has been shrinking distances of time and space. As this revolution is erasing venerable physical and intellectual boundaries, the process of globalization has begun and is leading to the emergence of a global village, which deeply affects many aspects of life. Ancient walls and barriers are being lowered, allowing world-wide utilization of comparative advantages in the production of goods and services as well as cross-fertilization of knowledge and ideas. Collaboration by individuals and by universities, firms, and governments has the potential of raising general well-being to new heights. Wide-spread collaboration in a virtually borderless world can stoke the engines of growth of new knowledge and understanding. Thus, it is likely that our time will be noted by historians for the emergence of a global village of trade, capital movement, and knowledge.

Not unlike the forces that generate positive results from trade globalization and free flow of capital are those that follow from the lowering of universities' internal and external walls. As a consequence, scholars and scientists of one discipline can readily cross-fertilize colleagues in others. They can do so not only within their own university and their own country, but also with respect to the outside world, including high-tech industry and cultural institutions as well as other universities. There exists, however, a fundamental difference between lowering barriers of trade and those of educational and scientific undertakings. Whereas globalization of world trade is an engine of progress and growth driven by all participants, that of globalization of education and science is driven mainly by universities. Their teaching and research, a celebration of the human spirit, are the instigators and incubators of society's progress. As both of these university functions are carried out, and the existing internal and external walls of academia are pierced and lowered, a global knowledge village emerges. Collaboration among scholars and scientists within the university and between it and the outside world plays a defining role.

Universities will have to perfect new mechanisms, at times even to adjust their structures, to become effective participants and even more pivotal key players. Particularly they must provide incentives to facilitate and nourish creative collaboration in teaching and provide opportunities for cross-fertilization. At the same time, they must transmit to students the value of these changes. Further, they must create an understanding among their students of the merits and efficacy of an interdisciplinary education. Clearly, this revamping of teaching and research toward greater interdisciplinary efforts should show respect, where appropriate, for teaching and research that concentrate on a single discipline. Much thought must be given to finding a flexible balance between the two thrusts.

While these technology-driven forces work on the supply side in stimulating the emergence of a global village, similar forces are at work on the demand side. For example, in the case of research universities, problems increasingly transcend the competence of single disciplines or departments. Therefore, researchers and students must become competent to engage in interdisciplinary undertakings if they are to meet societal and scientific challenges.

In the search for promising ways to find its place in the global village and raise the levels of collaboration and bordercrossing, the solemn mission of the university must continue to serve as a guiding light. New arrangements must assure that faculty remain, to paraphrase John Maynard Keynes, the trustees of the possibility of civilization. The quality of education and that of unbiased research must remain as high as ever. Moreover, as external walls are lowered and more collaboration with industry takes place, the university must be vigilant to safeguard its academic integrity and resist unseemly compromises.

AS WALLS ARE CRUMBLING

Movement toward a global village of knowledge coincides with and is driven by the lowering of four venerable walls or barriers. These are barriers within the university, between universities, between universities and industry, and a combination of barriers that can impede outreach programs.

Barriers within the University

For a long time universities have been predominantly concerned with imparting and advancing a liberal education—that body of knowledge and culture most worthy of knowing. At one time it was referred to as universal knowledge. Toward this end, they carved the large territory into discrete parts, which have evolved into independent fields and disciplines most often housed in separate departments. But as Clark Kerr, president emeritus of the University of California, has suggested, universities "could, however, provide some 'broad learning experience' that would help students think in terms of more than one discipline in approaching broad issues. Students' academic majors orient them toward vertical thinking, but throughout their lives as citizens and also at higher levels in their careers they need to think horizontally". Kerr offers as thematic examples the environment, Asian civilization, and the origins and impact of the city on human development (Kerr, 2001).

In short, as challenges facing society become increasingly complex, multidimensional, and multi-faceted, education must stimulate horizontal, thematic thinking and exploration. Emphasis on interdisciplinary curricula and research is thus in order.

Make no mistake, there was a rationale in carving up the huge knowledge territory. Using departmental subdivisions as building blocks has enabled universities to construct rather effective governance structures. Faculty with specialized interests join departments, which in turn are combined into schools or colleges. Department chairs report to the college's dean, who in turn reports to a vice rector or vice president concerned with academic affairs.

The lines setting apart departments are drawn on the basis of a common methodology, which has facilitated the formulation of a coherent core curriculum. At times though, it has led to overspecialization. More significantly, this structure tends to interfere with inquiries at boundaries of disciplines, just the area where important learning and world class research increasingly takes place. Crossing disciplinary boundaries and engaging in interdisciplinary undertakings, both in the classroom and in the laboratory, will enable universities to better meet tomorrow's challenges. Productive collaboration and interaction will enrich both teaching and research. It also will meet the expectations of the body politic, whose appreciation of academia is essential for the allocation of the necessary financial resources.

How can universities function in a world where their internal walls are becoming increasingly permeable and in some instances are being dismantled altogether? What changes in structure are needed to promote freer wandering over disciplinary divides in education and research?

Many universities are already facilitating academic border crossing in undergraduate education. Some offer thematic courses, team-taught by members of two or more departments. Others go further. For example, the University of California at Los Angeles has revamped its undergraduate program and has introduced a thematic cluster system of general education for the first two undergraduate years.

On the graduate level in Europe and the United States more interdisciplinary courses and programs are being offered. Examples are Law and Economics (at the University of Oslo and Oxford University), Neuro-chemistry, and Economic and Environment Sciences (at the University of California at Santa Barbara).

In regard to faculty, research team undertakings of multi-disciplinary faculty joined by graduate and post-doctoral students are becoming common. Such teams can tackle research problems at the border of a number of disciplines and at the same time train the next generation of scientists. In some areas teamwork is nothing new. For example, "clinical research is most often carried out by multi-disciplinary teams of investigators led by physician-scientists who can bridge the gap between basic research and the health of patient or the public" (Ceck et al., 2001). In some instances, these arrangements take a more formal shape, i.e., institutes and centers. Their faculty, drawn from a number of disciplines, explore subjects of mutual interest, at times with a thematic focus. The latter can be stimulated by offering financial support, which can be particularly helpful to faculty in the humanities and arts, who often have difficulty in finding funding. While the initial support tends to come from the university itself, success is often followed by outside funding. A particularly interesting experiment is the University of California BioSTAR Project. It is an industry-university matching grant program to support new bio-technical research on nine campuses and at three National Laboratories, and since 1996 it has awarded $23 million.

Inter-university Barriers

In the past, institutional barriers have impeded the mobility of students between universities. Other barriers, though less pervasive, have impeded faculty mobility, thereby reducing faculty's ability to collaborate with their counterparts in other universities and research institutes. There is much to be gained when students are exposed to different environments, experiences and faculty. By mingling with students in other institutions all gain intellectual stimulus and, at times, cross-cultural experience, so important in the global village. They also are likely to receive a better education if their university is relatively small and thus unable to afford a faculty of sufficient size and diversity. By joining forces with other universities these shortcomings can be remedied.

In regard to inter-university educational cooperation on the undergraduate level, Western European universities have taken many more initiatives than have American. Thus, one observes both regional cooperation and cooperation among European Union members. For example, since all four Scandinavian countries are relatively small, they have initiated regional collaboration—eleven universities in Sweden and Denmark have established Øresund University, a network of autonomous universities in Sweden and Denmark, including the Universities of Lund and Copenhagen (Smith, 2001). Joint programs as well as shared classes, libraries, and technical resources have been arranged. Students either commute or stay for a time. With the purpose of being exposed to the richness of cultural diversity in Europe, the European Union sponsors the Erasmus Inter-university Cooperation Projects and the Tempus Joint European Projects. Moreover, extensive institutional networks have been sponsored by universities, e.g., the Coimbra Group, UNICA, CAESAR and NATURA (Van Ginkel, 1999).

In the United States, a few cooperative efforts exist. One is the Claremont Colleges in Southern California, where a number of liberal arts colleges and one graduate school have joined forces. Many colleges and universities have a "Study Abroad" program, where some of their undergraduates spend a year at a foreign university. Drake University seeks to eliminate foreign language programs, which have been declining in enrollment and replace them with languages learned in their "Study Abroad" program (Smith, 2001). Some American medical schools place their students as interns in a number of affiliated hospitals.

The situation is much better in regard to research, where faculty mobility is significant. Collaborative arrangements, many informal, exist between faculty members of many universities and formal ones exist between some universities. Such collaboration has become necessary in the physical and natural sciences as well as in medical research, where very costly instrumentation is essential to carry out research. This precedent has spilled over to many other fields. An American example is the UCLA-UCSB California Nano-System Institute, a collaborative research effort by members of a number of departments on two campuses of the University of California (Robak, 2001). A Western European example is the Ferrara Health Industry Policy Forum in which faculty from a number of departments of the University of Ferrara, University of Bologna, and the University of California collaborate.

Barriers Between University and Industry

The place of universities in the global village and their contribution to it is being supported by their close collaboration and formation of alliances with the high-tech industry. This development has taken place as a result of universities' expanded research efforts and, more recently, their increasing reliance on private funds to support research (Kerr, 2001). At the same time, high-tech firms have begun to outsource cutting edge research to universities, thereby benefiting from contributions of top-ranked university scientists and engineers, whose services would otherwise not be available to them. This collaboration enables universities to better fulfill their societal responsibilities.

Collaboration is beneficial to both the university and the high-tech firm. The university gains from faculty joining in research with scientists in industry who are used to work on real world problems, who often have vast experience, and who have developed a unique culture and way of thinking. Industry often brings to the table expensive world-class equipment and instrumentation as well as financial resources. Such alliances also facilitate the placing of the university's graduates.

But industry also benefits from collaboration with research universities. The latter tend to have on their faculty world-class scientists who have made important discoveries and inventions, who own many valuable patents and have the distinction of having developed a creativity-stimulating environment. These assets are especially valuable to high-tech pharmaceutical, semiconductor and computer software firms. They have in common extremely high development and start-up costs, inordinately low production costs, and yet rapid obsolescence.

For example, bringing a new drug to market can cost between half and three quarters of a billion dollars. The high cost is related to the fact that for every 5,000 compounds evaluated for treatment, only five will make it to clinical trials, of which just one will make it to market. Usually this takes many years. The same holds for semiconductors and software, whose useful life is about a year and a half.

The greatest rewards in many knowledge-based enterprises go to those who innovate at a rapid pace and obtain the largest possible market share for their new product. Consequently, such firms are consumed with a defining drive to innovate and achieve monopoly power, however temporary it turns out to be. Toward this end, firms seek to collaborate with research universities and locate in their vicinity. Universities are thus increasingly surrounded by geographic clusters of symbiotic enterprises which benefit from synergies and positive externalities on the demand side and from cost savings on the supply side.

Benefits can accrue not only to participating universities and firms but can spill over into their region as well as to the nation, if not the entire world. To stimulate growth and wealth creation, for example, the United Kingdom has created the Higher Education Innovation Fund. It funds universities to work closely with firms in the private sector and transfer new knowledge to industry. However, removing barriers between research universities and high-tech industry, according to Donald Kennedy, president emeritus of Stanford University, leads to "some major benefits along with significant cost" (Kennedy, 2001). Among the costs are faculty's potential conflicts of interest as well as commitment. Both can significantly weaken the university's ability to carry out its core mission and endanger its integrity. The issue is so serious that recently the Association of American Universities formally called on its members to require of their researchers financial disclosures (Kaiser *et al.*, 2001). Moreover, the New England Journal of Medicine has been forced to relax its recently instituted conflict of interest review rules, since it cannot find enough qualified manuscript reviewers with no ties to drug companies. A further threat is curriculum imbalances between academic units that do and those that do not benefit from funding of collaborative research with industry.

Barriers to Outreach Programs

In the global village, everybody's knowledge, work, cultural experience and well-being are affected by everybody else's. Efforts to update knowledge culturally enrich citizens and assist communities in effectively fulfilling their responsibilities. Universities are increasingly seeking to meet these great challenges by offering continuing education and to work with communities and industry.

As the half-life of basic knowledge in more and more spheres is becoming shorter and shorter—today it is at most five years—yet the need to be up-to-date becomes ever greater, so lifelong learning opportunities must play an increasing role (Walshok, 2002). This need is reinforced by the fact that life expectancy is increasing and with it the population that seeks to be intellectually and culturally engaged during extended retirement.

In today's dynamic world, achieving a financially secure and intellectually and socially fulfilling life is becoming increasingly demanding. Challenges are becoming increasingly complex, multifaceted and multidimensional, particularly as breathtaking change makes today's knowledge and way of thinking obsolete tomorrow. Under these circumstances, interaction with the premier producer and interpreter of new knowledge and culture—academics—becomes a basic need of society. Thus, universities that once used to educate the young must tool up and address themselves to the educational needs of a mature and older clientele.

Some universities are experimenting with even more ambitious programs, which reach to the outside world to assist members of the local community to gain leadership and management skills needed in the private, public and not-for-profit sectors. A few have even developed programs to assist local residents in founding start-up high-tech companies and in aiding existing firms.

This need for local orientation can clash with the major goal and *raison d'être*, particularly of research universities. Their research and scholarship have a global orientation. It is the general community of colleagues with whom they interact and compete for distinction. This clash between local and global orientation can make it difficult to attract into the outreach programs the very best faculty. As a consequence, the esteem in which lifelong learning programs are held can be affected. This would be unfortunate, since successful efforts in this area require interests and skills that often are quite as scarce as are highly qualified scientists and scholars.

CONCLUSIONS

The world energized by the information and communication revolution is piercing venerable partitions and barriers. As a consequence, global villages are emerging. One is that of higher education and its institutions. Universities, though often loath to change, are beginning to realize that they increasingly operate in such a global village. They are extending themselves to meet the resulting challenges, by reorganizing themselves both internally and externally. While collaboration can work to their advantage, they can also incur costs associated with lowering their external walls and collaborating with industry. The latter has altogether different objectives, ethos and ways to carry out its function from the research university.

While universities face a number of risks as they collaborate with industry—e.g., intradepartmental imbalances, limiting faculty rights and compromising the university's financial stability and integrity—two further ones can be much more damaging—faculty conflicts of interest and commitment and interdepartmental imbalances.

Conflicts are best avoided by the university working with faculty to develop protocols and model master contracts. They can signal to firms seeking university research collaboration what the university's minimum conditions for collaborating are.

Major interdepartmental imbalances, which can result when industry finances research in the university, can skew priorities among academic units, usually to the disadvantage of the humanities and arts. It can be remedied by the administration taxing units with major research contracts to fund units that by their very nature cannot attract much outside funding. Moreover, the latter units might be encouraged to collaborate in interdisciplinary undertakings with financially favored units.

Taking such and similar steps to protect the integrity and excellence of the university in the global village of knowledge can assure net benefits from collaboration both within the university and with the outside world.

REFERENCES

Ceck, T. R. *et al.* (2001). "The Biomedical Bottleneck", *Sciences*, July 27, p. 573.

Hastings, R. (1958). *The University of Europe in the Middle Ages*, in Powicke, F.M. & London Emden, A.E., new ed., Oxford University Press, London.

Kaiser J. *et al.* (2001). "Science Scope", *Science*, October, p. 285.

Kennedy, D. (2001). "Enclosing the Research Commons", *Science*, December, p. 2249.

Kerr, C. (2001). *The Gold and the Blue*, University California Press, Berkeley, pp. 291, 403-404.

Robak, W. (2001). *UCLA-UCSB California Nano System Institute*, University of California, Los Angeles, December, pp. 1-2.

Smith, L. (this book). "Opening Up Departments", *As the Walls of Academia are Tumbling Down*, Economica, London.

Tien, C-L. (1999). "Future Challenges Facing Higher Education", in Hirsch, W. Z. & Weber, L. E. (eds.), *Challenges Facing Higher Education at the Millennium*, Pergamon, London, p. 162.

Van Ginkel, H. (1999). "Networks and Strategic Alliances within and between Universities and with the Private Sector", in Hirsch, W. Z. & Weber, L. E. (eds.), *Challenges Facing Higher Education at the Millennium*, Pergamon, London, pp. 88-89.

Walshok, M.L. (this book). "Facilitating Lifelong Learning in a Research University context", in Hirsch, W. Z. & Weber L. E. (eds.), *As the Walls of Academia are Tumbling Down*, Economica, London.

PART I

· · · · · · · · · · · · ·

The New 21st Century Environment and its Implications for Universities

CHAPTER 2

No Ivory Tower:
University and Society in the
Twenty-First Century

Henry Rosovsky [1]

"Ivory Tower", especially as applied to universities and academic life more generally is an odd description whose origins are not entirely obvious. The first usage appears to be in the Song of Solomon, an erotic biblical poem, though Jewish tradition sometimes claims that it is intended to describe the love between God and the people of Israel. In the poem we encounter the phrase: "thy neck is like a tower of ivory," (i.e. slender, round, and straight; cool and smooth)—obviously no relation to education.

In its more modern meaning—as in looking down on the vulgarities of every-day life, cool and elegantly detached, pure and austere—the sources usually refer to the year 1837, when the French literary critic Saint Beuve charged the poet Alfred de Vigny with evading the responsibilities of life by withdrawing to a *tour d'ivoire* (Hendrickson, 1987, p. 281). [2] Still no relation to universities, but the meaning is closer to modern usage.

The first application to universities or scholars appears to have taken place surprisingly recently. In a 1940 political tract, H. G. Wells (1940, p. 133)

1 I would like to thank Derek Bok, Richard Chait, and Lawrence Summers for many helpful comments. Matthew Hartley, who provided valuable research assistance, also made many helpful comments. None of these gentlemen are in any way responsible for the contents of this essay.
2 The best source on the general and complicated background of the expression is to be found in Erwin Panofsky's wonderful and erudite commencement address delivered at Harvard University on June 13, 1948. I am grateful to Prof. Bernard Bailyn for calling this source to my attention.

wrote: "We want a Minister of Education who can...electrify and rejuvenate old dons or put them away in ivory towers". No earlier example of the term applied to higher education seems to exist.

At least in modern times, the ivory tower always represented, on the part of our internal and external critics, more imagination than reality, and that must have included H. G. Wells. For example, in the United States it was the Morrill Act of 1862 that became the basis of many public institutions. The Act stressed agriculture and the mechanical arts: very much in the real world. Similarly, the first department of Tokyo University, founded in the 1870's, specialized in agricultural economics. More recently university scientists played major roles during World War II (on all sides), and many postwar "freedom movements" were closely tied to university faculties and students. These are just a few random examples to indicate that inactive "old dons" were not typical university inhabitants.

As defined pejoratively, the ivory tower is a myth, because in modern institutions of higher education there has always existed tension between service to the public and more contemplative scholarship. What the historian Bernard Bailyn (1991) wrote about Harvard a decade ago remains true for many universities in different parts of the world. "Harvard has never been an ivory tower, a closed universe of scholars talking to scholars and students. It has always been, has had to be, open to the world, responsible to its founding and governing community—hence in the service of society—and yet at the same time devoted to the demands of learning for its own sake. That balance between learning and service is the heart of the institution and it has shifted in emphasis from time to time".

EXTERNAL PERMEABILITY

The emphasis has, in the second half of the twentieth century, shifted sharply towards "service", if that term includes activities not confined to internal university tasks. The degree of university permeability to outside influences has increased tremendously since World War II, and at a rapidly and still rising rate. External influences on the university have multiplied and they are penetrating its activities with increasing frequency. Government and business are the major sources of influence. [3]

The following item from the Harvard University Gazette (2000) is a revealing example. The person being interviewed was a young professor who had just been granted tenure in the applied sciences. This is what she said:

---

3 Illustrations will come from the American experience, and many will be taken from Harvard University, but the issues are quite similar in other institutions and other countries.

"When I came here, the obvious goal was to get tenure. If things didn't work out, I thought, I could always get a job where I worked less and got paid more. That wouldn't have been bad. Now that the pressure's off, I've started to ask myself: What's my next goal? I won my black belt in karate a year ago. I've got tenure, a wonderful family, and a thriving business. It's time to figure out what's next".

Is there anything the least bit arresting about this statement? It may depend on one's age, but the seamless combination of a Harvard (or another university's) professorship and ownership of a thriving private business—this natural pairing—could seem odd to the more traditionally-minded. Of course, the current pairing of entrepreneurial and academic tasks is symptomatic of that fact that some of what we do matters more and more to society. Universities house intellectual assets that society needs; they also train the "workers" most needed by the knowledge economy. That favors some individuals and institutions, who control new techniques or ideas.

Recently, the president of the University of California asserted that fifty percent of U.S. growth since World War II has resulted from investments in R&D, the principal driver being federally funded research in universities (Atkinson, 1999-2000). No wonder that government and business have taken an ever more active interest in research universities. These days, institutions are frequently urged to focus on more relevant research, and to let the market rule. Critics urge universities to emphasize efficiency and bottom lines; sometimes mergers have been suggested, and also the ruthless elimination of "redundant units." Government and business care, because what institutions do is expensive and may have major economic consequences.

Just as the outside world has shown greater interest in university affairs, so have universities shown greater interest in the outside world. This can produce attitudes that Richard Chait labels "need and greed". [4] In the United States, both public and private universities operate under continual pressure to raise revenues. Those segments of the institution that are able to generate commercial backing can become "profit centers," much beloved by hard-pressed and/or ambitious administrations. Chait asks: will these so-called profit centers rule the roost? Will all our intellectual assets be for sale, and what is the fate of those activities that cannot produce revenues? That would surely include the basic sciences, the humanities, and access for underprivileged members of society.

Thus far, a combination of government, private philanthropy, and internal university resources have been the guarantors of these areas, but that could change. Even the basic sciences, that have received the most powerful public

---

4 The examples used by Chait are from the text of an unpublished talk: "Higher Education in a Commercial Environment."

backing since World War II, require continual protection. Vannavar Bush, whose ideas framed postwar U.S. science policy, understood "...that, in the short term, people would never grasp the true value of basic science. If basic science and applied science were to mix completely freely, the latter would inevitably drive out the former. The only way basic science could survive—something Bush wanted to ensure—would be to completely insulate it from that competition, leaving basic scientists to pursue their work in peace" (Mukherjee, 2002). The institutions created for that purpose were the National Institutes of Health and the National Science Foundation.

Much of this reasoning applies to the humanities and to access for underprivileged groups. The point is simple: some core university activities will always require subsidies and protection from the market. Investment in promising "profit centers" should not come at the expense of activities that have no appeal for the private sector.

Issues of commercial sponsorship that have received the most publicity—and deservedly so—concern preferential access to research results, as a condition of financial support. Especially prevalent in the biomedical sciences, this may involve various forms of conflict of interest, censorship, secrecy, delayed publication, etc. Although still not very large, industry is proportionately growing as a source of university research funding, while federal funding is—proportionately—declining. There is no reason to believe that these trends will change soon. In 1999, over seven percent of university medical research was financed by industry. It should reach ten percent very soon.

Increased external permeability is not confined to commercially sponsored research. Some other manifestations include use of company names for professorial chairs and sometimes associated obligations to funders, instruction designed for and confined to specific companies, and donor relations in general. Furthermore, the pressures associated with external permeability are not confined to commercial interests. The fact that government funds the overwhelming amount of scientific research affects how investigators select their career paths and research topics. Government financial aid policies also affect all of higher education. Political pressure groups also influence institutional behavior, especially in public universities, although it is not clear that these have increased in intensity since the 1960's. They are cyclical and ever-present.

It is not astonishing that under current conditions students are taking openly consumerist attitudes, surrounded as they are by increasingly "real world" influences. A humorous example was recently reported in *The New York Times* (Ayres, 2001). At Yale Law School, students during class used their laptops to play solitaire or to surf the web. Not surprisingly, the professor was somewhat displeased at these signs of boredom. When confronted, the students "said that the professor has an incentive to teach more effectively when he or she must compete against other more interesting claims on student's attention." You could not ask for a better example of market influence in the classroom.

Recently, increasing outside interest in university activities (and *vice versa*) has been supplemented by predictions of radical transformation in higher education, based largely on the presumed impact of the IT Revolution. Indeed, some observers predict the university's inability to adjust to this new world, and see complete failure in its future: the institution as we know it will have to be replaced by something quite different, perhaps unrecognizable.

James Duderstadt, former president of the University of Michigan, sees a future in which a few "academic celebrities" will become the main "content providers" and sell their "learning products" to students nationally and perhaps internationally, thereby eliminating the need for the majority of institutions to offer introductory subjects (Traub, 2000).

Arthur Levine (2000), president of Columbia Teachers College, forecasts a great diversification among providers of higher education. He sees a division into three categories: the "brick" institutions exemplifying all that is old-fashioned; the "brick and click" combining the old with the new distance learning; and finally the pure "click" enterprises that will confine themselves to virtuality. He also welcomes the possibility of much more individual programming, where students (consumers) set the agenda: in effect, "bespoke" educational programs for everyone. In his opinion, degrees will decline in importance and be at least partially replaced by certification for specific competencies.

The prince of darkness has to be Peter Drucker: "Universities won't survive. Higher education is in deep crisis. Already we are beginning to deliver more lectures off-campus via satellite or two-way video at a fraction of the cost. The college campus won't survive as a residential institution. Today's buildings are hopelessly unsuited and totally unneeded" (Lenzner & Johnson, 1997). Dimensions of educational quality or the likelihood that learning is a social activity have not been a major aspect of these visions.

Niels Bohr is supposed to have said that predictions are very difficult, especially those about the future. That can provide a certain amount of consolation. After all, the president of DEC said in 1977 that there is no reason for any individual to have a computer in their home. DEC is gone; computers are in most homes. Nevertheless, a recurring nightmare is suggested by these visions, at least to those with even slightly traditional orientations. The setting is Harvard University—the country's oldest—twenty-five years from today. [5]

The buildings of the Harvard campus—the venerable Yard—have been largely converted to condos. They have become redundant: faculty and students are scattered all over the world. Widener Library has become a Golden Age center, very much in demand because so many will live for a long time. The books have been burned; everything is on line. The former president's mansion is the largest McDonald's in the eastern United States. All of what once was Harvard University is now housed in one corner of the president's garage: that space is occupied by a big server. Lucrative "profit centers" have replaced non-performing assets.

Harvard e-university has become a branch of Microsoft Universal University. The president of its Harvard subsidiary is an eighteen year old computer "geek" whose education terminated with a certificate from the Nintendo Play Station Institute. All courses are commissioned nationally and internationally: computer sciences are provided by experts in Singapore; instruction in video game theory comes from Japan; and American scholars are responsible for research and teaching in sports medicine and personal injury law. In effect, Harvard has become an interactive cable station...and then the dreamer may wake up in a cold sweat.

To summarize: the ivory tower does not describe the modern research university: learning and service are always present. External influences are becoming more powerful for many different reasons: the power of government, the search by commercial interests for knowledge within the academy, the perpetual need for more resources within the university, and—not least—the opportunity for individual faculty members to make economic gains. Add to that the predictions just mentioned: unavoidable, fundamental, and quite possibly destabilizing restructuring of institutions. Can universities preserve their objectivity as disinterested researchers and social critics if current trends persist? Will our judgment be unduly affected by commercial considerations? Will even the appearance of outside influences—public and private—weaken the university's reputation for probity and with what consequences? Can anything be done?

The poet's voice provides the most elegant, yet cynical and dour summation. In a prophetic Phi Beta Kappa poem (*Under Which Lyre*), W. H. Auden (1946) contrasts the sons of Apollo who represent the establishment, officialdom, and external pressure, with the sons of Hermes, seen as contrarians, free spirits, and therefore perfect faculty members of the old school. Auden writes: "And when he [Apollo] occupies a college,"

---

5 The setting could just as easily be Stanford, Wisconsin, Tokyo or Oxford.

Truth is replaced by Useful Knowledge
He pays particular
Attention to Commercial Thought
Public Relations, Hygiene, Sport
In his curricula.

Athletic, extrovert and crude,
For him to work in solitude
Is the offence,
The goal a populous Nirvana
His shield bears this device: *Mens sana*
Qui mal y pense.

INTERNAL PERMEABILITY

None of the above is intended to imply that the impact of rising outside influences has mainly negative consequences. Additional resources are made available, valuable opportunities are provided for some professors and students, and the university becomes more directly useful to society. Faculty members who can or hope to take advantage of current trends do not wish to see any interference with the personal benefits potentially offered: to engage in joint ventures, to run businesses, consulting, and the like. They want maximum freedom; in the words of Deng Xiaoping, "To become rich is glorious." Administrations are equally eager to explore outside opportunities, and neither faculty nor administration have agreed-on senses of limits.

This enthusiasm is, in one sense, paradoxical. Welcoming increased permeability means tearing-down or lowering walls that have surrounded institutions. These have never been particularly effective, but—as already mentioned—the flows of funds and ideas are greater now than ever before in history. The paradoxical point is that what might be called "internal permeability" presents a rather different picture. Disciplinary barriers and defense of departmental turf remains strong, more so in the humanities and social sciences than in the natural sciences. "Interdisciplinary" is not a magic technique guaranteeing valuable and innovative research results, but it is possible to give examples where harm results from internal barriers, and where we would all benefit if the welcoming spirit to the extra-mural world were applied within our own borders. A good example is area studies.

Disciplinary barriers have hampered the progress of area studies, defined as the analysis of foreign culture and history using the tools of social science. Area studies combine knowledge of country, language, and culture with training in a social science discipline. Russian or Chinese or Latin American studies would be typical subjects. From the point of view of traditional departments, the marriage of "area" and "discipline" has never been very happy, and nowhere is this more evident than in economics—the queen of the social sciences.

Economists have fashioned an austere and rigorous discipline based—somewhat vaguely—on the model of the natural sciences. In their internal pecking order no one stands higher than theorists, today using almost exclusively the sophisticated language of mathematics. This methodology—this adoration of science—means that culture and history play almost no role in analysis. Business cycles are a worthy subject of study, but not Japanese or Argentinean business cycles. After all, one does not study Japanese or American physics; we simply study physics.

Economics has within its ranks very few regional specialists as a result of this internal disciplinary barrier: a very low value is placed on the cultural and historical skills that these scholars have acquired with great difficulty. As the other social sciences move to imitate economics—e.g., the growth of the rational expectations school in political science—this attitude will undoubtedly spread.

Does it matter? One cannot be certain, but the situation observed in recent years where social scientists offer advice to troubled countries while possessing minimal knowledge of local societies, combined with the frequently poor results, provides encouragement to question the intellectual *status quo*. It has to be admitted, however, that the record of those with deeper country knowledge is not obviously better. In any case, the issue is not economics, social science, or even interdisciplinary studies. The question is: why are academics so welcoming to the opportunities offered by the private sector, an activity frequently justified by the promise of expanded intellectual horizons, and so resistant to opportunities offered by their intellectual neighbors? Perhaps it is that *vis-à-vis* outsiders academics can pose as fountainheads of wisdom while hoping to gain money, excitement, and sometimes fame. Colleagues from other departments are more likely to cramp our style, and to offer uncomfortable criticisms with fewer tangible rewards.

Many—including the editors of this volume—believe that the increasing external demands on universities require internal adjustments: institutions must re-organize themselves to carry out new roles, usually of an interdisciplinary character, without sacrificing their values, and that requires lowered internal walls. How can this be achieved? It will not be easy.

DRAWING LINES

When one mentions disturbing predictions, nightmares, commercialization, and similar unpleasantness, there is an inclination to interpret these concerns as opposition to change; as reactionary; as quaintly old-fashioned. That would be a mistake. Universities have adapted throughout their long histories, otherwise they could not have survived for nearly a thousand years. Further change is and should be coming, but does change mean that anything goes?

There is a famous Chinese curse: may you live in interesting times; and we surely do. Living in interesting times while standing on a "slippery slope" describes the current situation for many universities, and to retain institutional balance requires the capacity to recognize old and also to draw new lines that define acceptable and/or desirable conduct and policy. These are lines that, in principle, we will not cross. Unfortunately, when it comes to institutional standards in higher education, there seem to be very few general principles that enjoy wide acceptance. We tend to believe that the lines we will not cross resemble Justice Potter Stewart's definition of pornography: "I know it when I see it." That will not work because the decisions that face universities are much too complicated. To produce a reasonably complete set of lines not to be crossed may not yet be possible, but a few examples may be useful.

The "four essential freedoms of a university" were cited over forty years ago by Justice Felix Frankfurter in the famous Sweezy v. New Hampshire case.[6] He wrote: "A university ceases to be true to its own nature if it becomes a tool of church or state or any sectional interest." Frankfurter then enumerated the four essential freedoms: *"to determine for itself on academic grounds who may teach, what may be taught, how it should be taught, and who may be admitted to study."*[7] Subject to legal constrains that may apply especially in public institutions—for example, the state may mandate aspects of admissions policy—this is a declaration of independence for higher education.

Secondly, another reference to Bailyn's article (1991) of a decade ago entitled "Fixing the Turnips." He begins with Bertrand Russell's visit to the University of Wisconsin in the 1930's. Russell noted, with some disdain, that in Wisconsin "when any farmer's turnips go wrong, they send a professor to investigate the failure scientifically." From the perspective of a Cambridge scholar, those were unworthy academic assignments. Bailyn, writing about Harvard, takes a different position: "In recent years we have had a rich and beneficial turn to public service, mainly in the professional schools. We are positioned as never before, in our powerful professional faculties, to fix the turnips when they go wrong, indeed to see to it that they grow properly in the first place. But as we begin a new transition, I hope we can conceive of

---

6 Frankfurter was quoting from a statement by a group of senior scholars in South Africa.
7 Italics supplied.

the balance shifting back toward the University's primary faculty—toward the magnet of learning, toward disinterested study, toward intellectual pursuits not for extrinsic purposes but for their own sakes. We are in no danger of forgetting the turnips. *The danger is that the University will become a mere holding company for highly publicized, semi-independent service institutes, its original core faculty still respectable but old-fashioned, diminished, and by-passed in importance.* I hope in the years ahead we will above all honor our first commitment, which an earlier Harvard president, Josiah Quincy, defined simply as "giving a true account of the gift of reason." [8]

Frankfurter and Bailyn may sound very abstract, but they do provide—indirectly —suggestions for lines that should not be crossed; at the very least they alert us to issues that should be carefully examined if the full implications of actions are to be understood. The relevance of these concerns can be demonstrated by some examples touching on collegiality, commercialization, and conflict of interest.

Increasing commercialization and conflict of interest are twins—Siamese twins—and current problems are especially noticeable in biotechnology and some other fields where technology transfer is promising, although the emphasis remains on promise. The total value of university technology transfer in the year 2000 has been estimated at only about $750 million, with 40 percent being biomedical and the rest in engineering. Symptoms of pathology are numerous, especially in biomedical research: secrecy, delayed publication, drugs tested by those with commercial interests in the product, etc. For example, studies of cancer drugs funded by pharmaceutical companies were 1/8th as likely to reach unfavorable conclusions as non-profit studies. (In part, this could be the result of selecting only those studies with the greatest commercial promise—but only in part.) Data show that scientists frequently fail to reveal their ties to industry in publications. In one very controversial case, Novartis received a voice inside a Berkeley department concerning the distribution of research funds that the company had donated (Press & Washburn, 2000). Few favor these abuses, much has been written about them, and there is growing agreement that stricter rules are needed. Responsible academic leaders agree that technology transfer and university collaboration with industry is needed and good for all. They also agree that transparency and monitoring should provide context. The dean of the Harvard Medical School, Joseph Martin, has been a leader in the movement to push for stricter rules (Martin, 2001; Moses III & Hamilton, 2002).

It is entirely reasonable for the biomedical sciences to be the center of attention when considering the potential benefits and difficulties of external permeability. In terms of research promise and public support, they rank at or

---

8 Italics supplied.

near the very top, and it has been recently suggested by President Lawrence Summers of Harvard and others that the next Silicon Valley will specialize in biomedicine. Even if this proves to be an accurate forecast, it is useful to consider some less obvious and perhaps less prominent issues, because the manner in which the university interacts with the world beyond its walls may eventually affect a much broader range of activities.

As an example, the Harvard Business School offered and may again offer advanced management courses exclusively for certain (large) companies. Perhaps the school was extremely well compensated for these offerings; it is not the most essential issue. The School is wealthy enough not to have to take assignments only for money, but do these exclusive arrangements violate any or all of the "essential freedoms?" Surely big "customers" can influence and perhaps even dictate who teaches; they will insist on, in their estimation, the very best instructors. Customer certainly can influence the curriculum, and will also largely determine who is in the classroom. Do these arrangements represent faculty decisions reached on academic grounds?

It is possible that the school engages in this practice because these programs open company doors and lead to original and valuable case-based research. But a university embodies many features of a public good: it is tax exempt, possibly tax financed, and the beneficiary of gifts representing generations of donors. In principle, its services should be available to all, with selection based above all else on merit. In the United States, flagship institutions have tried for many years to minimize the influence of students' ability to pay by awarding scholarships and loans. Do company-specific programs represent a retrograde step and a method of "buying your way into Harvard?" Are some students treated better than others? At the very least these are policy issues that deserve university-wide discussion that include ethical considerations.

"Drawing lines" can also become a concern in relations with donors, who—as a group—are becoming increasingly important to universities, and who also represent a growing source of outside influence. Today, even public universities depend heavily on private philanthropy, as the proportion of state support has fallen: state support in the range of 20 to 30 percent of total budget is not unusual. Private universities, of course, have always had to depend on individual non-governmental donations. Donors have their own priorities and agendas and sometimes they clash—or should clash if standards prevail—with internal university policies or plans. This is certainly not a new problem, but it is one that will grow in significance as all research universities become increasingly dependent on philanthropy. It is much more likely that explicit policies and rules will have been directed towards government funding, and perhaps that should be supplemented by more attention paid to acceptable rules for governing private philanthropy. What happened at Yale is an example of problems that may become more common in the future.

About a decade ago, Yale received a $20 million gift to fund an undergraduate program in Western Civilization. Aside from the inherent interest in the subject, at a time of great financial need Yale would have been able to support some non-incremental senior chairs and to appoint some new junior faculty members. All of this happened during a hiring freeze. The donation was solicited and accepted by the president and dean with minimal faculty consultation; at least that was the opinion of many faculty members.

Problems emerged very quickly and they were clearly related to political divisions. The president and dean were considered advocates of very conservative views. Many professors believed that a new program should have had prior faculty approval, because under a system of shared governance they should have the authority to determine on academic grounds "what is taught." The donor became exasperated by internal Yale fights and by ensuing severe delays, and ultimately asked for a voice in the choice of new faculty appointments for the proposed program. The new president of Yale immediately understood that a line had been crossed—who teaches is entirely determined by the university—and amidst much public astonishment the gift was returned.

The point is that this incident is not that unusual. Gifts should be returned when conditions develop that cross a line, and some should not be accepted in the first place, no matter how hungry the beneficiary. A transparent set of internal institutional standards would be very useful because subtle questions—more subtle than at Yale—surface quite easily. For example, what should be done if a donor is willing to give a professorial chair provided an individual of his or her choice becomes the initial occupant *and* assume that individual happens to be one of a number of reasonable choices? Or, assume that the donor is very knowledgeable about the subject of the chair and asks to be a member of the search committee? These examples are real and the answers are not entirely obvious and would be worthy subjects for the development of general policies.

Possible problems also arise every time a chair, a building, or a fellowship is named after a commercial enterprise. Chait's "need and greed" examples are arresting. Professorial chairs named after companies are now common: examples would be the FEDEX and Yahoo! professorships. What about the Bank of America Dean of the Haas Business School at the University of California at Berkeley or the Colgate-Palmolive Professor of Dentistry at the University of Queensland in Australia? Does using these names imply endorsement of the company, perhaps the University of Queensland's preference for Colgate over Crest? (After all, what is the incentive for a company to associate its name with a university?) At one time, Harvard did not allow positions to be named after commercial enterprises—e.g., a Henry Ford II professorship was possible, a Ford Motor Company chair was not permitted—but that policy was abandoned well over a decade ago. Sometimes chairs named after companies carry special obligations vis-à-vis that company. At Wayne State University the holder of the K-Mart Chair in marketing has the duty to provide some company training. In the current climate, drug companies might have a particular interest in featuring their names at universities.

Very recently, a former Harvard president asked the following provocative question: should the university accept a gift of $2 billion if the donor received the right to place a sign on the pedestal of the John Harvard statue that announced "Things go better with Coke." The answer is obvious, but why not? It is an awful lot of money that could be used for socially worthy purposes such as scholarships for needy undergraduates. Might one turndown $2 billion but accept $4 billion?

The answer lies in "giving a true account of the gift of reason." Advertising promotes many (mostly?) meaningless distinctions. Pepsi and Coke, Crest and Colgate, Ford and Chevrolet, Fidelity and Merrill may represent different consumer preferences, but those of us who travel under the banner of veritas—all universities—should avoid lending their collective authority to trivial or, at best, purely commercial distinctions and endorsements. It undermines our capacity for truth and objectivity, or at least the public's belief in our objectivity, and those are the characteristics that should distinguish universities in society. There are few reasons for a commercial company to put its name on (say) the Yale Bowl except to associate its services or products with the values or influence represented by Yale, enhanced by the growing public stake in higher education. And there is no valid reason for Yale to provide this particular endorsement—rather than to a competitor—save for a certain sum of money.

In an era when questions of this type will arise with increasing frequency, mainly as a consequence of rising external permeability, and when "lines" and "general principles" are few and unclear, the role of the faculty becomes particularly important. Their sense of academic values should be the university's first line of defense against potential abuses; because of obvious conflicts of interest, the faculty should not be the final line of defense: that role, all too often performed imperfectly, belongs to the president and to trustees. It is the faculty's responsibility to render judgments on academic grounds and that implies shared governance. It is the foundation of collegiality. A faculty is not an individual; it is a group of colleagues, and that is what gives authority to faculty opinion. Today, however, in many American universities some fifty percent of the faculty are adjuncts, frequently an underpaid, exploited, gypsy proletariat with minimal or no rights. That situation is antithetical to collegiality and thus another line has been crossed. At many of our proudest research universities, that same line has been crossed with the overuse of teaching fellows and post-docs. That they are used mainly as apprentice scholars has become a pretense. Just as with adjuncts, it has become a form of cheap labor and destructive of collegial values. Reducing the proportion of adjuncts, teaching fellows, and post-docs means moving back inside the line that delimits our basic values.

Enormous gaps in compensation between fields of specialization—another consequence partly related to increasing external permeability—also weakens shared governance and collegiality. The issue is not only the usual suspects of law, medicine, and business versus everybody else. What happens within the category "everybody else" is equally important. Not only are the average salaries of professors in the humanities and similar fields much lower—similar fields simply means no outside demand for a particular type of scholarship—but the large majority of its constituents has few opportunities for non-academic earnings. We have developed a two sector society: the haves who love market forces and the have—nots whose benefits from these forces are at best indirect and always small. The market creates and exaggerates differences. The "haves" get both higher salaries and outside income. Even if the numbers who benefit from the market are not very large, and that represents conventional wisdom although accurate facts are hard to obtain, the resulting psychological divide (read envy) does affect collegiality.

In general we deal with this problem by refusing to talk about it, and that is not surprising given its complexity and sensitivity. How can market forces be ignored without preventing a decline in faculty quality? How can market forces not be resisted if they undermine principles of collegiality that are fundamental to peer relationships? It could be claimed that collegiality in the American research university is already a lost cause. Research institutions are too large and too diverse, and it is simply not realistic to seek common ground between a business school and a divinity school or between a classics and a biochemistry department. And yet, a university should reflect some common values and standards, otherwise the future may lie in "...a mere holding company...for semi-independent service institutes..." that will be indistinguishable from commercially-based research centers. "Semi-independence" would endanger the special investigator freedom—"science driven by curiosity"—supplemented by superbly able graduate students, that characterizes university-based research and that has proved so innovative (Mukherjee, 2002). This applies not only to the sciences.

There is no wholly satisfactory answer. It is clear that market forces cannot be ignored in the American setting where competition between universities is an important element in raising quality. Competition may, in considerable measure, account for the internationally high standing of American higher education. Market forces have to be reflected in compensation and total faculty income. Yet there are ways to mitigate resulting distortions: higher subsidies for some activities and perhaps a tax on wealthy enclaves as a means of some income redistribution. It is a palliative, but valuable just the same.

Many different situations have been mentioned where old "lines" need to be remembered and new ones need to be created. There is a great deal of diversity among the problems, but there is a common denominator: university connection to the world beyond its walls creates the challenge to traditional values and practices. A balance of activities in a research university that is not sufficiently reflective of its fundamental purposes is one of the dangers. Bertrand Russell was wrong. We should fix the turnips and make sure that they grow correctly in the first place. One of our prime social purposes is, in Derek Bok's (1991) words, "to contribute the knowledge that will help society discover how to overcome its pressing problems." But neither lure of gain nor public clamor should allow the university to neglect "disinterested study...and intellectual pursuits not for extrinsic purposes but for their own sakes." Among other things, this means that the university's role as a preserver of culture is not just tolerated: it is generously nourished. There is room for optimism. In 1911, Max Weber warned that universities are becoming "state capitalist enterprises managed for purposes external to learning for its own sake and freedom of enquiry is beginning to give way to the production of knowledge useful to the state for technological and economic reasons...." That did not happen in democratic societies and if the external and internal changes are carefully considered, it will not happen in the future (Heyde, 2001).

FUTURE TASKS

Two tasks face institutions in light of the environment envisioned in this volume: first lowering internal barriers, and second the control of external permeabilities. The latter has already been discussed from many points of view. Essentially following the model of discussions within the biomedical sciences is a good first step: moving towards stricter rules with enforcement and transparency. In addition it would be useful to conceive the consequences of external permeability more broadly, with some attempt to implement changes that result from that broader scope.

Lowering internal barriers has received less attention even though they undoubtedly have a great effect on intellectual outcomes. A general policy prescription is impossible because institutional traditions vary so much, but an example may be helpful. Because of the author's experience, Harvard will, once again, provide the illustration.

Harvard is famous—infamous would be a more accurate term—for the autonomy with which its faculties or schools operate. The slogan "each tub on its own bottom" describes the management philosophy: each faculty responsible for its own expenditures, revenues, and endowments, with the central administration largely unable and temperamentally unwilling to shift resources from one faculty to another. At Harvard even the academic calendars differ by faculty!

This particular style has historically led to some very positive results: management more powerful and efficient at the faculty level, and entrepreneurship strongly encouraged because one cannot count on rescue from the center. However, the "tub system" does create obstacles for activities that need to reach across faculties and departments. If interfaculty and interdisciplinary needs are becoming more urgent, the Harvard structure could be—already may be—counter-productive. About a decade ago, this became a matter of concern and, without in any way abandoning advantages of tub-style management, steps were taken to draw the university closer together. The method was to select a number of broad research and teaching topics that obviously were beyond the intellectual capacity of any one faculty, and then to organize programs, with seed money, at the level of the central administration, responsible not to faculty deans but to the provost and president.

Four topics were selected: children studies; mind, brain, and behavior; environmental studies; and health care policy. The topics varied greatly in style and character. Environmental studies became a new interdisciplinary undergraduate major. Health care policy became a Ph.D. program. The initiative for children focused on interdisciplinary courses and research. Mind, brain and behavior was the originator of cutting-edge research. These were beginnings and some were more successful than others, but all drew on the intellectual capital of the entire university, and each interfaculty initiative became a place where one's tub identity ceased to be the most important name-tag.

Traditions vary from university to university. At some, interdisciplinary teaching and research will come more naturally than at others, but creating special facilitating structures will be needed in all universities.

We end as we started, with the ivory tower. As a general description of the modern university it was always flawed. As a description of the life-style of individual scholars, the term becomes much more valid. The art historian Erwin Panofsky (1948) in his defense of "tower dwellers" recognizes that they cannot be as active "as those who live on the outside." But perhaps from their high perch they can see farther and "signal along the line from summit to summit...In so doing they will automatically contribute to the making of our world." A pure mathematician friend of Panofsky's (1948) said to him with some concern: no one can prevent mathematics from being occasionally applied!

Therefore it is a great mistake to think of ivory tower in a pejorative sense as accurately applying to those university activities that appear of little immediate or practical importance: typically the humanities, history, and some basic sciences. The great triumphs and disasters of the twentieth century were less the product of technology transfer, applied sciences, or business schools, than the consequence of positive or deeply distorted human values.

To say it again, universities are among the oldest continuing institutions in the world, and that would not have been possible if they did not adapt to world conditions; and so it will be in the future. Periods of rapid change such as the present make it mandatory for institutions to operate within reliable internal rules, which have been referred to as lines that should not be crossed. The identification and development of these lines is an urgent task for faculty and administration. The difficulties of creating new norms are magnified by the competitive environment in which higher education operates. The price of virtue can be made prohibitive, especially for institutions whose resources are extremely limited. This is surely a case where the rich should lead by example. Yet if the dangers are understood, perhaps collective action that would not damage institutional interests would become a possibility.

REFERENCES

Atkinson, R. (1999-2000). "The Future Arrives First in California," *Issues in Science and Technology*, Winter Issue.

Ayres, I. (2001). "Lectures vs. Laptops," *The New York Times*, March 20.

Bailyn, B. (1991). "Fixing the Turnips," *Harvard Magazine*, March-April Issue.

Bok, D. C. (1991). "The Social Responsibilities of American Universities," *Harvard University Commencement Address*, June 6.

(The) Chronicle of Higher Education (2000). "The Future of Colleges: Nine Inevitable Changes," October 27.

Harvard University Gazette (2000). September 28.

Hendrickson, R. (1997). The *Facts on File Encyclopedia of Word and Phrase Origins*. (rev. ed.), Facts on File, New York.

Heyde, C. C. (2001). "The Changing Scene for Higher Education in Science: A View from the Statistical Profession," in Herzberg, A. M. & Krupka, I. (eds.) *Statistics, Science, and Public Policy*, Vol. V., Queen's University, Kingston, Ontario.

Lenzner, R. & Johnson, S. S. (1997). "Seeing Things As They Really Are," *Forbes Magazine*, March 10.

Levine, A. (2000). The Future of Colleges: Nine Inevitable Changes," *The Chronicle of Higher Education*, October 27.

Martin, J. B. (2001). "Are Policy Changes Needed to Address Conflict-of-Interest and Intellectual Property Issues Arising in University Research," Presentation to the Government-University-Industry Roundtable, Washington, D.C., March 28.

Moses III, H. (2001). "Academic Relations with Industry." Presentation to the Government-University-Industry Roundtable, Washington, D.C., March 28.

Moses III, H. & Martin, Joseph B. (2002). "Academic Relations With Industry: A New Model for Biomedical Research," JAMA, Vol. 285, No. 7.

Mukherjee, S. (2002). "Fighting Chance: The Case for Funding Curiosity," The New Republic, January 21.

Panofsky, E. (1948). "In Defense of the Ivory Tower," Harvard Alumni Bulletin, July.

Press, E. & Washburn, J. (2000). "The Kept University," The Atlantic Monthly, March.

Traub, J. (2000). "Online U," The New York Times Magazine, November 19.

United States Supreme Court, (1957). 354 U.S. 234.

Wells, H. G. (1940). The New World Order, Secker and Warburg, London.

CHAPTER 3

Scientific Advances and the ever more Complex Challenges facing Society

Jakob Nüesch

INTRODUCTION

E very year in December, the editors of *Science* select the ten most important discoveries of the year. Genomics led the year 2000 ranking, probably not a great surprise to most of us. That year, several milestones
had been achieved in deciphering genomes from drosophila to plants and,
finally, to man.

Number two in the ranking was the elucidation of the structure of ribo-
somes, as well as the confirmation of a hypothesis of the catalysis of the poly-
merisation of amino acids by RNA and not by proteins. Furthermore, the
discovery of two well conserved cranes from south of Trifles were ranked,
because they permit to conclude that our ancestors left Africa for Eurasia
some 1.7 million years ago. Remarkable progress was achieved with stem
cells, a very important domain of cell biology with a great theoretical as well
as medical potential. Also of interest was the announcement of cloned pig-
lets. In this connection, it was shown that cloning methods can be useful to
avoid the extinction of endangered species.

A final biological discovery concerned nuclear receptors. These elements
play an important role in the regulation of the functions of genes. From a
medical point of view, nuclear receptors are instrumental for the understanding of diseases of the cardiovascular system, as well as of cancer and of the
side effects of drugs.

Besides the winner in the field of biology, important discoveries in quantum physics, organic semiconductors and supraconducting polymers with

exciting properties were distinguished. Last but not least, research on planets showed, among other aspects, that our neighbouring planets might well hide some water reserves and that some four billion years ago, water could have been present on planet Mars in the form of lakes. Research in astronomy as well as in cosmology led to new insights.

This short description of the ranking list illustrates the dominance in interest in biology or life sciences over other scientific disciplines and shows growing interest in the physical sciences, in particular solid state physics and quantum physics, as well as astrophysics and cosmology. In conclusion, all the selected discoveries belong to knowledge-oriented, long term basic science. Several discoveries have an obvious potential for application. The selection made by the *Science* editors underlined not only one of the strong points of the past century, but pointed to the new century in which life sciences and information technologies might continue and even reinforce an important megatrend. As a matter of fact, this megatrend continued in the year 2001 at more or less the same pace (*Science*, 2001a).

Science is a key element of modern human societies. As it consumes considerable amounts of public money, it is influenced by science policy and political bodies. President Bush's first research budget was set to favour life sciences, with all its unforeseeable consequences for other scientific disciplines. The tragic events of September 11, 2001, however, had a deep impact on his second budget.

The European Union (EU), on its side, is making strong efforts to restructure the highly fragmented European scientific community. In addition, priority areas were identified and agreed for the sixth Research and Development Framework Program: Information technology, Genomics and biotechnology, Sustainable development and global change, Nanotechnology, Intelligent materials and new production processes, Aeronautics and space, Food safety (*Science*, 2001b). Whereas the EU programme is probably less focused on life sciences than US research, there is a major difference in funding. The EU nations invest 1.8 % of their Gross Domestic Produce in R and D, a very modest figure in comparison with the United States' 2.7 %, or Japan's 3.1 %.

Nevertheless, there are common traits between these nations or groups of nations belonging to the science- and technology-driven industrialised world. Since World War II, science and technology have been dominating the tertiary sector, whereas humanities, social sciences, or even economic sciences have been playing a minor role.

To conclude this introduction, let me pose a question. Since the time of Francis Bacon, human beings have had the idea that technical progress will provide happiness through unlimited mobility, freedom through unlimited communication, and the prolongation of life. The latter has been achieved in the course of the last centuries. But are we happier than before and do we have less problems?

SCIENCE AND TECHNOLOGY — MAJOR DRIVING FORCES OF MODERN CIVILISATIONS

The world we live in today is defined as post-modernist, or in a more simplistic way, as a 'Knowledge Society' or 'Risk Society' (Nowotny, Scott & Gibbons, 2001).

On the macro level, the following characteristic traits are worth mentioning:

- Profound changes in the world of labour
- Dematerialization of products
- Quantitative and qualitative enhancement of service activities
- Application as important as knowledge production and, as a consequence, an enormous increase in the speed of innovation
- The sources of scientific and technological knowledge are completely reshaped by processes of internalisation and globalisation.
- Changes in production systems, increased flexibility (just in time), lean organisations
- Increasing importance of information technologies (IT)
- Primacy of the economy, in other words, the market dominates the meaning of life.
- Innovation addiction and risk aversion characterise our hedonistic and pluralistic world.
- Despite a continuous oscillation between public hysteria towards risks, fear of science and certain technologies, indifference and attempts to reform, there is no serious awareness or will in politics and governments to counteract quantitative growth with its foreseeable negative impact on a sustainable development of our world. President Bush's decision to renege on his pre-election promise to regulate emissions of carbon dioxide is a saddening warning as to the low importance given to environmental and sustainability issues (*Nature*, 2001).
- Last but not least, the idea that knowledge is dangerous is deeply embedded in our society.

On the micro level of science and technology, several trends have appeared during the last fifty years or so. Science has moved increasingly from a knowledge-driven to a utility-driven system. As a consequence, the diversity of the scientific system has been reduced. This might lead to bud-

gets becoming out of balance, as is seemingly the case with the US administration's science budget, which favours to a great extent life sciences at the
expense of other disciplines. Or, far-reaching specialisation of a university
may have a negative impact on its potential for future and as yet unknown
developments.

During the past years, scientific organisations were accused of being resistant to change and of inefficient management, as well as of being reluctant to
collaborate with industry. These criticisms are partially justified and they
have to be taken seriously. The same is true for the ivory tower attitude. It is
obvious today that a scientific institution is no longer external to society. As
a matter of fact, it is part of it. The time is over when the communication
between science and society was unilateral. Today, society asks questions to
science, with an ever-increasing intensity. Indeed, nothing is more needed
for science than to win public confidence.

To conclude this discussion of the present situation, let us consider briefly
a problem internal to science: the relation among disciplines. Whereas the
scientific and technological world have long learned out of necessity to communicate with each other, the situation is very different concerning communication between science, technology on the one hand, and humanities and
social sciences on the other. As mentioned earlier, science and technology
have shaped the modern world. Their creative power is such that strategies
for exploring implications have to be developed. In other words, to solve a
practical problem or to acquire knowledge with far-reaching and often
unknown consequences once applied, demands dialogue with people who
have explored different ways of thinking and focused on questions of concept, methodological theory, epistemology, ethics and social impact. In view
of the ever-increasing complexity and unpredictability of science- and
technology-driven societies, the humanities must become partners of science
and technology, in order to contribute to ethical norm-setting, as well as to
pre- and post-action reflection on possible repercussions.

SCIENCE AND TECHNOLOGY FOR THE FUTURE

It is Frank H. T. Rhodes (2000) who wrote: *Universities are communities of
enquiry, discovery and learning, created and supported by society, with the convic-
tion that the growth and diffusion of knowledge not only enrich personal experience,
but also serve the public good and advance human well-being.* This statement
reflects in a pertinent way the goals and characteristics of the modern university. It is quite different from Wilhelm von Humboldt's vision of the university, which is centred on the idea of the formation of individuality as the final
goal of the universe (Rebe, 1995).

Without any doubt, in modern universities, science and technology play a dominant role. Real science, in the broad sense of the definition, will always produce ideas about how the world works. On the other hand, ideas in technology will result in usable objects. Nevertheless, technology is more and more science-driven and the relationship between science and technology becomes closer and closer and less hierarchical. What will the future pillars of the science and technology systems look like?

Basic or Knowledge-oriented science

Basic or knowledge-oriented science will still play a major role. It is part of our cultural inheritance. It cannot be planned and yet it is an important part of our value system. Notwithstanding its unpredictable nature and very loose goal orientation, this kind of science has to accept adequate criteria of productivity via appropriate quality assessment systems. Probably there will be a natural tendency to do research at the interfaces between the disciplines, with the consequence that in-depth knowledge will have to be combined with a horizontal language that allows communication with neighbouring disciplines.

In future systems, basic science will interact much more with the humanities, as well as with the social sciences. A good illustration is given by the neurosciences. In this field, in particular in brain research, very basic questions such as free will and personal responsibility will be discussed between philosophers and neurobiologists.

Finally, the contextualisation of knowledge production will become important (Nowotny, Scott & Gibbons, 2001).

Problem-oriented or applied sciences

If openness is already important in basic sciences, it becomes even more important and more complex in applied sciences, which by definition lay the ground for technological solutions to practical problems. Strategies for the exploration of implications will be of paramount importance. Interaction between scientists of various disciplines and belonging to the "two cultures" must thus become much more intensive than in the past.

New systems of participation and involvement—even from the public—will have to be considered. This part of the scientific enterprise depends heavily on public confidence. In view of the development and socio-economic and ecological state of our world, there is an urgent need to develop criteria and conditions in order to foster a sustainable development. In other words, universities of the future will have to go beyond their traditional tasks and participate in addition in the search for solutions to major problems of human societies. After all, humans are the world's greatest evolutionary force and it is part of our responsibility and accountability as scientists to contribute to the understanding of the consequences of our actions on future developments.

As Nowotny *et al.* (2001) mention, knowledge societies will have to become learning organisations in order to develop their human and intellectual capital. Universities will play a major role, provided that they are adaptable organisations and comprehensive institutions rather than highly specialised niche players. If we accept the opening of the university internally as well as externally by re-thinking the culture of communication and creating a new relationship with our partners from industry and society as a whole, we may create the prerequisites for a socially credible institution, able to alleviate people from the belief that knowledge is fundamentally dangerous.

Science is not only an activity leading to knowledge and, finally, to innovation. It is above all a cultural achievement of human creativity. Universities are places where science can develop its greatest potential. Their most important impact on society can be achieved through science-supported education. Therefore, research and education have to remain united. Nevertheless, there is an urgent need, in particular in Europe, to improve the concepts of education. We often forget that in a learning institution teachers as well as learners are learning. It might be necessary to re-evaluate and adapt this important process. It is important to leave the unidirectional teaching process and also to adapt to teaching interdisciplinarity in an interdisciplinary research environment without losing scientific quality.

Last but not least, many European universities are faced with an outdated concept of governance. The future university needs a great deal of autonomy coupled with a new communication culture and a new perception of accountability. The future research and education university will certainly have to face limited financial resources. It is therefore of paramount importance that concepts are developed in order to increase its productivity.

In this context, Europe offers interesting opportunities. There is a high degree of cultural diversity within a relatively dense distribution of qualitatively good institutions of higher education and research. This situation can be favourably exploited for the creation of complementary networks, provided the notorious particularism of the single institution can be overcome. Networking has another advantage, because it allows us to assemble monodisciplinary excellence within a high-performing transdisciplinary system.

CONCLUSION

Even if the university of the future will maintain its concept of research-supported education, it has to adapt and develop substantially in order to face successfully future challenges and needs.

The science of the future, applied or basic, must be based on reflections going beyond the sciences. This is where a true cooperation with humanities, social sciences and also economics and ecology will emerge. Beside its traditional tasks to create knowledge, to educate and to lay the basis for the responsible ecological, social and economic wellbeing of human societies, science has to act as an early warning system. This important task can be achieved only if a new contact between science and society is established.

REFERENCES

Nature (2001). 410, p. 499.

Nowotny, H., Scott, P. & Gibbons, M. (2001). *Re-Thinking Science*, Blackwell Publishers Ltd, Malden, 278 p.

Rebe, R (1995). *Denkerkundungen*, Georg Olms Verlag, Hildesheim-Zürich-New York, p. 69.

Rhodes, F. (2001). *The Glion Declaration 2000*, in Hirsch, W. Z. & Weber, L. E., *Governance in Higher Education*, Economica, London, p. 195.

Science (2000). 290, pp. 2220-2225.

Science (2001a). 294, pp 2442-2447.

Science (2001b). 291, p. 1676.

CHAPTER

Preparing for the Revolution: The Future of the University in the Digital Age

James J. Duderstadt

"The impact of information technology will be even more radical than the harnessing of steam and electricity in the 19th century. Rather it will be more akin to the discovery of fire by early ancestors, since it will prepare the way for a revolutionary leap into a new age that will profoundly transform human culture." (Attali, 1992, p. 11)

INTRODUCTION

One of the central topics of the third meeting of the Glion Colloquium concerned the eroding boundaries of the contemporary university as traditional constraints disappear and new arrangements are demanded by a changing world. The forces driving this restructuring of the higher education enterprise are many and varied: the globalization of commerce and culture, the lifelong educational needs of citizens in a knowledge-driven society, the advanced educational needs of a high performance workplace, the exponential growth of new knowledge and new disciplines, and the compressed timescales and nonlinear nature of the transfer of knowledge from campus laboratories into commercial products. This paper concerns itself with the impact of information and communications technologies on higher education, which are rapidly obliterating the conventional constraints of space, time, organization, monopoly, and even reality itself.

Modern digital technologies such as computers, telecommunications, and networks are reshaping both our society and our social institutions. These technologies have increased vastly our capacity to know and to do things and to communicate and collaborate with others. They allow us to transmit information quickly and widely, linking distant places and diverse areas of endeavor in productive new ways. They allow us to form and sustain communities for work, play, and learning in ways unimaginable just a decade ago.

Of course higher education has already experienced significant change driven by digital technology. Our management and administrative processes are heavily dependent upon this technology. Research and scholarship are also highly dependent upon information technology, for example, the use of computers to simulate physical phenomena, networks to link investigators in virtual laboratories or "collaboratories," and digital libraries to provide scholars with access to knowledge resources. There is an increasing sense that new technology will also have a profound impact on teaching, freeing the classroom from the constraints of space and time and enriching learning by providing our students with access to original source materials.

Yet, while information technology has the capacity to enhance and enrich teaching and scholarship, it also poses certain threats to our colleges and universities. We can now use powerful computers and networks to deliver educational services to anyone, at anyplace and anytime. Technology is creating an open learning environment in which the student becomes an active learner and consumer of educational services, stimulating the growth of powerful market forces that could dramatically reshape the higher education enterprise.

THE EVOLUTION OF INFORMATION TECHNOLOGY

It is difficult to understand and appreciate just how rapidly information technology is evolving. During the first decades of the information age, the evolution of hardware technology followed the trajectory predicted by "Moore's Law"—that the chip density and consequent computing power for a given price doubles every eighteen months (Deming & Metcalf, 1997). This corresponds to a hundredfold increase in computing speed, storage capacity, and network transmission rates every decade. Of course, if information technology is to continue to evolve at such rates, we will likely need not only new technology but even new science. But with emerging technology such as quantum computing, nanocomputers, and biocomputing, there is significant possibility that Moore's Law will continue to hold for at least a few more decades.

To put this statement in perspective, if information technology continues to evolve at its present rate, by the year 2020, the thousand-dollar notebook computer will have a computing speed of 1 million gigahertz, a memory of thousands of terabits, and linkages to networks at data transmission speeds of gigabits per second. Put another way, it will have a data processing and memory capacity roughly comparable to the human brain (Kurzweil, 1999). However, the computer will be so tiny as to be almost invisible, and it will communicate with billions of other computers through wireless technology.

This last comment raises an important issue. The most dramatic impact on our world today from information technology is not from the continuing increase in computing power, but rather from the extraordinary rate at which bandwidth is expanding, that is, the rate at which we can transmit digital information. In a sense, the price of data transport is becoming zero, and with rapid advances in photonic and wireless technology, telecommunications will continue to evolve very rapidly for the foreseeable future.

The nature of human interaction with the digital world—and with other humans through computer-mediated interactions—is also evolving rapidly. We have moved beyond the simple text interactions of electronic mail and conferencing to graphical-user interfaces and then through voice to video. With the rapid development of sensors and robotic actuators, touch and action at a distance will soon be available, i.e., "telepresence".

The penetration of digital technology into our society has proceeded at an extraordinary pace. Already the Internet links hundreds of millions of people. Estimates are that, by the end of the decade, this number will surge to billions, a substantial fraction of the world's population, driven in part by the fact that most economic activity will be based on digital communication. Bell Laboratories suggests that within two decades a "global communications skin" will have evolved, linking together billions of computers that handle the routine tasks of our society, from driving our cars to monitoring our health.

In other terms, over the next decade, we will evolve from "giga" technology (in terms of computer operations per second, storage, or data transmission rates) to "peta" technology (one million-billion or 1015). A petabyte of data is equivalent roughly to the capacity of a stack of CD-ROMs nearly 2 km high. We will denominate the number of computer servers in the billions, digital sensors in the tens of billions, and software agents in the trillions. We will evolve from "e-commerce" and "e-government" and "e-learning" to "e-everything"!

Of course, our world has experienced other periods of dramatic change driven by technology, for example, the impact of the steam engine, telephone, automobile, and railroad in the late nineteenth century, which created our urban industrialized society. But never have we experienced a technology that has evolved so rapidly and relentlessly, increasing in power by a hundred-fold or more every decade, obliterating the constraints of space and time, and reshaping the way we communicate, think, and learn.

There are several characteristics of information technology that set it apart from earlier experiences with technology-driven change: 1) its active rather than passive nature; 2) the way that it obliterates the constraints of space and time (and perhaps reality); 3) its extraordinary rate of evolution, relentlessly increasing in power by factors of 100 to 1000 fold decade after decade; and 4) the manner in which it unleashes the power of the market place. Furthermore, this technology drives very significant restructuring of our society and social institutions through what Brown and Duguid (2000) term the 6-D effects: demassification, decentralization, denationalization, despecialization, disintermediation, and disaggregation. Perhaps we should add a seventh "D", democratization, since the technology provides unusual access to knowledge and knowledge services (such as education) hitherto restricted to the privileged few. Like the printing press, this technology not only enhances and broadly distributes access to knowledge, but in the process it shifts power away from institutions to those who are educated and trained in the use of the new knowledge media.

Most discussions concerning information technology and higher education deal primarily with technology's impact upon instruction, for example, online distance education or virtual universities. But the roles of the contemporary university are broad and diverse, ranging from educating the young to preserving our cultural heritage; providing the basic research essential to national security, economic prosperity, and social well-being; training our professionals and certifying their competence; and challenging our society and stimulating social change. Knowledge is the medium of the university in the sense that each of its many roles involves the discovery, shaping, transfer, or application of knowledge. In this sense, it is clear that the rapid evolution of information and communications technologies will reshape all of the roles of the university. Thus, to understand the future of the university in the digital age, it is important to consider the impact of technology on each of its activities.

THE IMPACT OF INFORMATION TECHNOLOGY ON THE ACTIVITIES OF THE UNIVERSITY

The earliest applications of information technology in research involved using the computer to solve mathematical problems in science and technology. Today, problems that used to require the computational capacity of rooms of supercomputers can be tackled with the contemporary laptop computer. The rapid evolution of this technology is enabling scholars to address previously unsolvable problems, such as proving the four-color conjecture in mathematics, analyzing molecules that have yet to be synthesized, or simulating the birth of the universe.

The availability of high bandwidth access to instrumentation, data, and colleagues is also changing the way scholars do their work. They no longer need to focus as much on the availability of assets such as equipment or the physical proximity of colleagues, and instead can focus on hypotheses and questions. It has also changed the way graduate students interact and participate in research, opening up the environment for broader participation. In fact, information technology is "democratizing" research by allowing researchers and institutions that would normally not have access to the sophisticated facilities and libraries of research universities to become engaged in cutting edge scholarship.

The preservation of knowledge is one of the most rapidly changing functions of the university. The computer—or more precisely, the "digital convergence" of various media from print-to-graphics-to-sound-to-sensory experiences through virtual reality—will likely move beyond the printing press in its impact on knowledge. The library is becoming less a collection house and more a center for knowledge navigation, a facilitator of information retrieval and dissemination (*Daedelus*, 1966, pp. v-vii). In a sense, the library and the book are merging. One of the most profound changes will involve the evolution of software agents that will collect, organize, relate, and summarize knowledge on behalf of their human masters. Our capacity to reproduce and distribute digital information with perfect accuracy at essentially zero cost has shaken the very foundations of copyright and patent law and threatens to redefine the nature of the ownership of intellectual property (Barlow, 1994). The legal and economic management of university intellectual property is rapidly becoming one of the most critical and complex issues facing higher education.

The traditional classroom paradigm is also being challenged, not so much by the faculty, who have by and large optimized their teaching effort and their time commitments to a lecture format, but by students. Members of today's digital generation of students have spent their early lives immersed in robust, visual, electronic media—home computers, video games, cyberspace networks, and virtual reality. They expect—indeed, demand—interaction, approaching learning as a "plug-and-play" experience; they are unaccustomed and unwilling to learn sequentially—to read the manual—and instead are inclined to plunge in and learn through participation and experimentation. Although this type of learning is far different from the pyramidal approach of the traditional college curriculum, it may be far more effective for this generation, particularly when provided through a media-rich environment.

For a time, such students may tolerate the linear lecture paradigm of the traditional college curriculum. They still read what we assign, write the required term papers, and pass our exams. But this is decidedly not the way they learn. They learn in a nonlinear fashion, skipping from beginning to end and then back again, and building peer groups of learners, developing sophisticated learning networks in cyberspace. In a very real sense, they build their own learning environments that enable interactive, collaborative learning, whether we recognize and accommodate this or not.

Sophisticated networks and software environments can be used to break the classroom loose from the constraints of space and time and make learning available to anyone, anyplace, at any time. The simplest approach uses multimedia technology via the Internet to enable distance learning. Yet many believe that effective computer-network-mediated learning will not be simply an Internet extension of correspondence or broadcast courses. Since learning requires the presence of communities, the key impact of information technology may be the development of computer-mediated communications and communities that are released from the constraints of space and time. There is already sufficient experience with such asynchronous learning networks to conclude that, at least for many subjects and when appropriately constructed, the computer-mediated distance learning process is just as effective as the classroom experience (Bourne, 2000).

The attractiveness of computer-mediated distance learning is obvious for adult learners whose work or family obligations prevent attendance at conventional campuses. But perhaps more surprising is the degree to which many on-campus students are now using computer-based distance learning to augment their traditional education. Broadband digital networks can be used to enhance the multimedia capacity of hundreds of classrooms across campus and link them with campus residence halls and libraries. Electronic mail, teleconferencing, and collaboration technology is transforming our institutions from hierarchical, static organizations to networks of more dynamic and egalitarian communities. Distance learning based on computer-network-mediated paradigms allows universities to push their campus boundaries outward to serve new learners. Those institutions willing and capable of building such learning networks will see their learning communities expand by an order of magnitude.

In the near term, at least, traditional models of education will coexist with new learning paradigms, providing a broader spectrum of learning opportunities in the years ahead. The transitions from student to learner, from teacher to designer-coach-consultant, and from alumnus to lifelong member of a learning community seem likely. And with these transitions and new options will come both an increasing ability and responsibility on the part of learners to select, design, and control the learning environment.

IMPACT ON THE FORM AND FUNCTION OF THE UNIVERSITY

Colleges and universities are structured along intellectual lines, organized into schools and colleges, departments and programs that have evolved over the decades. Furthermore, the governance, leadership, and management of the contemporary university are structured also to reflect this intellectual organization, as well as academic values of the university such as academic freedom and institutional autonomy. The "contract" between members of the faculty and the university reflects the unusual character of academic values and roles, the practice of tenure being perhaps the most visible example.

Just as the university is challenged in adapting to new forms of teaching and research stimulated by rapidly evolving information technology, so too its organization, governance, management, and its relationships to students, faculty, and staff will require serious re-evaluation and almost certain change. For example, the new tools of scholarship and scholarly communication are eroding conventional disciplinary boundaries and extending the intellectual span, interests, and activities of faculty far beyond traditional organizational units such as departments, schools, or campuses. This is particularly the case with younger faculty members whose interests and activities frequently cannot be characterized by traditional disciplinary terms.

Beyond driving a restructuring of the intellectual disciplines, information technology is likely to force a significant disaggregation of the university on both the horizontal (e.g., academic disciplines) and vertical (e.g., student services) scale. Faculty activity and even loyalty is increasingly associated with intellectual communities that extend across multiple institutions, frequently on a global scale. New providers are emerging that can far better handle many traditional university services, ranging from student housing to facilities management to health care. Colleges and universities will increasingly face the question of whether they should continue their full complement of activities or "outsource" some functions to lower cost and sometimes higher quality providers, relying on new paradigms such as e-business and knowledge management.

It has become increasingly important that university planning and decision making take account not only of technological developments and challenges, but draw upon the expertise of people with technological backgrounds. Yet all too often, university leaders, governing boards, and even faculties ignore the rapid evolution of this technology, treating it more as science fiction than as representing serious institutional challenges and opportunities. To a degree this is not surprising, since in the early stages, new technologies sometimes look decidedly inferior to long-standing practices. For example, few would regard the current generation of computer-mediated distance learning programs as providing the socialization function associated with undergraduate education in a residential campus environment. Yet there have been countless instances of technologies, from personal computers to the Internet, that were characterized by technology learning curves far steeper than conventional practices. Such "disruptive technologies" have demonstrated the capacity to destroy entire industries, as the explosion of e-business makes all too apparent (Christensen, 1997).

IMPACT ON THE POST-SECONDARY EDUCATION ENTERPRISE

In higher education, digital technology is redefining the basis for competitive advantage and survival. It redefines boundaries and blurs roles. This technology, coupled with the emergence of competitive forces driven by changing societal needs (e.g., adult education) and economic realities (erosion in public support), is likely to drive a massive restructuring of higher education. From the experience with other restructured sectors of our economy, such as health care, transportation, communications, and energy, we can expect to see in higher education the mergers, acquisitions, new competitors, and new products and services that have characterized other economic transformations. More generally, we may well be seeing the early stages of a global knowledge and learning industry, in which the activities of traditional academic institutions converge with other knowledge-intensive organizations, such as telecommunications, entertainment, and information service companies.

The size of the education component of this industry, consisting of K-12, higher education, and corporate learning, is enormous, estimated at over $740 B in the United States and $2 trillion globally (Moe, 2000). It is growing rapidly, driven by the increasing importance of human capital to our knowledge-driven economies. Business leaders are united in their belief that there is no bigger challenge in the global marketplace than how to obtain, train, and retrain knowledge workers. The new economy is a knowledge economy based on brainpower, ideas, and entrepreneurism. Technology is its driving force, and human capital is its fuel.

A key factor in this restructuring has been the emergence of new aggressive for-profit educator providers that are able to access the private capital markets (over $4 billion in 2000). Examples include the University of Phoenix, Sylvan Learning Systems, the British Open University, the Western Governors University, and a growing array of "dot-coms" such as Unext.com and Blackboard.com. It is important to recognize that while many of these new competitors are quite different than traditional academic institutions, they are also quite sophisticated in their pedagogy, their instructional materials, and their production and marketing of educational services. They approach the market in a highly sophisticated manner, first moving into areas characterized by limited competition, unmet needs, and relatively low production costs, but then moving rapidly up the value chain to more sophisticated educational programs. These IT-based education providers are already becoming formidable competitors to traditional postsecondary institutions.

Although traditional colleges and universities will also play a role in such a technology-based, market-driven future, they could be both threatened and reshaped by shifting societal needs, rapidly evolving technology, and aggressive for-profit entities and commercial forces. Many of the predictions about the growth of demand for distance learning are overly optimistic, at least for the near term. But, clearly the university will lose its monopoly for students, faculty, and resources, and it is likely to lose market share as well, as commercial competitors position themselves to address the rapid need for adult education. The successful penetration of this market for most universities will involve partnerships with the commercial sector.

The research university will face particular challenges in this regard. Although rarely acknowledged, most research universities rely upon cross-subsidies from low-cost, high profit-margin instruction in general education (e.g., large lecture courses) and low cost professional education (e.g., business administration and law) to support graduate education and research. Yet these high margin programs are just the low hanging fruit most attractive to technology-based, for-profit competitors. In this sense, the emergence of a significant technology-based commercial sector in the post-secondary education marketplace could undermine the current business model of the research university and threaten its core activities in research and graduate education.

As a knowledge-driven economy becomes ever more dependent upon new ideas and innovation, there will be growing pressures to commercialize the intellectual assets of the university—its faculty and students, its capacity for basic and applied research, the knowledge generated through its scholarship and instruction. Public policy has encouraged the transfer of knowledge from the campus to the marketplace. But since knowledge can be transferred not only through formal technology transfer mechanisms such as patents and licensing, but also through the migration of faculty and students, there is a risk that the rich intellectual assets of the university will be stripped away and commercialized by its own faculty, even as support for graduate education and research erodes.

THE CHALLENGE OF UNIVERSITY LEADERSHIP IN THE DIGITAL AGE

Today's college and university leaders face myriad important questions and decisions concerning the impact of information technology on their institutions. For example, they need to understand the degree to which this technology will transform the basic activities of teaching, research, and service. Will the classroom disappear? Will the residential campus experience of undergraduate education be overwhelmed by virtual universities or "edutainment?" How should the university integrate information technology into its educational programs at different levels? Will information technology alter priorities among the different university activities?

What kind of information technology infrastructure will the university need? How will it finance the acquisition and maintenance of this technology? To what degree should an institution outsource the development and management of IT systems? How should the university approach its operations and management to best take advantage of this technology? How can institutions better link planning and decision making with likely technological developments and challenges? How can one provide students, faculty, and staff with the necessary training, support, and equipment to keep pace with the rapid evolution of information technology? What is the role of universities with respect to the "digital divide", the stratification of our society with respect to access to technology?

How do colleges and universities address the rapidly evolving commercial marketplace for educational services and content, including, in particular, the for-profit and dot.com providers? What strategies and actions should they consider? What kinds of alliances are useful in this rapidly changing environment? With other academic institutions? With business? On a regional, national, or global scale? Should colleges and universities join together to create a "best practice" organization that provides assistance in analyzing needs and opportunities?

How can colleges and universities grapple with the forces of disaggregation and aggregation associated with a technology-driven restructuring of the higher education enterprise? Will universities be forced to merge into larger units, or will they find it necessary to outsource or spin-off existing activities? Will more (or perhaps most) universities find themselves competing in a global marketplace, and how will that square with the regional responsibilities of publicly supported universities? Will new learning lifeforms or ecologies evolve based upon information technology that will threaten the very existence of the university?

The list of questions and issues seems not only highly complex but overwhelming to university leaders, not to mention the many stakeholders who support higher education. Yet, surveys suggest that despite the profound nature of these issues, information technology usually does not rank high among the list of priorities for university planning and decision making in the United States (Government-University-Industry Research Roundtable and National Science Board, 1997). Perhaps this is due to the limited experience most college and university leaders have with this emerging technology.

It could also be a sign of indecisiveness and procrastination in the face of complexity and uncertainty. Yet, as the pace of technological change continues to accelerate, indecision and inaction can be the most dangerous course of all.

As information technology continues to evolve, organizations in every sector are grappling with the need to transform their basic philosophies and processes to collect, synthesize, manage, and control information. Corporations and governments are reorganizing in an effort to utilize technology to enhance productivity, improve quality, and control costs. Entire industries have been restructured to better align with the realities of the digital age.

To date, the university stands apart, almost unique in its determination to moor itself to past traditions and practices, to insist on performing its core activities much as it has done for decades. In spite of the information explosion and the profound impact of digital communications technology, the use of information and dissemination and learning remain fundamentally unchanged in higher education. Most universities continue to ignore the technology cost learning curves so important in other sectors of society. They insist that it remains simply too costly to implement technology on a massive scale in instructional activities—which, of course, it does, as long as we insist on maintaining their traditional character rather than re-engineering educational activities to enhance productivity and quality. Our limited use of technology thus far has been at the margins, to provide modest additional resources to classroom pedagogy or to attempt to extend the physical reach of our current classroom-centered teaching paradigm. It is ironic indeed that the very institutions that have played such a profound role in developing the digital technology now reshaping our world are the most resistant to reshaping their activities to enable its effective use.

A NATIONAL ACADEMY PROJECT

In the United States, the National Academies (i.e., the National Academy of Sciences, the National Academy of Engineering, and the Institute of Medicine) have a unique mandate to monitor and sustain the health of the nation's research universities as key elements of the national research enterprise and the source of the next generation of scientists, engineers, and other knowledge professionals. This role becomes particularly important during periods of rapid change. It was from this perspective that the presidents of our National Academies launched a project in 2000 to understand better the implications of information technology for the future of the research university. I was asked to chair the steering group for this effort, comprised of leaders with backgrounds in technology, higher education, and public policy.

The premise of the National Academies study was a simple one. The rapid evolution of digital technology will present many challenges and opportunities to higher education in general and the research university in particular. Yet there is a sense that many of the most significant issues are neither well recognized nor understood by leaders of our universities or those who support and depend upon their activities.

The first phase of the project was aimed at addressing three sets of issues:

- To identify those technologies likely to evolve in the near term (a decade or less) that could have a major impact on the research university.
- To examine the possible implications of these technology scenarios for the research university: its activities (teaching, research, service, outreach); its organization, structure, management, and financing; and the impact on the broader higher education enterprise and the environment in which it functions.
- To determine what role, if any, there was for federal government and other stakeholders in the development of policies, programs, and investments to protect the valuable role and contributions of the research university during this period of change.

Our steering group met on numerous occasions to consider these issues. We visited major technology laboratories, such as Bell Labs and IBM Research Labs, and drew upon the expertise of the National Academy complex. In 2001, we convened 100 leaders from higher education, the IT industry, and the federal government, and several private foundations for a workshop at the National Academy of Sciences.

There was a consensus that the extraordinary evolutionary pace of information technology is likely to continue for the next several decades and even could accelerate on a superexponential slope. Photonic technology is evolving at twice the rate of silicon chip technology, with miniaturization and wireless technology advancing even faster, implying that the rate of growth of network appliances will be incredible. For planning purposes, we can assume that within the decade we will have infinite computer power, infinite bandwidth, and ubiquitous connectivity (at least compared to current capabilities).

The event horizons for disruptive change are moving ever closer. The challenge of getting people to think about the implications of accelerating technology learning curves as well as technology cost-performance curves is very important. There are likely to be major technology surprises, comparable in significance to the appearance of the personal computer in the 1970s and the Internet browser in 1994, but at more frequent intervals.

The impact of information technology on the university will likely be profound, rapid, and discontinuous—just as it has been and will continue to be for the economy, our society, and our social institutions. It will affect our activities (teaching, research, outreach), our organization (academic structure, faculty culture, financing and management), and the broader higher education enterprise as it evolves into a global knowledge and learning industry.

Yet, for at least the near term, the university will continue to exist in much its present form, although meeting the challenge of emerging competitors in the marketplace will demand significant changes in how we teach, how we conduct scholarship, and how our institutions are financed. Universities must anticipate these forces, develop appropriate strategies, and make adequate investments if they are to prosper.

Over the longer term, the basic character and structure of the university may be challenged by the IT-driven forces of aggregation (e.g., new alliances, restructuring of the academic marketplace into a global learning and knowledge industry) and disaggregation (e.g., restructuring of the academic disciplines, detachment of faculty and students from particular universities, decoupling of research and education).

Although information technology will present many complex challenges and opportunities to university leaders, procrastination and inaction are the most dangerous courses of all during a time of rapid technological change. To be sure, there are certain ancient values and traditions of the university that should be maintained and protected, such as academic freedom, a rational spirit of inquiry, and liberal learning. But, just as it has in earlier times, the university will have to transform itself once again to serve a radically changing world if it is to sustain these important values and roles.

Although information technology will continue its rapid evolution for the foreseeable future, it is far more difficult to predict the impact of this technology on human behavior and upon social institutions such as the university. It is important that higher education develop mechanisms to sense the changes that are being driven by information technology and to understand where these forces may drive the university. Because of the profound yet unpredictable impact of this technology, it is important that institutional strategies include: 1) the opportunity for experimentation, 2) the formation of alliances both with other academic institutions as well as with for-profit and government organizations, and 3) the development of sufficient in-house expertise among the faculty and staff to track technological trends and assess various courses of action.

To conclude, for the near term, information technology will drive comprehensible if rapid, profound, and discontinuous change in the university. For the longer term (two decades and beyond), all bets are off. As noted, implications of a million-fold or billion-fold increase in the power of information technology are difficult even to imagine, much less to predict, for our world and, even more so, for our institutions.

THE FUTURE OF THE UNIVERSITY IN THE DIGITAL AGE

The digital age poses many challenges and opportunities for the contemporary university. For most of the history of higher education, we have expected students to travel to a physical place to participate in a pedagogical process involving tightly integrated studies based mostly on lectures and seminars by recognized experts. Yet, as the constraints of time and space—and perhaps even reality itself—are relieved by information technology, will the university as a physical place continue to hold its relevance?

In the near term, it seems likely that the university as a physical place, a community of scholars and a center of culture, will remain. Information technology will be used to augment and enrich the traditional activities of the university, in much their traditional forms. To be sure, the current arrangements of higher education may shift. For example, students may choose to distribute their college education among residential campuses, commuter colleges, and online or virtual universities. They may also assume more responsibility for and control over their education. In this sense, information technology is rapidly becoming a liberating force in our society, not only freeing us from the mental drudgery of routine tasks, but also linking us together in ways we never dreamed possible. Furthermore, the new knowledge media enable us to build and sustain new types of learning communities, free from the constraints of space and time. Higher education must define its relationship with these emerging possibilities in order to create a compelling vision for its future as it enters the next millennium.

For the longer term, the future of the university becomes far less certain. Although the digital age will provide a wealth of opportunities for the future, we must take great care not simply to extrapolate the past, but instead to examine the full range of possibilities for the future. There is clearly a need to explore new forms of learning and learning institutions that are capable of sensing and understanding the change and of engaging in the strategic processes necessary to adapt or control it.

While the threats posed to traditional roles and practices by emerging information and communications technology may serve usefully as a warning shot across the bow of our institutions–particularly their faculties–university leadership should not be simply reacting to threats but instead acting positively and strategically to exploit the opportunities presented by information technology to improve the quality of education and scholarship. Technology will allow colleges and universities to serve society in new ways, perhaps more closely aligned with their fundamental academic mission and values. It will also provide strong incentives for building new alliances among diverse educational institutions, thereby providing systemic opportunities for improving the quality of higher education.

Hence, while college and university leaders should recognize and understand the threats posed by rapidly evolving information technology to their institutions, they should seek to transform these threats into opportunities for leadership. Information technology should be viewed as a tool of immense power to use in enhancing the fundamental roles and missions of the university as it enters the digital age.

REFERENCES

Attali, J., (1992). *Millennium: Winners and Losers in the Coming World Order*, Times Books, New York.

Barlow, J. P. (1994). *"The Economy of Ideas: A Framework for Rethinking Patents and Copyrights in the Digital Age"*, *Wired*, 2.03, March.

Bourne, J. (ed.) (2000). *On-Line Education Learning Effectiveness and Faculty Satisfaction*, Center for Asynchronous Learning Networks, Vanderbilt University, Nashville.

Brown, J. S. & Duguid, P. (2000). *The Social Life of Information*, Harvard Business School Press, Cambridge.

Christensen, C. M. (1997). *The Innovator's Dilemma*, Harvard Business School Press, Cambridge.

Daedelus (1996). *"Books, Bricks, and Bytes"*, 125, no. 4.

Deming, P. J. & Metcalf R. M. (1997). *Beyond Calculation: The New Fifty Years of Computing*, Springer-Verlag, New York.

Government-University-Industry Research Roundtable and National Science Board, National Academy of Sciences (1997). *"Convocation on Stresses on Research and Education at Colleges and Universities"*, Washington, D.C. <http://www2.nas.edu/guirrcon/>.

Kurzweil, R. (1999). *The Age of Spiritual Machines: When Computers Exceed Human Intelligence*, Viking, New York.

Moe, M. T. (2000). *The Knowledge Web: People Power–Fuel for the New Economy*, Merrill Lynch, New York.

CHAPTER 5

The ever Increasing Demands Made on Universities in the United States by Society and Politicians

Harold M. Williams

The public university is the focus of increasing demands by society and politicians and there is no doubt that this trend will continue. In fact, one can predict that new issues will arise, promoted by new advocates and critics, adding to the pressures.

THE DEMANDS ON THE PUBLIC UNIVERSITY

The public university is expected by its constituents to provide a college education for the greatest number. It is caught between two conflicting realities.

- The number of applicants has dramatically increased as the perception that a college education is essential to upward economic and social mobility has become more widespread among young people.
- At the same time, funding from the public sector is more limited given the increasing demands on public funding to meet society's various and pressing other needs. The consequence of greater and more diverse demand for access far in excess of state funding available to accommodate it presents an unprecedented crisis. For example, the demand in California is expected to increase in excess of 30 % by the year 2010, with no commensurate increase in funding. Nonetheless, the political expectation is that access will be maintained and education of at least the present quality will continue to be delivered.

Well into the 20th century, higher education consisted primarily of colleges and universities that were elite and predominantly religious. The rise of the research university, coupled with the enactment of the GI Bill at the end of World War II, fundamentally altered the role and presence of higher education in the United States. It went from being the limited privilege of the few to an institution of central importance to the economy and society, a center for research and for the education of any student able to benefit from it.

In the century just ended, the percentage of college graduates increased from 3 % to over 30 % of high school graduates. If the anticipated demand for access is met, that percentage will increase significantly. The challenge is how to meet that demand in order to afford students the increased economic opportunity and lifetime benefit of a college education.

Every state has the responsibility to assure its residents of an opportunity for college. With 78 % of college students enrolled in public colleges and universities, the state's involvement in higher education is significant and growing. State appropriations for higher education exceeded $63 billion for the academic year 2001-2002 (*Chronicle of Higher Education*, 2002).

Nevertheless, since 1980, the percentage of state spending represented by higher education has declined from 44 % to 33 % in fiscal year 1997, according to the United States Department of Education. Since the mid-1990's, this structural trend has accelerated and is expected to continue. Other priorities, especially health and welfare, human services, correctional facilities and K-12 education, have increased, at the expense of higher education.

At the same time, the cost of higher education continues to grow at a rate greater than inflation and, in an economic environment where welfare and health care have been fundamentally reordered and corporations in the private sector have gone through painful restructuring, higher education is perceived as unchanged and unresponsive.

THE CRITICISM OF THE PUBLIC UNIVERSITY

As higher education becomes an increasingly important public good, and as the competition for state resources makes it increasingly difficult to finance, it follows that the state in both political and social terms will be increasingly concerned about issues of access, quality and efficiency. Will all qualified students be accommodated? Will quality be maintained? How well is higher education using the resources provided by public funding and serving the needs of the state and its people? What is the return?

The criticism that higher education fails to deliver on its perceived responsibilities will become louder and the demand that existing funding be used more efficiently will increase. The issue of establishing priorities for available funding will become more pressing. Particularly in light of increasing public skepticism about how well higher education serves the concerns of its various constituents. Parents expect their children to be prepared for careers and a viable economic future, the state expects civic engagement from an educated citizenry that also contributes to economic growth; and the business community is looking for a skilled work force. The criticisms target a range of issues: graduates who are unprepared to enter the workforce and have no concept of citizenship; emphasis on research at the expense of undergraduate education; the quality of undergraduate curricula and teaching; policies on admissions and academic standards, grade inflation; failure to address the critical issues facing society, inefficient use of facilities, and costs continually rising beyond inflation.

THE RESPONSE BY HIGHER EDUCATION

Given that the pressures and demands of society and politics on the university are inevitable, the critical issue is how to respond in a way that preserves the most important and enduring values. What are these values, and what are the issues that brook no compromise? How can the university take the initiative to stake out a position and prevail? What can the university do to ameliorate the pressures, maintain its integrity, and still respond to economic and societal realities?

Tuition

Given the inability or unwillingness of the states to fund increasing costs adequately, tuition charges will inevitably be higher. It will become increasingly difficult for students from lower income families to gain access to the university, unless student aid is adequate and readily available. A study conducted by the Detroit News (2002) on the rising cost of higher education found only five states where all the four year public colleges are affordable for low income students and in many of those the students still need to borrow money to get by.

However, many students are from families able to afford substantially higher tuition. The state and the public university will need to consider moving from a low tuition policy for all, to one of high tuition for those who can afford it, while providing adequate aid to those who cannot. The effect would be that the educational "bargain" represented by the public university would be reduced significantly—though it need not be eliminated—and the cost to the individual student would accord with means.

Defining the Future

While raising tuition may cushion the financial pressure, it will not address the fundamental issue—indeed, it may divert institutional attention from doing so. The issue is that the university has not sufficiently defined its educational mission so that it can resist the pressure from external forces to follow the marketplace. Higher education is being dangerously pushed in the direction of market responsiveness, which can undermine its purpose. The future of the university will be determined by whether institutional changes are driven by the educational mission and are educationally justified or by the marketplace to capitalize on the latest trend.

Yet the marketplace cannot be ignored. Balancing between the two in order to protect the mission requires a level of leadership from within the university. Traditionally, the major developments in higher education in the U.S. have come from outside the higher education establishment, i.e. the Morrill Act land grant college legislation, the model for the contemporary research university, the GI Bill, and Sputnik. More recently, shared governance, the devolution of the university president from public intellectual to fund-raiser and the faculty's primarily loyalty to the disciplines rather than to a larger institutional vision, result in a lack of internal leadership and of address to the fundamental issues critical to the future of the institution. Sadly, the faculty's narrow focus not only keeps them from addressing the bigger picture, but also may lead them to delay or prevent movement or change in direction. While it would be far preferable that the public university be proactive in shaping its own future, will it be able to do so under the present leadership and governance structure?

If the university is to survive substantially as we know it, it will have to make its case more clearly and effectively. The university has difficulty articulating the basic values that justify its own existence. While the university tends to see itself as an end, the public sees it as a means.

What is the university's responsibility to our society? What is the place of higher education within the social fabric? What are the moral, political, economic, or other justifications for the university as an institution? Who is the primary beneficiary of higher education? Are universities instruments of public good or do they merely provide service to the individual consumer?

If the university does not answer these questions satisfactorily, someone else will, and the answers may compromise the university's definition of itself. How much is the public willing to pay for the public good, i.e. for activities that do not directly relate to students' education? If the public does not pay, who does?

What is a "College Education"?

A college education used to mean a general liberal arts curriculum, exposing students to diverse disciplines and general knowledge of literature, history and culture. But increasingly, students are customers, primarily concerned with finding a job after college and less committed to learning for its own sake and to learning how to think as one of education's primary goals. The late futurist, Herman Kahn, foresaw that one of the principal threats to progress in the postindustrial economy and the postindustrial society would be what he called "educated incapacity." He defined it as an acquired or learned inability to understand or see a problem, much less a solution. He predicted that this kind of functional handicap would increase in proportion to a person's academic education and expertise.

With many, if not most, students not pursuing a career in the subject of their major, and with less of a liberal arts education to provide a basic framework, we have college graduates without the skills to adjust to the learning needs of a working lifetime, much less in a position to meet the responsibilities of citizenship. This has important consequences for our country and our society. Has the idea of a college education become so open ended as to be all but meaningless?

If the university leaves its graduates generally unprepared for the responsibilities of citizenship, what will be the consequences? College graduates should be prepared to lead lives of civic engagement in addition to individual success. If we are ignorant of our history, government and the fundamental ideals and values that distinguish our society, we cannot be good citizens. Education has been the best predictor of civic involvement, and higher education now serves as the nation's most important common ground and is essential to the future of a democratic society.

Will the public university pick up the gauntlet and educate students for citizenship as well as for a life in the workplace? Will it redefine its mission to include opportunities for lifelong learning through non-degree offerings as integral to its programs? Or will the university remove itself from public life, isolate itself from the public interest, and leave the playing field?

The Public Research University

The university's research contribution in science, technology and medicine will continue to be of critical importance to a healthy economy. While the American research university is admired for its ability to create wealth through new ideas and technologies, it is criticized for failing to address the contemporary intellectual issues, human concerns and social problems of our society.

The need for financial resources will lead to an ever-greater emphasis on collaboration with industry and government in basic and applied research and exploitation of the economic value of commercialization of university-sponsored research. According to the Association of University Technology Managers, universities received more than 3,760 patents in 1999, earned at least $850 million in license fees, and formed over 300 start-up companies.

States are also encouraging public universities to turn their laboratories into engines of economic development, on the model of Stanford and Silicon Valley. They are investing significant funds in information technology, biotechnology and nanotechnology research.

Will the integrity of the university's research efforts be preserved as the researchers become increasingly involved with industry and the private sector? The issues and conflicts inherent to such collaboration are numerous and serious and will need to be resolved in order to further the growing collaboration while endeavoring to preserve the integrity of the university's role and contribution.

As the research of the public university becomes more commercial and involved with the private sector, how will the society and its politicians react to the perceived neglect of research on the issues facing society that cannot be commercialized?

The research university is a combination of two separate entities — a research institute and an undergraduate college or university. The research institute involves graduate students working essentially as apprentices as in European universities or American research laboratories. Undergraduate education, on the other hand, raises questions about teaching, learning and the meaning of general education as well as the social and political issues of access, diversity, equity, etc. As long as the research university chooses to offer undergraduate education, it will not be able to disengage itself from the issues facing higher education in general.

When it comes to how to allocate limited funds, political and social forces will press for the allocation to undergraduate education whereas the research university would place its priority on graduate education and research. This raises two questions. First, should a research university provide undergraduate education, or should there be a separation between the research "institute" with only graduate study, and the undergraduate institution? What would be the public funding implications of this? What is the compelling logic that combines undergraduate education with the research mission? Indeed, are they compatible? Second, and related, if the public research university maintains its role in undergraduate education, can it ever hope to compete with the private research university?

Given the pressures for access to undergraduate education and limited public funding, can a public research university any longer realistically aspire to compete with the private research universities? The pressures related to access and quality do not have the same impact on the private institutions. They are not under public pressure to increase access and, therefore, can apply the enormous growth in their endowments to improving quality. A study at the University of Illinois reported that the salary gap between full professors at the country's best private universities and its best public ones has grown from $4,300 in 1980 to $21,700 in 1998. The private universities can offer larger research budgets, smaller teaching loads and tuition reciprocity programs, which the report characterizes as "a quarter of a million dollar jackpot if you have three children." The article goes on to conclude that the nation's public universities are at risk of becoming training grounds for private universities with bigger check books. Are society and its politicians prepared to accept that, given the pressures for access and limited public funding, a public research university can no longer realistically aspire to compete with the private research universities?

Student Learning

A major challenge facing higher education is that it cannot tell the public, or politicians, anything meaningful about the most important result of a college education, i.e. what students learn. The tension between research and teaching, a faculty issue, detracts from this more important concern. The focus on teaching methodology rather than on what enables students to learn better is also misplaced. If the focus were on learning, the role of technology, of group learning and of other than the classroom lecture would be incorporated to the approach to teaching.

The view is increasingly expressed that higher education has an obligation to develop better measures of student achievement. The traditional measures of how much students learn — seat time and grade point averages — do not seem to satisfy employers, politicians or the public any more. They want to know more specifically what kind of competencies students have. Some say that degrees are already beginning to fade in importance in favor of transcripts that document each student's competence, including the specific knowledge and skills the student has mastered. If degrees become less important, how will the university continue to attract students in a world offering limitless educational choices? Why would a student stay in college for five years if the value of a degree gives way to a specific measurable competence? As an example of this trend, in 1998, the United States Congress passed legislation requiring all colleges wishing to receive federal funds for training teachers to submit a report documenting their graduates' performance on state licensing and certification exams. Although it may make sense when degree programs are specifically geared to job training, it is harder to visualize the measure of accountability for a liberal arts education with all its desirable diversity from one student to another. Could this becomes another nail in the coffin of the liberal arts education? If measures of accountability were to be part of the university's future, it would be important for the university to be part of their definition. If not, the concern about what is a college education and why it is a public good will have to be satisfied in some other way.

CONCLUSION

It is clear that, in view of the significant role of the university in modern society, demands upon it will continue to grow. These will be determined by changing priorities and needs of society itself, as higher education is increasingly perceived to be a right of the many rather than a privilege for the few.

It is crucial that higher education not wait for demands to be imposed, but rather try to anticipate the legitimate needs of the public and the politicians, so that society is satisfied without jeopardizing the educational integrity of the institution.

REFERENCES

Chronicle of Higher Education (2002). January 18.
Detroit News (2002). January 8.

CHAPTER 6

Universities' Responsiveness and Responsibilities in an Age of Heightened Competition

Luc E. Weber

INTRODUCTION

I t has become a banality to affirm that the world is changing at an increasingly rapid pace and that this affects the environment of all social, economic and political activities. Although perhaps less visibly, this evolution concerns also education, and in particular, the higher education sector and its institutions (Weber, 1999). However, the implications for the missions and the governance of higher education institutions, and in particular of research-intensive universities, as well as for national and even regional policies, differ significantly from those of other organizations, in particular business firms. If, in order to survive, firms have practically no alternative other than to be responsive to the changing environment, research-intensive universities should not only be *responsive*, but also *responsible* towards the community they serve, that is, they should protect the long term interests of society. Although they converge in the long run, these two sides of universities' missions can well be contradictory in the short run. Obviously, a period of rapid change, as we experience now, creates a growing tension between the necessities to be *responsive* in the short run and *responsible* in the long run. Whereas universities can often be blamed for being too conservative or even neglectful, in other words not responsive enough to the changing environment, they may also, under pressure, make decisions without paying due attention to their long term responsibilities.

This paper has two aims: first, to show why research-intensive universities have to be *responsive* to their rapidly changing environment, but also assure a long term *responsibility* towards society; second, to examine how the main characteristics of the changing environment are increasing the tensions between *responsiveness* and *responsibility*, making it more difficult than before to govern a university and to design a national or a regional policy. Without a clear understanding of the mechanisms of change, as well as of the missions of a university, it is hardly possible to identify what the correct attitude and policy should be.

Responsive and responsible universities

Whatever the nature and rhythm of change, there is a duality in the missions of universities. It is useful to consider the challenges in terms of two concepts: *responsiveness* and *responsibility* (Grin, Harayama & Weber, 2000).

On the one hand, universities are expected to be *responsive* to short-term needs of the private economy, the State and their main stakeholder, the students. This means that universities should respond to what society demands at any one time. This influence is in general positive: universities cannot pretend that they are the only institutions with knowledge and offer only what they like; they should pay careful attention to the aspirations and needs of their students, the economy and the public sector. Today, these pertain in particular to:

- rising enrollments, which is still the situation in many countries,
- safeguarding equality of access and encouraging the enrolment of underrepresented groups,
- maintaining the "purchase" price of education as low as possible,
- diversifying course contents and increasing the range of courses offered,
- guaranteeing efficient and transparent operations,
- all this while, of course, ensuring relevance and quality in teaching and research.

In addition, universities are expected to fulfill an ever-expanding list of missions that have less to do with teaching and research, and more to do with the provision of fundamental aspects of quality of life and general education. Meeting these multi-faceted demands is the "responsiveness" side of the role of universities. Universities should take these needs or requests very seriously as they are legitimate pubic demands (Glion Declaration, 1998).

On the other hand, while *responding* to society's needs and demands, universities have also to assume a crucial *responsibility* towards society. Universities are one of the oldest surviving institutions, clearly older than modern States. Moreover, they remain practically the only institution able to secure and transmit the cultural heritage of a society, to create new knowledge and to have the professional competences and the right status to analyze social problems independently, scientifically and critically. The great difference between being responsive and being responsible lies in the fact that, in the first case, universities should be receptive to what society expect from them; in the second case, they should have the ambition to guide reflection and policy-making in society. While universities excel at making new discoveries in all disciplines of science and technology, they must also scrutinize systematically the trends that might affect soon or later the well being of populations, and, if necessary, raise criticism, issue alarm signals and make recommendations.

It is precisely this responsibility that justifies why universities have been granted "autonomy", which is unique in the whole education sector, not to speak of other sectors or the State. This responsibility used to be a strong mission of the press; however, the political and economic pressures of our time push the media to be too responsive to the tastes of their audience, their government or the business world. Therefore, the responsibility of universities is even greater.

This responsibility, as well as the principles necessary to allow universities to assume them, has been repeated with strength by a thousand rectors and presidents of European universities gathered in 1988 in Bologna for the ninth centenary of the oldest university in Europe. In "The Magna Charta Universitatum" signed on this occasion, it is first of all stressed that Universities "must also serve society as a whole" and "must give future generations education and training that will teach them, and, through them, others, to respect the great harmonies of their natural environment and of life itself". Secondly, it is stated that "the university is an autonomous institution at the heart of societies" whose "research and teaching must be morally and intellectually independent of all political authority and economic power".

"Because society is changing, it needs references and frames for social, political and economic debate, construction of meaning, identity, and consensus on policies. The universities have a key role to play in providing these. We have noted that some of the duties that higher education is entrusted with can quite easily conflict with each other. In these cases, higher education must exercise its sense of responsibility vis-à-vis society, by adopting solutions that maintain and reassert the intellectual, ethical and social values on which it is built. This reassertion precisely constitutes one way of exercising its leadership role in society. It can sometimes mean selecting ways in which change should take place, sometimes encouraging and advancing change, but also sometimes resisting change" (Grin et al., 2000). These two responsibilities can obviously be contradictory in the short run, as the pressures of the market and of politics require from universities to respond to immediate needs or to business or political opinions which are too often basically utilitarian, reflecting short term, or even partisan needs, as well as sometimes temporary fashions, or possibly also the result of pubic hysteria in some particular topics such as nuclear power and genetically modified food. Therefore, it is crucial that universities have the freedom and the strength to pursue their search for knowledge away from undue pressure, political or financial, and to have the last word in designing their teaching or research programs. This does not mean that they should ignore their changing environment. On the contrary, universities have shown for centuries an extraordinary capacity for adaptation and change; otherwise, they would have disappeared. The reality for them is that they are situated at the center of forces, between the necessity to be responsive to the short term needs of their stakeholders and to be responsible for the long term interests of the society they are serving. In other words, a *responsible* society is also *responsive*, but in the long run, and universities incarnate the type of institution best suited to maintain this long term perspective, necessary for the society.

The tension between *responsiveness* and *responsibility* has been increased by the accelerating changing environment Hence, meeting the challenges of permanent change and engineering the corresponding changes require recurring arbitration between the requirements of *responsiveness* and *responsibility*. However, examining these challenges, it is difficult to escape a feeling of dizziness. "Seldom has any institution been required to meet so many challenges, each of them so demanding and specific in its implications, all at the same time. The State itself, of course, is one of those institutions that has to discharge a large number of complex duties, but the latter do not seem to be socially defined in such an exacting manner. Furthermore, the state apparatus normally enjoys the use of a wider range of instruments (not to mention authority itself) to act upon the situation; by contrast, the universities have much more restricted courses of action at their disposal" (Grin *et al.*, 2000).

CHARACTERISTICS OF THE CHANGING ENVIRONMENT AND THEIR CONSEQUENCES FOR UNIVERSITIES: AN ECONOMIST'S POINT OF VIEW

The economists' focus

Economists are, like the other social scientists, particularly interested in changes taking place in society due mainly to the process of economic growth and its main determinants, to demographic and social transformation, and to the changing political and economic organization of the world. They observe and analyze their impact globally on the standard of living of nations, the distribution of income and wealth between and within nations, as well as in a more focused manner, their impact on business and governments, regional development (at continental as well as national levels), on the labor and financial markets, on exchanges of goods and services and on the welfare of human beings. Even if they do not put as much emphasis on the question, they are also interested in the impact of change upon the world of education and research.

The key transformations of our time

The key events, the source of deep transformation, are well known: the collapse of the Communist regime and the apparent end of the Cold War, the intensification of scientific discoveries and breakthroughs, the revolution of the information and communication technologies, the liberalization of world trade of goods and services and the simultaneous creation of regional economic or even political power blocks, the increased mobility of tourists and workers, the ever growing divide between those who have and can and those who have not and cannot, as well as the demographic imbalances between West and East.

These events, as well as related ones, are generally quoted under one heading: globalization. The movement of globalization has multifold and deep political, economic and social consequences. To the economist (but this should also be true for political scientists and sociologists), by far the most important one is increased competition in all aspects of social, political and economic life.

This obviously concerns business firms. Big firms have to play globally to survive, and merge with other firms if they are not the right size. In merging, they try to reach some sort of monopoly position and also to exploit a situation of decreasing cost per unit of production or service, which might be originated by the growing importance of the initial investments necessary to market a new product or service. Under the increased pressure of the financial market, firms have also not only to secure their profitability, but to aim at a higher return on capital. Among the many consequences are that they have more than ever to employ a quality labor force, to implement good strategies and provide better goods and services, thanks to a greater incorporation of advanced knowledge in their products and services, as well as in the production process.

This concerns also the State and other governmental organizations. The climate of strongly increased competition is pushing the public sector to pay more attention to its efficiency, and less to social justice, nationally and internationally. This has led to the privatization of utilities like telecommunications, electricity, collective transport or even postal services and water services, as well as to the search for increased efficiency in the provision of public services.

The climate of increased competition affects deeply the relationship between States. The necessity to assure the competitiveness of a country has become one of, if not the first, policy priorities of many governments. It has led to the creation of regional alliances, the main aim of which is to increase the competitiveness of the alliance towards other leading countries or regions. This has certainly become the most frequently quoted target of the European Union in order to counter or to match the threatening economic, political and military hegemony of the United States, as well as the industrial capacity of Japan.

Globalization and the climate of severe competition that it provokes does not spare the university sector from transforming itself in order both to take advantage of new opportunities and to adapt its provision of services to changing needs. Three developments are essential, as are their immediate consequences for universities, in particular research-intensive universities, pushing them to be responsive without weakening their responsibility towards society. These developments are: first, that universities are increasingly confronted with competition; second, that their activity will be increasingly dependent on the business sector; and third, that they should respond to an increasing need to be critical towards some social, political and economic developments. In fact, there is a fourth impact: as the movement of change has accelerated, the governance of universities must significantly become more pro-active and requires more and more clear and unpopular decisions.

The increasingly competitive university environment

In many respects, universities used to benefit from a quasi monopoly situation. In countries like the USA or the UK, this is certainly true for the national university system, as the immense majority of students study within the country. The pool of recruitment becomes even regional for more professionally-oriented institutions. In continental Europe, despite the great visibility of the Erasmus and Socrates programs of the European Commission, there is still little mobility. The majority of students choose to attend an institution in their own city or region, and spend their whole study time in the same institution. This is going to change gradually, due to the great efforts made to create a European Higher Education Area as well as a European Research Area, and due to globalization. The main forces at work will strongly reduce the quasi monopoly situation of universities, in particular for teaching, which has always been more local than research. Although the increased competition has also an impact on research, we shall examine this question under another angle in the second point.

Regarding the teaching mission of universities, multifold developments are reducing the monopoly position of universities:

- The increasing demand of students to do part or all of their studies abroad and multinational agreements like the Bologna process in Europe, which aims at eliminating all administrative barriers to free movement from one university to the other and one country to the other over a ten-year period in order to create the European Higher Education Area (Bologna Declaration, 1999).
- The increased demand for continuing education, due to the fact that the length of validity of knowledge is decreasing rapidly and that everyone is now forced to change job several times in a professional life.
- The improved information from universities, which is the fruit of a broad genuine effort, and which is supported thanks to the elimination of time and distance made possible by Internet.
- The implementation of new technologies for teaching and research is at a starting point. If teaching has been done for centuries basically with the same chalk and blackboard, and with students remaining rather passive, the new technologies, in particular CD, DVD and Internet, will offer very attractive teaching material and methods locally or at a distance.
- The accelerating creation of new, more specialized, teaching institutions, some of them run as "for-profit" businesses, will increasingly provide on a location or at a distance attractive teaching programs, which can be completed more rapidly than in traditional universities or in parallel to a professional activity. This development is not yet significant in Western Europe, seems to speed up in the USA and runs at full steam in the East and Central European states, where, over a 10-year period, 600 so-called universities were created, for example, in Russia, and 180 in Poland. However, things are changing in the West too and the number of new, often very specialized, institutions will greatly increase in the years to come.

These developments will soon be considered as serious and even threatening competition for traditional public or private not-for-profit universities. It is therefore in the interest of the latter to react in order to improve their offer, in particular the relevance and quality of their programs and of their teaching methods. Moreover, they are pushed to do so by their governments and/or by the business world, which is fast to complain that universities are not providing the qualifications that they need.

It is precisely here that the tension between being responsive and being responsible appears. Yes, universities will more and more have to pay attention to the market, i.e., to treat their students as customers, in the sense that they have to serve their perceived needs and not only offer them what faculty pleases. The more the higher education market will become competitive, the more it will become transparent, and the easier it will become for students to choose the program and the institution best adapted to their needs and most prominent.

However, does this mean that universities should reduce or abandon the disciplines providing a general education without specific professional knowledge or that they should transform their teaching programs to make them more professionally oriented? They should not do so, because of their long-term responsibility towards society. If they were to do so, they would only promote disciplines like information and telecommunication technologies, life science, material science, business management and law. These sciences are critical for the competitiveness of the national business sector, but they are not the only ones. The welfare and cohesion of a society depends also on knowledge, the rate of return of which cannot be evaluated in terms of economic growth. This is obviously true for the humanities, as they contribute greatly to the timelessness of our cultural heritage. But it is also true for social sciences like sociology, political science or economics, as they help to understand the deep rooted transformations that affect society, as well as to pinpoint the sources of tensions and, consequently, to suggest policies to overcome them. In this context, ethical issues raised by the development of science, the consequences of economic development on the environment, or the increasing divide between those who have and can and those who have not and cannot, require that programs aim not only at providing knowledge to the students, but also a better general education and a sense of their responsibility towards the long term interest of society and not only the essentially short term targets of the business world.

Moreover, providing professionally-oriented programs might be quite tempting in disciplines like law, business or education. This would probably make it easier for young graduates to find a job. However, this would mean giving less importance to pure intellectual training and to the study of related, more cultural, disciplines, which will rapidly appear as a great loss, making it more urgent and difficult to correct afterwards. And more than that, as soon as one learns that half of graduates, after 5 to 10 years, do not have a professional activity narrowly related to the discipline they studied, one is forced to realize how much the university provides, above all, intellectual training and not fixed knowledge that can be used indefinitely.

The increasing financial dependence and decreasing intellectual autonomy

The second main consequence of globalization, and of the climate of increased competition which follows, is to decrease the financial independence and intellectual autonomy of universities. In the nineteen sixties and seventies, universities benefited from a generous budget allocation from the public sector, because politicians were convinced that higher education was a crucial investment. In the eighties and particularly in the nineties, the State financing of public universities changed significantly on both sides of the Atlantic. Universities have become the target of increasingly numerous critiques emanating principally from right wing politicians and from the business world, and their budgetary allocations have suffered deeply from the higher priority given in particular to social security and redistribution policies, health and agricultural policy. This competitive climate has a negative impact on the quality of teaching and condemns the leaders of research laboratories to search for compensatory or additional financial resources outside of the public sector, entering increasingly into contracts with industry.

Moreover, the ever increasing complexity of the research topics and the sophistication of research methods contribute to make research more and more expensive in many fields: sophisticated equipment and the creation of multidisciplinary teams or networks have become indispensable. More than ever, advanced research in the hard and life sciences, and even for some projects in the social sciences and humanities, is strongly impeded by tight budgetary constraints. On the industry side, the transfer of new knowledge into new products is also becoming a real challenge. The hard competitive environment makes it crucial to shorten the lapse of time between a scientific discovery and its application to a new product or a new service.

These two developments push industry and universities to collaborate more closely and to create a true university-industrial complex. There are clear gains of trade for both parties:

- Industry is generally lagging behind in basic research and avoids investing in free basic research because its financial return is hypothetical. On the other hand, the world of universities and independent research laboratories provides an immense reservoir of knowledge, with leading teams in most fields of scientific enquiry.
- Industry finds it generally easier to secure the necessary financial means for investigating what it considers as a priority.
- In addition to that, the challenge of the transfer of technology makes it important that there is a much closer collaboration between fundamental and applied research, in other words that university and industry create together effective knowledge networks.

The developments in public universities described above can also be observed, however in less dramatic terms, in private not-for-profit institutions, which are numerous in the USA and hardly existing in Western Europe. They have also to collaborate much more closely with the business world in order both to secure adequate funding and to have the opportunity to remain an important, or better, a leading actor in some domains of research.

The fact that both parties are more and more demanding, as they both gain from the collaboration, explains the intensification of the university-industry links and cooperation. However, the deep difference of culture, missions and aims of these two types of organizations makes of this complex a "marriage against nature", which is very difficult for both parties for the following reasons:

- Industry is inevitably thinking in terms of return on research investment. The necessary condition is therefore to commercialize the result of successful research, in other words to become the private owner of the knowledge discovered. As industry is providing the financial means to the complex, it is in a position to impose a great deal of the contractual conditions.
- University and independent research laboratories, on the contrary, have a mixed motivation between the sheer disinterested curiosity to do a piece of research on a topic and hopefully make discoveries which will make them known, and the necessity to find the funding to buy expensive equipment and to secure the payroll of the research staff.

In summary, the reinforced competition, which makes it crucial for industry to have a knowledge lead and for universities to find the necessary financial means for their research activity, despite a lack of adequate public financing, places the university in the middle of its dilemma between being responsive and being responsible. The dangers are obvious as universities may try to reach their research objectives, more or less whatever the means. This implies mainly two things: universities are tempted to accept more contracts in applied research than they should, and/or they could accept contractual conditions that impinge upon their academic freedom. Moreover, some laboratories could be tempted to arrange somehow the results of their research to please their sponsors or would accept to reserve the results of their research for their sponsors, which would then commercialize them if they are of interest to them (Nature, 2001). This might be profitable for the laboratory and/or the researcher, at least in the short run, as in the long run, he (or she) could also lose his (or her) reputation. But, it is against centuries of tradition where research results are a pure public good, made available to everyone through scientific publications or communications.

Moreover, the consequences may be even deeper for the whole institution. Berdhal (2000), chancellor of the University of California Berkeley, has observed that the fact that only some sectors of the university are partners of industry creates many serious imbalances and tensions within the institution.

Increased need for universities to be critical observers of society

The fact that universities benefit from a large autonomy regarding the choice of their staff, the object and content of their teaching and research, does not guarantee that they take advantage of this unique privileged position to be pro-active as a fine and critical observer of societal developments. Conservatism, conformism, as well as the lack of consciousness of independence, a lack of civil courage, or even of financial independence, mean that the academic community is often too hesitant or too passive to embrace serious societal questions, therefore not assuming fully the responsibility society has given to it in guaranteeing autonomy and academic freedom.

This is rather disappointing, because the key transformations described above, and in particular the climate of fierce competition affecting business, governments and the media, are dramatically increasing the need for people or organizations (why not universities?) to act responsibly towards the long-term needs of populations. This implies above all that they should pay more attention to societal developments and, if necessary, be more openly critical.

The challenges for universities and research are immense and include: the increasing disparity of wealth and access to education and new technologies at the world level, the inversed relationship between population and economic development, the degrading environment, the increasing importance of money and capital as a criteria of political and social decisions, the incapacity of the world to solve long lasting regional conflicts, the relative inefficiency of social policies and of the provision of public services. These questions, and many others, would deserve more attention on the part of researchers and a larger place in the teaching of many disciplines. Obviously, universities cannot change the facts, even force changes of policies. However, researchers, thanks to their scientific training, are in a better position to foresee the consequences of different trends and to see the possible interdependence between separate events. Moreover, the freedom and independence which is given to the academic community allow it to express publicly its views, and, if these are critical towards an enterprise or a government, with much less risk than for anyone being part of the business or political word. This is why that it is part of the responsibility of a university to watch critically what is going on and issue alarm signals if necessary.

CONCLUSION

Universities must permanently strive to adapt to their changing environment, in order to be more responsive to the needs of the community they serve. They have been granted autonomy to allow them to be responsible towards society by identifying present and forthcoming difficulties and helping to solve present and future problems.

However, there is obviously a tension between these two aspects of their fundamental mission. The recent development of the world, in particular the phenomenon of globalization and the climate of increased competition it creates, is increasing this tension within the university between responsiveness and responsibility. Not only is it ever more important that universities take seriously their responsibility as the main critic of social, political and economic development, it is also important that they avoid to be fully submitted to the increased pressures of the market and of politics, among other reasons, to secure alternative sources of funding.

If universities are unable to balance their two missions, they will lose the justification for the autonomy granted to them, which, in the long run would be a great loss, not only for them, but for society as a whole. This is why the fact that universities spend relatively little time on societal issues, compared with more abstract questions, deserves to be at the top of the list of criticisms addressed to universities today—not the fact that they are not responsive enough to the short term needs of society.

REFERENCES

Berdahl (2000). *The Privatization of Public Universities*, Conference given in Erfurt, Germany, 23 May.

Bologna Declaration (1999). (*http://www.unige.ch/cre/activities/Bologna%20Forum/Bologne1999/bologna%20declaration.htm*)

The Glion Declaration (1998). *The University at the Millennium*, The Glion Colloquium, Geneva and Los Angeles. (*http://glion.org/text_en.htm*)

Grin, F., Harayama, Y. & Weber, L. (2000). *Responsiveness, responsibility and accountability: an evaluation of university governance in Switzerland*, Dossiers 2000/4f, Office fédéral de l'Education et de la Science, Berne.

Nature (2001).Vol. 409, 11 January.

The Magna Charta Universitatum (1998). Bologna.
(*http://www.unibo.it/avl/charta/charta12.htm*)

Weber, L. (1999). Survey of the Main Challenges Facing Higher Education at the Millennium. In Hirsch, W. Z. & Weber, L. E., *Challenges Facing Higher Education at the Millennium*, ACE/Oryx, Phoenix and IAU/Pergamon, Oxford.

PART II

• • • • • • • • • • • •

Lowering Walls inside
the University

CHAPTER 7

Strategies to Foster Interdisciplinary Teaching and Research in a University

J. William Schopf and Werner Z. Hirsch

INTRODUCTION

In tomorrow's world, universities, and in particular those with a strong research orientation, will face a new environment that carries new challenges to their traditional way of doing business. Already, the Information/Technology (IT) Revolution is having a profound influence on universities, as is the ever-greater complexity of social and scientific problems facing today's world, developments that can only be expected to become more pervasive in the future. In the near-term future, both the society in general and academia's prime product, the students it is charged with educating and helping to develop into knowledgeable contributing citizens, are likely to make new and increasing demands on the teaching, research, and public service functions of universities. In response, universities will of necessity be forced to adjust to a decidedly new set of circumstances. Some such changes are already underway. In particular, the past decade has witnessed new emphasis, evident at virtually all levels of academia, on multidisciplinary, or even truly interdisciplinary, teaching and research. While this new thrust carries with it the promise of providing importantly increased understanding of problem areas that previously "slipped through the cracks," it embodies also the potential for unforeseen deleterious results—the production of students, of teaching programs, and of research results that, though broadly based, are intellectually shallow, lacking in the depth of knowledge fundamental to proper understanding.

There can be little doubt that throughout the academic world, walls between disciplines and departments are becoming increasingly permeable. But as this development takes place, as universities organize themselves to carry out this nontraditional role, it presents a potential peril that can be offset only if institutions of higher education find means to avoid sacrificing their commitment to in-depth excellence while at the same time meeting their mission to educate effectively the future leaders of society and its citizenry. It is easily predictable that the societal and scientific problems of tomorrow will be even more complex and multifaceted than those of today. In recognition of this, academia has begun to prepare the next generation to address such problems by establishing programs, both in teaching and in research, that combine knowledge of two or more of the conventional disciplines with an understanding of how such multidisciplinary concepts intermesh. In the future, the crossing of boundaries between conventionally academic disciplines, and comfortably doing so, will have become commonplace. The prime questions are: how best can this transition be eased, and how, in a university setting, can the potential pitfalls inherent in interdisciplinarity be avoided?

THE CASE FOR (AND AGAINST) INTERDISCIPLINARITY [1]

Most would agree that the defining mission of a university is to contribute to the understanding, advancing, and transmitting of knowledge and culture. In carrying out this all-important (if daunting) task, those who are engaged in the effort have carved the huge territory of human knowledge into a set of seemingly discrete subdivisions, each of which have themselves developed into independent fields, the various disciplines that define a university's departmental structure. Yet in many cases, these supposedly disparate fields are not truly independent. The natural world, for example, is made up largely of biology, chemistry, and geology—but taken together, not as separate entities as they are represented by the traditional departmental structure. Indeed, the real world is composed neither solely of the "life sciences" nor of the "physical sciences"—it is an interlocking mix of both. Yet on almost all university campuses, the natural sciences are divided into these same two great tribes—each with its own "homeland" and each with its own set of lore, rules, and a common understanding of what, for it, constitutes "good science." With the exception of an occasional student (but almost never a member of the faculty), few forage from one homeland into the other. There can be no doubt that this tribalism makes things simpler for all—learning the

---

1 This section has benefited from discussions with Professor Daniel Kivelson, Department of Chemistry & Biochemistry, University of California, Los Angeles.

ropes in a single subject is far easier than grappling with many. And it is undeniable that this structure has returned great dividends; the strategy of learning more and more about less and less has worked well. But in the process, a price has been paid, and the cost has been particularly high for those studying the natural world, where the life and physical sciences and their numerous component disciplines are intimately interconnected. In essence, the academy has fooled itself by partitioning Nature into intellectually manageable units that because of their constrained focus have served to inhibit understanding of how the units come together to form the whole. Over time, traditional boundaries both of fields and of departments change, sometimes leading to the emergence of new hybrid disciplines—biochemistry, biophysics, geochemistry, geophysics, and biogeology are good examples. The need for and very existence of such hybrids well illustrates the inability of traditional academic structures to address adequately important interconnections in the world around us.

The boundaries defining departments and the subject matter that each explores have developed over a long history. Fostered by the traditional conservatism of the academic community, this structure seems to have been maintained largely by a commitment on the part of its practitioners to protect their discipline-defined turf and, hence, to preserve the status quo, even when the structure thus protected has come to be outmoded and less than optimal. By and large, dividing lines between departments have been based on a combination of discipline and methodology, a means of subdivision that brings together faculty and students having shared interests and that enables them to communicate with one another and to formulate a coherent core curriculum. But, as intellectual interconnections between disciplines become increasingly recognized as salient and important, the traditional departmental structure and its inherent lack of flexibility will more and more be seen to be wanting. Turf fights, already not uncommon, will become an accepted cost of academic life; conflicts between nontraditional young turks and the firmly ensconced old guard will increasingly become prevalent.

A lack of flexibility is not the only weakness of the traditional departmental structure. Indeed, some would argue that an even more pernicious aspect is that it fosters rampant overspecialization. As such, it is unable to accommodate, let alone encourage, promising efforts in areas overlapping among two or more interrelated disciplines. This is not to deny that throughout much of the post-World War II period, markedly specialized single disciplinary endeavors have produced beneficial results, both in education and in research. Yet, again, a price has been paid. It is of course important to "see the trees" and even to know the workings of a given tree in cell by cell detail; but, if in that process the forest and the surrounding landscape are overlooked, then only a miniscule part of the picture will have been viewed and important understanding—knowledge easily accessible were relevant questions asked—will have needlessly been lost.

In many respects, the discipline-defined departmental structure has served academia well. But it has also failed, most notably in its lack of flexibility and its inherent drive toward ever-increasing specialization. Clearly, a move away from a structure based solely on single-discipline methodologically defined studies to one that is more flexible, inclusive, and that provides elbow room for interdisciplinary broad-picture investigations, is very much in order. Our call for such a move echoes Glion colleague, Hans van Ginkel's catchphrase that "life is not divided into disciplines," a perceptive admonition to which we would add that great intellectual challenges are not neatly divisible, either.

In recent years, interdisciplinary teaching and research have been encouraged widely, and though this plea has obviously been heard, the product generated can most generously be characterized as mixed (a not unlikely outcome of single discipline-trained faculty having to retool themselves to deal with ancillary disciplines in which they previously had little knowledge and only limited interest). Yet such interdisciplinary scholarship can be, and in some universities already has been, stimulated in major ways. Viewed from the vantage point of an economist, on the input, "supply side" of the equation are included such factors as the rapid increases in scientific knowledge and technology (developments part and parcel of the IT Revolution), as well as those in molecular biology, biotechnology, and the exploration of space. And on the outcome, "demand side," is the increasingly growing need to educate government officials, scholars, and the population at large so that they can more fully understand and effectively formulate solutions to already emerging problems of tomorrow's world. In such a view, both the supply side and the demand side of the equation constitute stimuli—one pushing and the other pulling toward the same result—and taken together, they are likely to be reinforced by other pressures emanating from the body politic, as well as an overall concern that the system be cost-effective. The world of tomorrow will require broad-gauged men and women, knowledgeable not only about particular "trees" but about the forest such trees comprise and the landscape in which they thrive—contributing members of society who can see and understand the interconnectedness of the world around them and adapt themselves readily to new circumstances and challenges.

Let us hasten to stress, however, that it would be an error to view interdisciplinary scholarship as something totally new, some novel, heretofore unimagined breakthrough in higher education. Indeed, breadth of knowledge has been a prime goal of educated societies over the millennia, just as breadth of scholarship has been a principal goal of universities worldwide. Even today, the modern "Renaissance Scholar", broadly educated and able to apply that breadth to great multifaceted problems, is both a hallmark and icon of Western cultural imagery. The Leonardo DeVincis of the past, and the Carl Sagans and Stephen Jay Goulds of modern times, have distinguished themselves by being able to draw on the knowledge of a number of disciplines and to bring together and interconnect the diverse concepts and insights those disciplines encompass.

So, breadth of knowledge is not an attribute newly valued in academia. Nor are collaborative efforts among scholars and scientists of differing backgrounds. What is new is the drive toward more and more productive interactions and a realization that however desirable such interactions may be, they are actively discouraged by the current department-dominated structure of universities and can be accomplished effectively only if the interacting parties are conversant with, and appropriately knowledgeable about, the differing disciplines involved.

Given the current structure of universities, and the deeply ingrained loyalties of university faculty to their disciplines, it is abundantly clear that the transition toward increasing interdisciplinarity must take a form that is consonant with the continued important role of departments in university affairs. Indeed, the transition can be eased only if it is seen to enrich departments in ways they regard as beneficial and supportive, rather than being viewed as irrelevant fluffery that occupies faculty time and effort to no good cause or, even worse, as a tangible threat to the continued existence of the department structure. In other words, the transition should be evolutionary, rather than revolutionary, based on the realization that because universities are ruled largely by what Frank Rhodes, President emeritus of Cornell University, has aptly termed "the tyranny of the department," to gain a foothold any new structure must not only coexist with departments, but must be viewed by faculty as being overtly supportive of departmental goals. And though to some traditionalists it may seem counterintuitive, it is in fact true that in many respects interdisciplinary programs can benefit departments in important ways. Carried out properly, such programs can not only broaden and deepen departmental perspectives and enhance the effectiveness of departments by playing the role of an effective symbiotic partner, but they can also provide a useful vehicle for exploration of previously uncharted territory, of intellectual *terra incognita* that, if explored successfully, can lead to establishment of new departments and new structures that benefit the university as a whole. Altogether, heightened interdisciplinarity can help universities not only to better prepare students for the world of tomorrow, but by advancing the dynamic character of a university can help it to achieve its full potential.

A few caveats, however, are in order. Although interdisciplinarity clearly is not a passing fad, it is not a panacea, either. Teaching and researching subjects at the heart of a discipline should, and no doubt will, continue to be basic to the finest in higher education, even as the crossing of academic boundaries gains increasing acceptance.

For the good of the academy, and the benefit of the society as well, the steps taken in this new direction should be deliberate, measured, and—above all—designed to assure academic excellence. As universities pursue this new path, academic rigor must continue to be the gold standard by which such institutions are judged. A great challenge will be to foster a sound flexible balance between the already well-founded efforts within a given discipline and the newer ones that seek to expand the scope of inquiry in an interdisciplinary direction, and at the same time assure the maintenance of rigor and excellence in both.

WHAT CAN WE LEARN FROM EXPERIENCE TO DATE?

While attempts to introduce full-blown interdisciplinary programs in a university setting have to the present met with rather mixed results, it would be a mistake to overlook the lessons learned. Indeed, some such arrangements have worked reasonably well, though given the single-discipline backgrounds of most of the faculty involved it would be naive to imagine that in the not-so-distant future even better programs having far better results will be in the offing. The successes with which we are most familiar are those that have taken place at our home institution, the University of California, Los Angeles (UCLA). There, for example, the departments of Chemistry and of Biochemistry, both widely regarded as world-class, merged some years ago into a single interdisciplinary department. Similarly, the Departments of Botany and Zoology merged to become Biology, later to be reorganized into two decidedly interdisciplinary units, the Departments of Organismic Biology, Ecology & Evolution and of Molecular, Cell & Developmental Biology. In other instances at UCLA, members of previously established departments have expanded their allegiances to form the core of new interdisciplinary organizations. Examples include the Molecular Biology Institute, the Institute of Geophysics and Planetary Physics, the Institute for Social Science Research, the Institute of the Environment, and numerous centers (e.g., the notably interdisciplinary Center for the Study of Evolution and the Origin of Life). Other universities have established similar structures—for example, in 1996, Stanford University founded its Center for Comparative Studies in Race and Ethnicity, an interdisciplinary unit that by 2001 had attracted from various departments nearly one hundred faculty engaged partly or wholly in interdisciplinary teaching and research (Stanford University Center for Comparative Studies in Race and Ethnicity, 2001). Examples such as these are not uncommon and often involve faculty of the professional schools—of business, planning, engineering, medicine, law, and education—, teachers and researchers who themselves have backgrounds in diverse academic disciplines.

Thus, while at least limited opportunities for interdisciplinary teaching and research already exist in many universities, in years to come more and more internal walls will be breached. The shift toward greater interdisciplinarity must be gradual rather than abrupt, a natural evolutionary development that reflects the changing times rather than being a structure put in place by fiat. Indeed, for such a transition to come to fruition, it cannot simply be mandated by a university's administration or by such bodies as a Board of Regents or a state legislature. Rather, the impetus for such a shift should come ideally from those who are destined to carry it out—the teaching and researching faculty. In great American universities, it is usual for the decision-making process to be shared by administrators and faculty, an arrangement termed "shared governance" that is not only common but is universally accepted as being necessary for the assurance of academic excellence. Thus, now, at the beginnings of the transition, the collective wisdom of the administration and faculty, both, should be marshalled to define an appropriate balance between single discipline and multidisciplinary units, and to begin to chart a path by which this balance can most fruitfully develop in the future. Because a university administration controls the purse strings of the institution, advocacy of the transition by university administrators will prove crucial to its success. It will be important for the university administration to assume a strong leadership role by providing a climate favorable for faculty to engage increasingly in interdisciplinary endeavors. But, as in virtually all changes in academia, even more significant is the faculty's support, since it is they who will need to rethink their traditional allegiances, retool themselves to effectuate the change, and, most importantly, carry it out.

Encouragement of the changes envisioned can take a variety of forms. Perhaps the least intrusive and least controversial approach is that involving activities of individual faculty who seek out others in one or more other departments with whom to carry out interdisciplinary teaching and/or research. A second approach can be more formal and take place under the aegis of an umbrella organization, such an an interdisciplinary institute or center, giving rise to collaborative activities in teaching and/or research that break down traditional barriers. Under an arrangement such as this, faculty members may either retain their departmental association or be members solely of the interdisciplinary unit (the latter affiliation being preferable in some situations, inasmuch as it serves to negate misgivings rather common on the part of departmental colleagues that those involved in such endeavors have "divided loyalties"; are engaged in scholarship beyond the scope the departmental faculty can comfortably evaluate; and are likely to be "jacks of all trades but masters of none," scholars less able than full-fledged department members). In this regard, young faculty are particularly vulnerable. Because the youngest in academia are often closest to the society from which they have only recently emerged, they are also often the most insightful about the emergent trends and needs of that society. But if such young members of the academic community fear that formal association with multi- or interdisciplinary endeavors or units may interfere with their promotion within a department, they may be reluctant to assume such a risk—an understandable position that nonetheless is detrimental to themselves, the future of their university, and the society in general.

ACADEMIC BORDER CROSSING IN UNDERGRADUATE EDUCATION

Despite the recent upsurge in multidisiplinary or interdisciplinary activities in academia—or, perhaps because of this very upsurge, and the threat it is perceived by some to represent—we use here the more neutral phrase "academic border crossing," a terminology that we hope can be viewed as devoid of the negative connotations associated with the more commonly used buzzwords. As stated earlier, it is our view that the world of knowledge is not neatly divided into distinct compartments, the academic disciplines that form the basis of modern university departments. Thus, it seems to us that a forward-looking undergraduate education requires that significant parts of its curriculum be interdisciplinary, and we see this as being particularly important both at the beginning of undergraduate education—when a student is most likely to be open to new ideas and new ways to explore the world and can most profitably be made aware of the interconnectedness of the various disciplines—and at the conclusion of that education, preferably in a small-class seminar format where the disparate fields and facts to which a student has been exposed can be brought together into a meaningful whole. And we think also that such courses must be taught by a new breed of faculty who have been educated in, and are themselves knowledgeable about, the diverse disciplines involved. In short, we believe that in this or some similar manner, universities can begin, now, to prepare students to function effectively in tomorrow's ever-changing multifaceted and increasingly complex world, where they will be confronted with a need for understanding knowledge that often crosses today's traditional disciplinary boundaries.

Such a curriculum would begin to give students the sort of solid foundation they are certain to require, not only in their professions but for their development as productive, contributing citizens equipped to lead richly satisfying lives. Toward this end, we think that undergraduate education should expose students to the knowledge and workings of the natural and social sciences, as well as the humanities and the arts. In particular, undergraduates should in the sciences become acquainted with paradigms, tools, and their analysis, so they can appreciate their usefulness and apply them as critical thinkers; in the humanities, be introduced to and inspired by "primary sources," particularly works of enduring value; and in music and the visual arts, be stimulated to value and understand how the beauty and aesthetic power of such creative contributions give life meaning and pleasure. Moreover, we think it important that programs be established to enable students to gain appreciation of the defining values, necessary rigor, and inherent excitement of participating in a learning/discovery environment in which they are stimulated to make a logical assessment of qualitative and quantitative information and to define not only the contours but the center of challenging problem areas and to engage in their analysis.

Further, and while we envision an appropriate undergraduate curriculum to be based on, and in great measure to be keyed to the core knowledge of the basic disciplines, we think that it is imperative also for it to include thematic courses that emphasize intellectual interconnections. A pilot program that involves just such an approach has recently been introduced at UCLA, a Freshman-Year "Cluster System" of courses that received its impetus from a 1997 faculty-administration study that sought to update and improve undergraduate education. Its centerpiece is a First-Year Cluster Course, a integrated, team-taught, interdisciplinary series of three courses to be taken sequentially over the three academic quarters of the Freshman year. Students are permitted to select one such course from among ten or more offered each year, with each cluster being devoted to a broad theme.

This endeavor provides a vehicle for emphasizing such fundamental intellectual principles as the interconnectedness of the traditional academic disciplines; the importance to sound scholarship of critical thinking, integrative learning, and use of primary scholarly works; the overriding need to an educated person for mastery of basic communication skills, both verbal and by use of the written word; and the value to a participatory democracy of cultural diversity, pluralism, equality of opportunity—citizenship. It is common for these courses to present the fundamentals of as many as four or five traditional disciplines, providing an introduction to the subject matter that forms the basis of various departments and thus serving as a potent departmental "recruiting tool." Moreover, at their best, the courses are designed to stimulate the students' imagination and intellectual creativity, factors crucial to their development that too often have been largely expunged during pre-university years by its emphasis on memorization and "learning to pass the test." During the first two academic quarters, instruction consists of lectures by faculty taught in concert with graduate student-led discussion sections and intensive English composition tutorials. In the final, third, course in the sequence, each student enrolls in one of a number of small "satellite courses"—each of which focuses on topics that radiate from a cluster's theme and which most commonly take the form of a "graduate level" seminar experience but, depending on the subject matter, may involve hands-on laboratory studies (e.g., in clusters centered on aspects of biology, chemistry, or computer science) or involve extensive fieldwork (e.g., in those focusing on geology or archaeology) (University of California at Los Angeles, 1997).

A prime example of such a cluster course is that entitled "Citizenship and Ethnicity in the United States," a course that takes as its central problem the question of what it means, and has meant, to be an American. (The faculty involved approach the subject from perspectives that link sociological and anthropological theory with literature interpretation, constitutional law, and historical analysis. In preparing and teaching the course, faculty with backgrounds in sociology, anthropology, ethnic studies, English, foreign languages, law, and history collaborate in an effort that emphasizes the points of convergence, as well as those of conflict, among their various fields).

Other such recent examples have focused on the immigrant experience (from the perspectives of literature, anthropology, law, history, and various social sciences); the theater as a projection of political power (an examination of Greek drama, French drama during the reign of Louis XIV, and the Chinese dramatic tradition—a cluster taught by faculty from theater arts, history, political science, classics, and various language departments); the meaning and nature of democracy (involving faculty from the arts, humanities, social sciences, and law); and a cluster entitled "Origin and Evolution of the Cosmos and Life" (encompassing subject matter extending from the origin of the universe to the origin and evolution of life, including humans, and taught by faculty with expertise in astronomy, geology, atmospheric sciences, biochemistry, genetics, biology, and anthropology—a subject and faculty quite effectively bridging the gap between the physical and life sciences).

Altogether, these cluster courses are designed to stretch students' minds beyond the confines of any single discipline and to encourage them to consider a more global and inclusive view of key events, phenomena, concepts, and methods. The joint efforts of the faculty involved emphasize both the points of intersection and of opposition among the various fields considered. Where such theory, methods, and findings diverge, students can learn how different approaches may complement one another and investigate the implications of the intellectual dissonances that separate them." (University of California at Los Angeles, 1997).

Teaching of interdisciplinary cluster courses can and often does have far reaching side-effects for the faculty participating. In particular, their horizons can be broadened markedly, as they become increasingly knowledgeable about other interrelated disciplines and the concerns, theories, and methods of analysis typical of ancillary fields. Moreover, the teaching experience can have a "spillover effect" by fostering useful interactions that lead to productive interdisciplinary research collaborations. In short, given the balkanization typical of today's universities, involvement in such a program can have decidedly beneficial results.

MOUNTING A UNIVERSITYWIDE EFFORT TO FOSTER ACADEMIC BORDER CROSSING

As we suggested earlier, it would be both inappropriate and unwise for a university president or other high administrator to mandate the adoption of interdisciplinarity; in most excellent universities, any such order "from on high" would be met with unrelenting stiff resistance. Indeed, in American universities, shared governance has become such a major driving force that no self-respecting faculty would permit itself to be so dictated to. This is not to suggest, however, that the aims of the university administration are not only salient, but are crucial to the success of such a venture. In fact, an administration convinced that such a move is in the best interest of its university could—and we think, would, if that administration is sensitive and perceptive—offer its faculty enticing opportunities and funding that would encourage them to voluntarily join and participate in such an undertaking. Encouragement would have to be public, advocacy strong, and funding would have to be at a level high enough to command the attention of a critical mass of the university's most distinguished faculty.

However, raising the overall interest of a university faculty in interdisciplinary undertakings requires more than public encouragement and more than mere funding, even at a generous level. The leadership of the university must generate enthusiasm—for key faculty, in particular, an enthusiasm probably best shown by example. Thematic focuses must be found and effectively articulated. Faculty of the highest quality, especially those having multiple talents and diverse interests, must be attracted to the program, so that the bar delineating success is set high and academic excellence is upheld. Success will be facilitated as the value and rigor of the program become generally appreciated across the university, and as departments see both that their participating faculty have benefited from involvement in the program and that students emanating from it are appreciably more perceptive, insightful, and better able to tackle the standard academic disciplines than those who have not participated.

Given what we perceive to be academia's certain answer to the needs of tomorrow's society—an inexorable shift toward increasing emphasis on interdisciplinarity in university education—yet coupling that perception with what we view to be a natural reluctance on the part of departmental faculties to embrace this changing emphasis, we suggest that special impetus may be required to bring this change to fruition. In particular, it seems to us that the change could be facilitated, and encouraged to occur in a way that would assure the success both of departments and of new interdisciplinary initiatives, were a structure established to coordinate, guide, and fund faculty-initiated interdisciplinary incentive centers. The principal goals of such a coordinating unit would be two-fold:

- To foster increased interdisciplinary collaboration among faculty of diverse academic disciplines, both in undergraduate and graduate teaching and in scholarly research, and to thereby break down long-established departmentally defined barriers.
- To foster innovation in education and research by encouraging dissemination of understanding about, and investigation of, emergent fields of knowledge, novel areas of inquiry that do not fit comfortably into the traditional discipline-defined structure.

To attain the first goal, faculty from diverse departments could construct courses and teaching programs that bring together, "coalesce," traditionally disparate areas of inquiry, and by doing so, show the interrelatedness of such areas and the commonality of the various approaches needed to achieve firm knowledge of the subject matter addressed. Such team teaching would pay special attention to the interconnections among the disciplines involved, and the emphasis of the course and curriculum thus constructed would be thematic rather than primarily methodological. The same would hold for the collaborative research, where such coalescence of investigative efforts by faculty and graduate students from diverse backgrounds would be fostered. In both teaching and research, work at the peripheries of the traditional disciplines, and in their many areas of overlap, would be emphasized and encouraged.

Attainment of the second goal—that of stimulating deeper understanding and active investigation of areas of knowledge that because of their very newness are far removed from the heart of the traditional disciplines—would be more difficult. Yet progress in this direction is achievable, if the right set of people from the right set of disciplines can be brought together at the right time and place. Clearly, there would be a need to engage faculty who represent diverse disciplines. But the faculty involved would also have to be able to "think out of the box," able to identify emerging fields, to place those fields in the context of a future that is as yet unknown, and on such bases to outline how academia might best prepare for that future, however it develops. (Clearly, this is asking a lot. Many academics are reasonably skillful at thinking about and understanding the past. But what is required here—a matter of looking toward the future—is a rare talent. Still, it is just such thinking that academia now needs. The future is sure to be different from the past or present, and academia must adjust. Those universities that have the foresight to now become prepared will have placed themselves in a position to make a difference in the years to come.) Difficult and as unorthodox as such thinking may be, the intellectual adventure it entails—crucial to the ability of academia to respond to the needs of tomorrow's world—could be encouraged by administrative funding of novel thematic undertakings that represent promising terrains for future intellectual development.

Initially, arrangements toward such ends would necessarily have to rely on voluntary participation of the faculty involved and be understood to be both experimental and (in terms of normal university operations) relatively risky. Thus, we suggest that from their inception, such arrangements be viewed as pilot projects, programs from their start are established as having firm "sunset clauses" that call for their disestablishment at dates fixed. From the outset, therefore, such programs would have only a temporary charter, and could not become permanent fixtures of the university structure. And though formally disestablished at the end of their tenures, if rigorous and thorough review were to show that one or another of these centers had during its existence proved all but indispensable to meeting the goals of the university (or, perhaps, if it had attracted sufficient extramural funding to justify its continued existence), it would be permitted to evolve into a new more permanent unit—the relatively few such projects judged worthy of having permanent status would become transformed into regular academic units, departments or some other construct more consistent with future university organization. An arrangement such as this carries the potential for no less than a rebirth of higher education, for providing a mechanism that not only copes with but enhances in an appropriate and innovative way the need of academia to adjust to the changing world.

Other requirements of the arrangement we envision include a symbiotic relation between any such newly established construct and existing departments; a robust mentoring of students who join faculty in exploration of the novel, "risky," research areas involved; participation of faculty of the highest quality; and sufficient funding to support the enterprise. One example of such a program is a recent undertaking at the University of California, Irvine, which addresses the novel question of whether—and if so, how and in what specific ways—music contributes to development during childhood. Broadly interdisciplinary, the research carried out has involved physicists, chemists, psychotherapists, musicians, and others. Additional examples could be cited (e.g., a study at UCLA of the policy implications of genome research, which brought together geneticists, ethicists, biochemists, psychologists, political scientists, and economists), but the point seems clear—as the title of this volume suggests, the walls of academia are tumbling down; like a tsunami, emphasis on interdisciplinarity is the wave of the future; universities that have the foresight to now become prepared will have placed themselves in a position to make a difference in the years to come.

REFERENCES

Stanford University Center for Comparative Studies in Race and Ethnicity (2001). *News Letter*, Spring.
University of California at Los Angeles (1997). *General Education at UCLA—A proposal for change*, Los Angeles, June 12.

CHAPTER

Opening up Departments

Lucy Smith [1]

INTRODUCTION

" T raditional disciplines... impose constraints on broader inquiry. Strong departments, for all their benefit—may restrict the aims and limit the scope of critical investigation." These wise words are taken from the Glion Declaration (1998). The division into faculties, departments and disciplines is not God-given, and as Hans van Ginkel has pointed out, life is not divided into disciplines. If the universities wish to contribute to the development of society—which most universities expressly state that they do—they have to deal with the major societal issues. And all the great challenges that the world now faces, like sustainable growth, migration and refugee problems, provision of health care, the inequality of North and South, globalisation, big-city problems, make it necessary to have an interdisciplinary and/or multidisciplinary approach in the analysis of problems and issues, in teaching and research, and in working life.

Further, new developments, either in the society or in research, may lead to the formation of new subjects across the boundary of two existing subjects, or lead to new definitions of borderlines within a discipline or between disciplines. An example of formation of a new subject is molecular biology, which was created between genetics and biochemistry, but also involving physics and chemistry. Thirty years ago, it did not exist; now it is a well-established discipline, with its own methodologies, journals, scientific societies, etc. The new discipline can then be said to be the result of cross-disciplinary research and co-operation. In Norway, we talk about the so-called hyphen-disciplines, like socio-biology or bio-informatics, which are now emerging in steadily

---

1 I thank Dr. Ken Edwards, who has read a draft of this article and given valuable comments.

growing numbers. After a while, when the new discipline is firmly established, the hyphen will probably disappear.

An example of traditional borderlines becoming less meaningful is the main border between public and private law—formerly considered almost as an iron curtain in European law. This borderline is now less clear, and somewhere practically disappearing. Public law principles, which often originate even from international organisations, play a part in the framework and evaluation of business contracts, whereas public entities more and more seek to promote their aims by use of agreements in the market instead of official directives.

Steven Chu (2000), a Nobel laureate in physics, noted recently: "Our strength and our weakness is the departmental structure. The department is the guardian of its field. It trains students and promotes intellectual excellence. But the departmental structure means that we must carve up all intellectual pursuits into quasi-well-defined segments". Many of the recent reforms, new research and study programmes and new interdisciplinary projects demonstrate, in my opinion, that the disciplines and faculties are not always perceived as a straitjacket. More often, it will be budget restrictions that are the main obstacle.

The organisations into departments or faculties will vary from institution to institution, and from nation to nation (the concepts in themselves do not have the same meaning in the different countries); they are more or less constructions that at particular times have appeared functional to the individual institution. Consequently, I will not in this chapter restrict myself to the opening up of departments; my theme is opening up traditional boundaries, be it boundaries between disciplines, departments or faculties. The theme has relevance both for research and teaching, and I will first look at the research, before discussing the content of the study programmes.

RESEARCH

In research universities, research is the basis of the teaching. Traditionally, it has been the teaching that has decided the main structure of the university, not research. The division into faculties was linked to the professional (vocational) studies, like medicine, law or theology. The modern research university emerged in the latter part of the nineteenth century (Wittrock, 1993). But as research gained importance and was becoming equal with teaching, it was the researchers who decided the curriculum inside each discipline. What should be taught was—and still is—to a great extent determined by the interest of each faculty member, and sometimes quite specialised interests. So if the research is primarily monodisciplinary, there will also be primarily monodisciplinary curricula and teaching.

Research across existing disciplinary boundaries can be conducted in different ways, either by a team of researchers from different disciplines or by a single researcher who has knowledge or training in two or more disciplines. It will often involve several people from different disciplines working in parallel, with more or less interaction between them. Sometimes it involves very close interaction, where the boundaries between disciplines are crossed and a new understanding developed. It is common to distinguish between three types of research involving several disciplines. These definitions were introduced by the OECD in 1972:

- Multidisciplinary research: research where there is autonomy of the different disciplines, and where the research does not lead to changes in the existing disciplinary and theoretical structures.
- Interdisciplinary research: research which involves formulation of a uniform, discipline-transcending terminology or common methodology; co-operation within a common framework shared by the disciplines involved.
- Transdisciplinary (or cross-disciplinary) research: research based on a common theoretical understanding and accompanied by a mutual interpretation of disciplinary epistemologies.

Interdisciplinary research is very often used as a common term for all three types of research across the traditional disciplines. The problem with the OECD definition is that it does not offer a term that encompasses all three types. In the following, I will therefore do as has been done by others; I will use the term interdisciplinary research to refer to all three. When I use interdisciplinary in the restricted sense, I shall place it in inverted commas.

Most research programmes across disciplines will belong to the two first categories: transdisciplinarity research is looked upon as more difficult to obtain. It may sometimes be difficult to decide when the transdisciplinary co-operation has resulted in a new discipline.

Interdisciplinary research is connected with several problems. One problem has been quality and the assessment of quality. There have been many examples of interdisciplinary research that are regarded as superficial and not up to the accepted standard of academic excellence. (One reason for this may be that interdisciplinary research is quite often policy-driven applied research, with expectation of quick results.) But, there have also been examples of interdisciplinary research that has not been assessed in a satisfactory way. This is connected with the general problem of who shall judge the quality of interdisciplinary research, and by what standards. The problem may be that the accepted reviewers of research and publications are likely to come from existing disciplines and find it difficult to assess the standards of interdisciplinary work.

There is still a rather widespread scepticism within the traditional research communities towards interdisciplinary research. It is also a fact that interdisciplinary journals generally have a lower status than the other academic journals, at least initially. The interdisciplinary research and their journals seem to live their own life without the traditional disciplines paying heed to either. An example is area-studies specialists, who to a very limited degree have published in the major journals of political science (Political Science & Politics, 2001). My own experience is that researchers from both law and economics often will be sceptical when other social scientists venture into their fields. They believe, and not always without reason, that people from other fields will not master their methods. One thing that has surprised me is often what seems to be random choice of reference literature, especially when one single researcher is conducting an interdisciplinary project. Some social scientists have the same scepticism towards economists, but partly for other reasons: "They study behaviour, but ignore motivation, conceptualisation and culture. They have an obsession with precision above relevance and realism. ...Economists too often acquire a superiority complex with reference to other social sciences." (McNeill, García-Godos & Gjerdåker, 2001). The scepticism between the natural sciences on the one side, and the social sciences and humanities on the other, will be even more difficult to overcome. Economics will, in many ways, be in between these two cultures.

Interdisciplinary programmes will have a greater chance to succeed if they are built on strong disciplinary research. Consequently, it will usually be desirable for a researcher to train and work in depth inside one single well-established discipline before turning to interdisciplinarity. Only then will he or she obtain the necessary experience in research standards and the reputation as a researcher of high quality. The standing of the involved researchers will of course also in itself have a bearing on the reputation of an interdisciplinary project. We have all seen examples of how an interdisciplinary research or study programme will be more easily accepted when initiated by a researcher of high reputation in one discipline. Having worked in depth with another discipline, a researcher will, however, have developed certain methods and a certain language, and it will often require a great effort to be able to have fruitful co-operation with researchers from another field. Interdisciplinary research is obviously more time consuming than monodisciplinary research. And so far, conducting interdisciplinary research has seldom been an advantage in an academic career, which means that many ambitious and promising researchers will be hesitant of venturing into interdisciplinary projects.

Behind research across disciplines is not only a quest to understand complex societal problems; the aim will usually also be to resolve or contribute to the resolving of such problems. Research across disciplines will often be aimed more at problem-solving than publishing. It will frequently be part of a large framework program initiated from funding agencies and/or policy-makers, sometimes governments, with the intention to solve special problems. For the researcher in this type of applied research, there will often be a difficult balance between social relevance and academic quality. It seems to be a rather widespread opinion that the results of large programmes initiated by policy-makers have not always be in proportion to the money spent. Probably it has first of all been these types of "interdisciplinary" or multidisciplinary projects that have led to the rather mixed opinions regarding interdisciplinary research. Experience has shown that this type of research will have the best chances to succeed if it is researcher-initiated and based on teamwork between two or more researchers with a firm standing in their own field (Schopf & Hirsch, 2002).

It is a general opinion—at least outside the universities—that the university faculty usually are very loyal to the traditional disciplines, and that although most universities now emphasise—at least in public—the importance of research and teaching across the disciplines, nothing much is happening in this field. There is some truth in this, but there are great variations, from discipline to discipline, and from university to university. Quite a number of universities now organise themselves in a way to encourage interdisciplinary research. Some do this by eliminating the faculties, or having a few very large faculties and instead organising their activities around "themes" (an example is Lindköping University). Virtual solutions make interdisciplinary research possible without changing the organisational structure of the university. Universities like these regard interdisciplinary collaborations as a plus in the academic career.

Almost all European universities now have centres that promote an interdisciplinary or at least a multidisciplinary approach, both in research and teaching, like centres of women studies, of development and the environment, of human rights and so on. Sometimes these centres belong to a faculty, sometimes to a department, and sometimes they exist outside and alongside the faculty structure. There are good reasons for having these types of centres inside the faculties. The "pure" faculties must get used to having interdisciplinary or multidisciplinary activity within their walls. The problem will often be that the universities are building up new units without reforming the traditional ones. These centres have often been met by considerable resistance from the established disciplines, because they will entail draining of both personal resources and budget.

Crossing the discipline border seems appealing to many young researchers and teachers, maybe because the challenges that make interdisciplinary work necessary, are new and exciting. Quite often, though, lack of resources is the great obstacle when the university leadership wishes to encourage an initiative to start a new interdisciplinary project.

STUDY PROGRAMMES

Teamwork is getting more and more important, both in research and in working life. One reason for this is the enormous cost of some types of research. Genomics, where most scientists work in groups, is an example of this. But it is also because of the great complexity of the problems the world is facing to day. Employers also ask for people who are able to work in teams. Interdisciplinary activities will most often involve teamwork. This must have consequences also for the way students work. It is important that the students acquire the ability to work in teams, also with people from other disciplines. They must be able to make problems and solutions from their own field intelligible to people with another background, and to understand and also to appreciate other methods than their own to approach a problem. These should be basic requirements. It is also an advantage if the students combine two or more disciplines in their study programs, but it should be a requirement that all the students study one discipline in some depth.

A student will normally have a much stricter timetable than a researcher. It is therefore a clear limit to how broad a student can be within a normal university and consequently there will be fewer possibilities of real interdisciplinary study programmes. There is a difficult balance between the wish for breadth and interdisciplinarity on the one side, and the requirement of in-depth and structured studies on the other, especially as regards the Bachelor degree. At the same time, there is a pressure in many countries for shorter studies. One way to include both teamwork and interdisciplinary studies in the Bachelor degree will be to let the students do an interdisciplinary project in their last term. It is my belief, however, that multi- and interdisciplinary teaching is more appropriate at the Master level than for a Bachelor degree. In the undergraduate studies, the intellectual requirements of the rigour of a well established discipline are crucial; provided this has been achieved, there will be more room for interdisciplinary studies in a Master degree.

Many European universities now offer multi- and/or interdiciplinary Master degrees. The European Master degree programs differ considerably in length, profile and purpose. There are degrees for further specialisation, broader competencies, professional preparation or preparation for doctoral studies. Efforts are now being made to achieve a greater coherence in the nomenclature of postgraduate degrees and to distinguish between the different types.

Liberal Arts and professional studies

In most continental European universities, an important dividing line runs between the professional studies that are organised in fixed study routes with built-in academic progression, and the non-professional studies with the so-called liberal arts degrees. The liberal arts degrees are only to a limited extent organised in fixed and organised study routes. They may in some ways be compared with the Bachelor degree in the United States.

Traditionally, there have in most universities been rich opportunities for the students to combine different subjects in a liberal degree. In a faculty of humanities, the students usually may combine different disciplines like history, languages and religious studies. In a faculty of natural sciences, the students study for instance biology, chemistry and physics. Traditionally, the subjects chosen in one degree will all be within one faculty/department (this depends of the definition of departments), and usually the students will move from one institute (department) to another when they start a new subject. The different subjects are in these cases taken in series, and the approach does not imply "interdisciplinary" studies; the degree or study programme will rather be multidisciplinary. There are also many multidisciplinary courses that involve taking two or more subjects in parallel, like, for example, the Cambridge Natural Science Programme. Many European universities now also offer an interfaculty degree, where the students combine subjects from different faculties, for example physics, biology and philosophy, law and languages.

The words "faculty", "department" and "institute" have different meanings in different countries. What in Scandinavia are institutes, will in the U. K. and the U. S. often be departments (like a department of chemistry). Faculties in the U. S. will often be larger entities than in Europe (like the Faculty of Arts and Science at Harvard), and the departments may be compared with the Scandinavian institutes.

The problems inherent with such a flexible, multidisciplinary "cafeteria" model (some are talking about a "boneless" model) are apparent and acknowledged. It has been criticised for atomisation of subject matters and for undermining sequential learning. In the American universities, there will always be defenders of a core curriculum, as we have seen recently at the University of Chicago, where there now will be a reduction of the famous "common core curriculum". "They want to attract not only more students, but less brainy students who will make more money and give it to the university", a professor from the university complains.

A university course shall ensure both academic depth and breath. But, within a limit of three years, this is not easy to combine, and at least it requires a more strict structure than one will find in many lower degree study programs today. I am aware that the new slogan is "more freedom of choice to the students to set up their own study program." The sense behind such a slogan will of course depend on the actual situation in the different institutions. It is my experience, however, that there is a limit to how much freedom the average student wants, at least the undergraduate student. I have seen from surveys that many students prefer the firm structure they often will get in the state colleges to the bewildering, manifold choices they may meet in the traditional universities. This will of course depend on the maturity and personal aims of the individual student. My answer would be that we should offer the students several choices of structured studies with progression, but also with elective parts. One must try to accommodate both the requirement of progression and intellectual development and the freedom of choice. But for me, the first is more important than the last. One could, however, also have an offer for the atypical students who wish to construct academic paths of their own, with combinations that seem unworldly and purely academic.

Our challenge in the undergraduate studies is to develop in all students a taste for independence and critical thinking. This is not an easy task in a setting with limited money per student, combined with stronger demands for efficiency, relevance and an increasingly diverse student population. And it will not be possible if the student does not study in depth one discipline.

As a rector, it was my goal to make the liberal arts degree more structured, with a progression, core courses and a more restricted choice of electives, and with a mandatory thesis, preferably project-based. In a way, this is a step backwards when it comes to freedom of choice for the students (and some of the students protested against this). For me, the main point in this connection is the progression and intellectual development, preparing students to become independent critics of a discipline. This is not easy to secure with a more or less unregulated system of credit accumulation. It was also a goal to make the students more employable, both after the first and second degree.

There are still in many European universities long study programmes with rather inflexible and monodisciplinary curricula. But several countries have either recently reformed—or are in the process of reforming—their degree structure. In the message from the European universities to their ministers at the Salamanca Convention in 2001, it is stated *inter alia*: "There is a broad agreement that first degrees should require 180 to 240 ECTS points [three to four years] but need to be diverse, leading to employment or mainly prepare for further, postgraduate studies. Under certain circumstances, a university may decide to establish an integrated curriculum leading directly to a Master degree." There is, however, a clear trend in Europe towards a three-year Bachelor.

The professional studies are traditionally integrated studies, with a continuous progression in subsequent, often mandatory courses, and with a more restricted choice of electives. Sometimes, they also contain a required general education component. These studies are often inflexible, with few possibilities of choosing subjects from other fields. In many countries, there exists a need for more flexibility and freedom of choice.

Traditionally, two of the oldest professional subjects, law and medicine, have been introvert and self-sufficient, closed, not to the society, but to other disciplines. Now the faculties feel a strong pressure to opening up. In a Swedish national evaluation of law studies from 2000, the law faculties are criticised for a low degree of interdisciplinarity, and they are recommended to enlarge their contact with other faculties, and to increase the possibilities for the students to choose non-legal courses. I feel certain that many other European law faculties could meet with the same criticism.

In most European countries, the study of law lasts from five to six years, with medical studies lasting about the same. This is quite different from the system in the U. S., where professional studies like law and medicine start after the bachelor level, and without any special requirements as to the content of the bachelor. The American J.D.s will thus have achieved an all-round, liberal education before they start Law School. This is not the case with the Scandinavian law candidates, and they do not get such education in the Law School (nor at high school, like, for example, French students do.) But, within a framework of five or six years, there should be room for a semester of non-legal studies, like languages, economy, psychology or other fields.

The reorganisation of law studies at the University of Oslo a few years ago illustrates how a professional discipline can be made more open. The main purpose of this reorganisation was to make it easier to combine parts of law studies with other disciplines and studies. The law study now consists of two parts. The first part is divided into two courses of minimum one year each (60 ECTS credits), one in private law and one in public law. Each of these courses may be combined with non-legal subjects as part of an interfaculty degree, a bachelor. It is, for example, quite common to combine the course in public law with courses in political science or economy. The second part of the law study, the professional part, is of minimum three and a half years. Of these, one and a half year is an elective section, where the student can choose among around 30 subjects. Parts of both the mandatory and the elective sections may be taken at universities abroad. The students also get credits for non-legal courses, but only half of the credits of the course in question.

This is an example of a system that makes it possible to combine law with other studies, and I suppose that there are other law schools with similar arrangements. What characterises the system of the Law faculty at the University of Oslo is, however, that we understand well enough that other faculties find it useful to study law, but we do not really encourage our own law students to take non-legal subjects—which I think we should do. Languages, economy and psychology are examples of subjects that may be very useful to combine with law.

Credit systems and modularisation

A growing number of European higher education systems have adopted systems for the transfer and accumulation of academic credits. This makes opening up much easier. All credit systems are seen as compatible with the European Course Credit Transfer System (ECTS), which is based on student workload. ECTS was developed in the wake of the European Union programmes for co-operation and mobility in higher education. But it will also be an important tool to reform universities' curricula and to facilitate multidisciplinary study programmes.

There are still problems to overcome with credit transfer between systems made up of modules, compared to systems that are organised in integrated studies and continuous academic progression in subsequent, obligatory courses, which have to be followed in more than one semester. There are, however, very few studies where it will be impossible to organise a system of credits, even in the professional studies. It is, for instance, now more and more common with elective parts in this type of studies, and these elective parts can easily be taken in another discipline, at another faculty or another university for that matter. Modularisation is also now introduced in a growing number of universities. In this connection, it should be emphasised that there is a difference between a credit transfer system and modularisation on the one side and an accumulation system on the other. Since it is the university that decides to validate study programmes and award a qualification, credit-based curricula are not incompatible with a structured, progressive study programme.

Restructuring of higher education systems

An example of the reform process we now witness in many European countries—partly based on the Bologna process—is the reform of the Italian higher education system. This system has been quite conservative and inflexible with few possibilities of multi- or interdisciplinary study programmes. The whole education system is now dramatically reformed. The university studies have been changed in the direction of the "Bologna system" with a three-year bachelor degree at the base. One important change is the flexibility, both in the plurality of courses of different length, which can freely be juxtaposed, and in the adoption of the credit system, built upon the ECTS system. These changes will make it easier to offer interdisciplinary study programmes, "elements that are very important in the contemporary world of work" (Modica & Stefani, 2002).

Interdisciplinary study programmes, some examples

There are now all over Europe many examples of innovative thinking in the structure of study programmes, also within traditional structures. There are many reform projects, several of which are built on some type of matrix organisation, with a co-ordination of activities across established structures, and with independent leadership. Here are some examples.

The ESST Master degree is transnational and transdiciplinary. The European Inter-University Association on Society, Science and Technology (ESST) is an association of universities that jointly teach and research in the field of social, scientific and technological developments. Universities from across Europe are members of the association, which is registered as a non-profit making organisation in Belgium. ESST has been running a Masters programme in 'Society, Science and Technology in Europe' since 1994. This degree — "Society, Science and Technology in Europe" — aims to develop informational resources, analytical skills and conceptual frameworks for researchers and students in technological change and innovation. The course is designed to provide post-graduate training for academics of all backgrounds: social scientists, engineers and humanities scholars. The approach is interdisciplinary, based on recent results from studies of science/technology and economy/society. The course aims to apply such research to the social and economic analysis of innovation, to strategic decision-making and management of sciences and (new) technologies, to ethical issues in sciences and technology, and to political and cultural analysis of modern science- and technology-based societies. The teaching of the Masters course is carried out by teachers at the member universities (and by teachers exchanged between the universities) and involves active participation by people from industry and engineering, as well as policy-makers from all over Europe.

An example of a study programme that meets the needs of the new society and therefore appeals to young scholars is the programme Corporate Governance, Contracts and Incentives at the Centre for Business Research, Cambridge University. One current research programme focuses on ethics, globalisation and regulation. It studies the business ethics issues raised by globalisation, the incentives for increasingly large, multi-national firms to be ethical, and the ways in which public policy might be altered to encourage more socially responsible behaviour by businesses—particularly in the developing economies, where bribery and child labour are all too common. This programme brings together researchers from law, economics and management studies.

Interdisciplinary informatics is a transdiciplinary degree at the University of Oslo, where a general course of informatics is combined with a choice of courses from other faculties, like social sciences, law, pedagogy. As regards informatics in general, it will usually be both a discipline of its own, often with a professional degree, and an important part of other disciplines and degrees.

Economics is, in the same way, becoming a part of several interdisciplinary studies, either forming a new subdivision, as part of a multi-disciplinary program, or in connection with interdisciplinary study programmes. Environmental economics is one example.

Economic analysis of law has expanded dramatically in recent years. Law and economics is especially strong in the United States, but many European law schools also have law and economy courses. At the Law faculty in Oslo, these courses are mandatory. There are several journals of law and economics, and there are law and economic associations in Europe, North America and Latin America. Still, as Richard Posner has pointed out, there are few judges and lawyers who seem to be aware of this scholarship and are using it actively in their practise. And in most European law schools, a very small part of the established faculty members are using law and economics in their scholarship. However, it is interesting to note that that many of the PhD theses in the law faculties these last years have been wholly or partly on law and economic character. The task for these young scholars will now be to convince lawyers and judges that law and economics is an important tool and a useful supplement to traditional law.

The national health services are having great problems in most European countries, with the combination of growing demands and a shortage of resources. Thus, there is a great need for result-oriented leaders with competence in medicine, economy, financial management and modern leadership. A tailor-made bachelor and a master for leaders in the health service is now being established in a few European universities. This is an example of how the universities can meet new needs of the society by a co-operation between the departments.

Human rights is an interdisciplinary and multidisciplinary field, with researchers primarily from law, philosophy, political science and anthropology. Many universities have a Centre of Human Rights. In other universities, human rights are part of the curriculum in the individual faculties with more or less co-operation between the researchers from the different disciplines. It is a field, however, where co-operation between the different milieus is absolutely necessary, and experience shows that it may be very fruitful to combine different academic approaches to problems, and sometimes even establish new structures. In a centre of human rights, the co-operation between the different disciplines will perhaps most often be multidisciplinary, but there are also many examples of real interdisciplinary research. In my opinion, however, it is still to early to consider human rights as subject/discipline of its own. The teaching of human rights will be both monodisciplinary, in the individual disciplines, like law, philosophy, social science and anthropology, and interdisciplinary in centres or programmes.

CONCLUSION

There is no doubt that in most European countries it is politically correct—among politicians and research foundations and funding agencies, but also among university leaders—to call for more study programmes across the traditional disciplines. A lack of resources and a conservative culture may be a hindrance to achieve this, and in some universities it seems that the institutes and departments have not to a sufficient degree been able to develop new study programmes and courses across disciplines. It is obvious that not all European universities have the required capacity for change. But, in some cases, the scepticism towards all these demands for interdisciplinarity from the funding agencies and political authorities may be sound, especially if it will be achieved at the expense of the necessary basic research in established disciplines.

However, as I have tried to show above, there is more innovative thinking in European universities, both in research and in teaching, than most people seem to be aware of. Many of the new initiatives involve interdisciplinary activities. There are, in almost all the universities, individual leaders who are thinking anew, and there are hundreds of examples of new interdisciplinary study programmes—more or less successful, it might be added.

Some think that ICT will solve all problems, also those that follow from division into disciplines and subjects. George Haddad (2000) writes in an article: "Teaching must quickly integrate the transdisciplinary dimension. Indeed, the compartmentalisation of disciplines made necessary in the 19th and 20th century by needs of progress of knowledge, will quickly give way to a new approach which enables one to grasp what transcends the different disciplines and links them in a common dynamic. The perception of complexity and totality will be made possible through new communication and information technologies."

Few university heads will have such a radical view on the possibilities of the new technology. The new technology has an immense influence in what is happening at the universities at the moment, and it will have an even greater influence in the years to come. But still it is only a tool. Let us not forget our history and our responsibilities: "the university is the trustee of the European humanist tradition." (The fourth fundamental principle of the *Magna Charta Universitatum* of the European universities.)

In contrast to the above quotation from Haddad, I now cite Joseph Bricall, keynote speaker at the Salamanca Convention of Higher Education Institutions in March 2001: "Humanism had a pervasive influence on all disciplines, and their teachers. Its dissemination helped universities give a meaning to the unity of knowledge, envisaging different disciplines as part of knowledge taken as a whole. This humanist tradition also needs reintegration into present day reality, if our world is to cope with the fragmentation of specialised demands for studies and research".

The division between disciplines will not always stay the same, and it will sometimes be diffuse, but it will always be a necessary tool in research and teaching. "Academic departments based on disciplinary fields of knowledge will go on being important, their disciplinary competence is essential, too valuable to throw away, and they have much power to protect their own domain." (Clark, 1987). The point is that the disciplines and the departments must not "impose constraints on broader inquiry".

Whether or not the faculties or departments will survive in the future, I do not know. Most likely, they will survive in most institutions, while some already have eliminated them, and others will do the same. The main point is that departments are not enough; the universities need another way to group academic work in order to take care of the interdisciplinary initiatives and activities. Most universities have also in the last decades taken a number of initiatives to organise research activities across the established structures, *inter alia* through the formation of centres of excellence or strategic areas with forms of network organisations.

The strength of a comprehensive university is exactly that it is comprehensive, that it has a breadth of subjects that makes it possible to offer to the students a wide choice of different fields, and a possibility to choose between them, also in combination. "Universities will play a major role, provided they are adaptable organisations and comprehensive institutions rather than highly specialised niche players." (Nuesch, this book). Each researcher and each student must not necessarily be interdisciplinary. But all universities must be both. They must be able to offer to the individual student and to the researcher the possibility of addressing difficult problems in an interdisciplinary way, and to do in-depth disciplinary research and training.

REFERENCES

Bricall, J. (2001). Keynote address to the Salamanca Convention of Higher Education Institutions, European University Association, Brussels and Geneva.
Chu, S. (2000). "Interdisciplinary Research and your Scientific Career", *The Chronicle of Higher Education*, September.
Clark, B.R. (1987). "Creating Entrepreneurial Universities", New York.
Glion Declaration (1998). The Glion Colloquium, Geneva and Los Angeles.
Haddad, G. (2000). "University and Society: Responsibilities, Contracts and Partnerships", in Neave, G. (ed.), *The Universities' Responsibility to Society*, Pergamon, Oxford.

McNeill, D., García-Godos, J., & Gjerdåker, A. (2001). *SUM Report*, no. 10, Oslo.

McNeill, D. (1999). "On Interdisciplinary Research: with particular reference to the field of environment and development", *Higher Education Quarterly*, Vol. 53, no. 4, October.

Modica, L and Stefani, E. (2002). "The 2000 Reform of University Teaching in Italy", Document from The Italian Rector's Conference to the European University Association Council.

Nuesch, J. (this book). "Scientific Advances and the ever more Complex Challenges facing Society", in Hirsch W. Z. & Weber, L. E. (eds.), *As the Walls of Academia are Tumbling Down*, Economica, London.

OECD, (1972). *Interdisciplinarity: Problems of Teaching and Research in Universities*, Paris.

Political Science and Politics, (2001). *The Future of Area Studies*, December.

Schopf, J. W. and Hirsch, W. Z. (this book). "Strategies to foster Interdisciplinary Teaching and Research in a University", in Hirsch W. Z. & Weber, L. E. (eds.), *As the Walls of Academia are Tumbling Down*, Economica, London.

The *Magna Charta Universitatum* of the European universities, (1988). Bologna. *(http://www.unige.ch/cre/activities/Magna%20Charta/magna_charta.html)*

Wittrock, B. (1993). "The modern university; the three transformations", in Rothblatt, S. & Wittrock, B. (eds), *The European and American university since 1800*, Cambridge University Press, Cambridge.

PART III

•••••••••••••

Lowering External Walls
of Universities

CHAPTER 9

University High-Tech Alliances: Promising Economic Opportunities as well as Dangers

Werner Z. Hirsch

In the long run, only more scientific technologically driven innovation can provide the new, more powerful tools required to help ensure a better future for all. Fostering collaborative partnerships in scientific research has emerged as a critical imperative to sustaining this innovation (Hasselmo & McKinnel, 2001).

INTRODUCTION

Just as the pace at which science, mainly in universities, has advanced at breath-taking speed, so has the desire of industry to benefit from the new knowledge. Collaboration is taking many forms. Such venerable collaboration as teaching and training firms' personnel, including managers and executives, and faculty serving as directors and consultants is being greatly expanded. However, individual consultancies are increasingly replaced by team efforts, at times by entire university departments. A relatively new form of collaboration, a manifestation of the high-tech revolution, seeks to benefit directly from universities' unique research capabilities. Today, high-tech firms seek to "contract out" to universities specific research undertakings by providing corporate funding. These arrangements between universities and high-tech firms, to be referred to as research alliances, are the focus of this paper, together with the collaborative efforts spawned by them.

The attractiveness to industry of such alliances is directly related to the excellence and breadth of research universities and their comparative advantage in effectively carrying out high quality research. In the United States, overall university research budgets have grown steadily, and so has corporate funding, which in 1998 reached $2.6 billion or 9 percent of all research performed by U.S. universities and colleges. It about equaled the contributions made to them by state and local governments combined (National Science Foundation, 1998, Table B-35). State governments have also increasingly realized the value of the research done by their universities and by their alliances with industry. For example, already in 1990 the Georgia Research Alliance was founded. While the state invested $242 million in its six universities during the 1990s, private matching funds amounted to $65 million. Such states as Michigan, Wisconsin, and Ohio have taken similar steps, but they have been dwarfed by California. In 2000, California established its Institute for Science and Innovation, earmarking $300 million in state moneys to fund three institutes, which are to carry out high-tech research programs for four years. These state funds must be matched by more than twice that amount from corporations (Markoff, 2000).

WHY ALLIANCES?

A major reason for forming research alliances is clearly the self-interest of both high-tech firms and research universities. Not only do the two benefit from collaboration; so do regional and national economies, as well as society at large.

For universities, positive driving forces include the quest for new revenue sources and intellectual gains from collaborating in research with scientists in industry who work on real world problems, who often have vast experience and who have developed a distinct culture and way of thinking. As a consequence, the quality and scope of the research can be enhanced, while costs are reduced. Industry (and government laboratories) brings to the effort expensive state-of-the-art equipment and instrumentation, as well as financial resources. Alliances also facilitate the placing of the university's graduates.

Industry benefits, since universities bring to the table world-class scientists and a well-educated staff, as well as patents and an environment that stimulates inquiry and creativity. For example, the top 173 American universities' 1996 royalty and license fee earnings were $592 million. Industry benefits further, since outsourcing of research enables it to engage the very best scientists who are often unwilling to work in the private sector. Firms thus gain greater flexibility in manning their research efforts.

Society at large can benefit, since alliances tend to stimulate the creation of new knowledge, innovation and inventions, particularly when they lead to the formation of high-tech industry clusters.

Additionally, university research, especially if carried out in cooperation with high-tech industry, can generate regional as well as national economic benefits. Thus, when California Governor Gray Davis announced the establishment and funding of the California Institutes of Science and Innovation, he said, "It's my hope to replicate Silicon Valley...The most important thing a state government can do to improve local economies is to support research universities." (Markoff, 2000). Corporate funding has followed rapidly. For example, one of the institutions immediately received $140 million from companies such as IBM, Sun Microsystems, Qualcomm and Sony. Regional and national economies benefit when alliances generate innovations, which stimulate synergies from complementary integration and productivity gains from vertical disintegration through outsourcing, as well as scale economies from horizontal integration. Universities and their research alliances can have a seedbed effect stimulating the emergence of high-tech clusters, which further raise productivity and foster innovation.

REGIONAL ECONOMIC IMPACT

Research alliances can benefit not only the partners—they can also affect the economic health of the region in which they are located, with spillovers to the rest of the state and nation. For an analysis of the effects on expenditure and employment, regional impact analysis can be applied (Caffrey & Isaac, 1971). The analysis can be extended to three stages, as presented in Figure 1. Thus, in stage I we have the direct impact on the regional economy from the university's spending the funds of the corporate research contract on labor,

Figure 1: Three Impact Stages of University High-Tech Industry Research Alliances

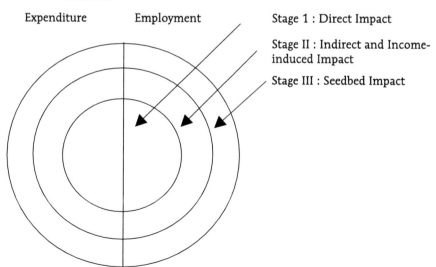

Expenditure   Employment   Stage 1 : Direct Impact

Stage II : Indirect and Income-induced Impact

Stage III : Seedbed Impact

material, and services. Stage II reflects the indirect and income-induced effects, and stage III the seedbed effect of the research grant. All of these effects have significant geographical dimensions, so that the alliance's total impact on local and regional economies is significantly greater than the sum of direct expenditures funded by the research contract.

Thus, two major interrelated forces are responsible for the regional economic impact of the university-high tech industry alliances. One force involves the inter-industry multiplier effect of money expended by the alliances on labor services and material, as they cycle through the economy several times. A second force relates to the emergence of high-tech clusters, which stimulate innovation and economic growth.

Inter-industry multiplier effect

Economists refer to the recycling of monies spent on labor, material and service in an economy as the indirect and income-induced "multiplier effect", so crucial in Stage II. The impact of each unit spent is "multiplied" as it is spent again in the economy. For example, the salaries paid by the university to faculty members and staff are spent by them to buy food, transportation, clothing, schooling, etc. To produce these and other goods and services, producers must buy a host of inputs, including labor. The extent of the effect can be estimated by using inter-industry multipliers, which have been calculated by modeling regional economies and making econometric estimates of their magnitude (Jaffe, 1989).

High-tech clustering and its effect

The economic impact of the research alliance does not stop here. The alliance's activities, especially those in the high-tech arena, often spawn new economic activities that benefit from proximity to the university. This is the seedbed effect, which is associated with clustering (agglomeration) of commercial activity and has further indirect and income-induced effects (Stage III).

The study of agglomeration has a long history. Alfred Marshall, the renowned 19th century English economist, provided insight into the advantages of what he called "localization" and therefore, agglomeration, of economic activity. He declared (in 1885):

"The Localization of Industry promotes the education of skill and taste, and the diffusion of technical knowledge. Where large masses of people are working at the same kind of trade, they educate one another.
Again, each man profits by the ideas of his neighbors: he is stimulated by contact with those who are interested in his own pursuit to make

new experiments; and each successful invention, whether it be a new machine, a new process, or a new way of organizing the business, is likely when once started to spread and to be improved upon.

In a district in which an industry is localized a skilled workman is sure of finding work to suit him; a master can easily fill a vacancy among his foreman; and generally the economy of skill can be carried further than in an isolated factory however large. Thus both large and small factories are benefited by the localization of industry and by the assistance of subsidiary trades."

Thus, just as Marshall's localization effects are long term, cumulative and depend on cooperation in knowledge creation and innovation, so does high-tech clustering.

To be a player in the knowledge-based high-tech economy (which is often referred to as a crucial part of the New Economy), requires successful and timely innovation and inventions for which there will be a responsive demand. Significant parts of this New Economy, especially pharmaceuticals and computer software, show two defining characteristics: 1) exceptionally high development costs of new products and therefore very high start-up costs of new companies, while production costs are extremely low, and 2) exceptionally rapid obsolescence of new products and processes.

As a result, the rewards in knowledge-based enterprises go to enterprises that innovate quickly and then capture the largest possible market share before being pushed aside by new innovations. Moreover, many innovative products in the New Economy have a very short life expectancy, for example 12-16 months for a typical semiconductor product (Hall & Ziedonis, 1999).

Today, firms in many high-tech industries are consumed with the defining requirement of achieving monopoly power, however temporary it turns out to be. Achieving this condition is significantly facilitated by locating near great research universities, which thus become increasingly surrounded by growing clusters of symbiotic enterprises. These clusters benefit from synergies and positive externalities on the demand side and from cost savings on the supply side. In turn, they attract human capital of the highest quality while providing an environment conducive to the lively exchange of knowledge and ideas.

Reflecting these defining characteristics of knowledge-based high-tech economic activities and effectively responding to them, high-tech clusters have emerged. They facilitate expeditious creation of new ideas, knowledge, processes and products, all very costly to create and yet frequently short-lived.

A high-tech cluster is thus a geographic concentration of horizontally and vertically interconnected companies and associated institutions, which have located themselves around research universities and other research centers. All these activities are linked by commonalities and complementaries, and benefit from positive externalities. Physical proximity among those who work on the cutting edge of knowledge continues to be extremely valuable, even in an age where the cyberspace revolution has shrunk distances in space and time. Thus, according to *The Economist* (1999, p. 71): "Even in the days of instantaneous communication, there is no substitute for researchers pressing flesh...and the ability to sit in the bar and chew the fat with colleagues and rivals."

Demand-related horizontal interactions tend to be crucial for initiating the clustering process. Benefits from these interactions include the ease and timeliness with which information, knowledge, ideas and novel concepts are exchanged between cap and gown and among high-tech industries. Many of the interactions are informal and unplanned and at times the idea exchange might not be recognized until much later.

In addition to horizontal, demand-related forces, there exist also significant vertical, supply-related ones. As firms form clusters, they need inputs, not only scientists and staff, but also products and services so that they can efficiently carry out their missions. This supply-related growth follows the demand-related one, but in due time both tend to interact. Being located in a high-tech cluster, and thus having access to a large labor pool and to specialized inputs, can raise a firm's productivity and competitiveness. Much of a firm's outsourcing can be local and thus involve lower transaction costs than non-local outsourcing does, but only up to a point. When clusters get too large and too cluttered with enterprises, negative externalities tend to raise their ugly heads and with them transaction costs tend to increase.

Horizontal and vertical interactions sooner or later affect each other. For example, as suppliers of inputs exchange information and ideas with high-tech firms and universities, they in turn contribute knowledge and ideas to their scientists and their students, and consequently in the long run improve the productivity of suppliers of goods and services. Because of these manifold interactions, technological developments, dynamics of the market and government regulation, high-tech clusters are in a continual state of flux.

The fact that research alliances can have a major impact on the regional economy is borne by some estimates of the 1998 economic impact of California's twelve research universities. It was estimated that their $254 million in corporate research contracts may have increased California's level of economic activity by perhaps as much as $1.4 billion. Employment may have increased by as much as 18,200 jobs (Hirsch, 2000).

THREATS, RISKS AND REMEDIES

When research universities lower their walls to the outside world, a variety of collaborative efforts with high-tech industry can follow. Among them, research alliances stand out because of their financial size and impact, but also because of the risks and controversies they can generate. Other forms are joint ventures of universities with high-tech firms and faculty assuming a financial interest in start-up companies or serving as directors, managers, lead scientists or consultants. While collaborative efforts with industry can be rewarding, they move universities far away from the cloistered environment, which in the earlier years was considered so essential to the creative pursuit and transmission of knowledge. Research alliances, in particular, carry with them the seed of commercialism in the university. This can pose serious threats to the institution's ethos and culture. Alliances can compromise its academic mission and, most importantly, interfere with its traditional role as honest arbiter of knowledge and guarantor of undisputed objectivity in the public interest.

This threat can become even more serious when corporate research funding brings to university administrators a business background and ethos, which can profoundly conflict with the venerable academic culture and mission.

Research universities must be concerned with the following major dangers:

- Inter-departmental imbalances, i.e. skewed priorities among departments, schools and research centers,
- Intra-departmental imbalances,
- Faculty conflicts of interest and commitment,
- Curtailment of faculty rights, and
- Financial risk of the universities.

Inter-departmental imbalances

Universities consider it their mission to offer a broad, balanced liberal education, particularly on the undergraduate level. However, massive corporate support for the sciences and engineering can have a seriously distorting effect. The humanities and arts go begging and serious frictions between them and the rest of the university have become common.

In the hope of mitigating such imbalances, a percentage of financial gains from corporate contracts could be allocated to disciplines important to a great university, yet hard to fund by contracts and other outside sources. Such a tax could be levied especially on corporate research funding in recognition of the fact that the quality of research that accrues to the firm is made possible by the breadth of the overall academic excellence of the university.

Intra-departmental imbalances

Not only the disciplinary priorities become distorted and imbalanced, so can priorities within academic units. Are not faculty members likely to be drawn to research areas in their discipline where funding is plentiful? Equally promising and deserving specialties, and perhaps those which might bring tomorrow's breakthroughs, can wither on the vine. As a consequence, serious conflicts can arise within departments and schools. The effects of departmental imbalancing, which result from large corporate contracts funding interdisciplinary research, could be mitigated by transferring these contracts into a research center. As a result, mono-disciplinary research would be carried out mainly in departments, while inter-disciplinary research with corporate funding would move into a research center.

Conflicts of interest and commitment

The nature of research in the sciences and engineering is changing at a rapid pace and so are collaborative efforts. The ever more complex research environment has led to ambiguities about the rights and responsibilities of faculty. Attractive funding opportunities offered by collaborating firms and the prospect of financial gain can skew faculty decisions, erode interest in university affairs and weaken commitment to the university's mission.

> A 'conflict of interest' arises when an academic staff member is in a position to influence either directly or indirectly University business, research, or other decisions in ways that could lead to gain for the academic staff member, the staff member's family, or others to the detriment of the University's integrity and mission of teaching, research and public service (University of Illnois, 1998).

Increased entrepreneurship by faculty and the rising financial influence of industry can become a combustible mixture, which can readily lead to short-changing undergraduate and graduate students. Collaboration with industry can result in faculty employing, and perhaps exploiting, graduate students in outside research in which faculty have a financial interest. Conflicts of interest can also arise when a faculty member assumes an executive, managerial, salaried or consulting position in an outside organization, conducts a professional practice, or uses university facilities and equipment for non-university research. In these circumstances, bias in research results can come about in return for special favors.

The challenges facing universities are especially grave in relation to drug companies—paid drug studies. Pharmaceutical companies often fund the studies, and then pay faculty for delivering lectures and for consultancies. They even list academic scientists as lead authors of papers, although the studies are actually designed and the data analyzed by drug company employees. How common such practices are is revealed in a recent study, which finds a third of one medical school's investigators have such relationships (Boyd & Bero 2000).

Separately, there is the risk of institutional conflicts of interest. It occurs when universities have financial interests in the corporate sponsors of their research. Such investment can color decisions and attitudes towards collaborating faculty and should be avoided. Universities have experimented with a number of policies designed to help check faculty's conflicts of interest. Devising such policies tends to run into difficulties, since not infrequently faculty and administration views differ. They conflict most decidedly in regard to two crucial areas: 1) maximum level of financial interest in a company that a faculty member can have while engaging in a university activity which involves that company and 2) circumstances under which the university administration is to be merely informed or formal approval is required by faculty, and when this step is to be taken, i.e., *ex ante* or *ex post*.

In relation to the first issue, for example, the University of California, San Diego (UCSD) adopted in 1999 the following policy. Financial interests in a company cannot amount to:

- Annual income in excess of $10,000 from the company, or
- Equity interest of more than 5 % or $10,000 in the company, or
- Management responsibility in the company.
- This standard for determining a significant financial interest should be applied to:
- Acceptance of contracts, grants, and gifts from companies in which the Principal Investigator has a financial interest,
- Acceptance of UC grants whose industrial partner is a company in which the Principal Investigator has a financial interest,
- Conducting clinical trials for companies in which the Principal Investigator has a financial interest,
- Acceptance of federal contracts and grants whose Principal Investigator or other researcher has a financial related to the project,
- Subcontracting of work by UCSD to a company in which the Principal Investigator or other researcher has a financial interest,
- Employment of a graduate student or postdoc in a company in which the student's or postdoc's advisor has a financial interest.

A second, somewhat lower, but still onerous, level of conflict relates to faculty's commitment to the University.

> A 'conflict of commitment' exists when the external activities of an academic staff are so substantial or demanding of the staff member's time and attention as to interfere with the individual's responsibilities to the unit to which the individual is assigned, to students, or to the University (University of Illinois, 1998).

In the hope of addressing the risk of conflicts of commitment, most universities limit the number of days faculty can spend on external activities. These policies are all too often ambiguous and tend to be disregarded by faculty, particularly since no penalties are usually invoked.

Not unlike policies to rein in conflicts of interest, so also those addressing conflicts of commitment face the two challenges of defining the maximum time faculty can devote to outside work, and in what form, and when notification of the administration is required.

Engagements of the following sort are the concern:

- Consulting,
- Assuming an executive or managerial position in a for-profit or non-for-profit business,
- Administering, outside the University, a grant that would ordinarily be conducted under the auspices of the University,
- Employing students in outside research projects in which the faculty member has a financial interest,
- Conducting a professional practice.

Faculty who staff research alliances tend to establish working relations with their counterparts and officers in the sponsoring firm. Consulting opportunities often follow and, at times, even part ownership, part-time positions as senior scientists and board membership. These roles can reduce commitment of time and devotion to the university, leaving the university facing a difficult choice. Either it can seek to rein in activities that short-change it and thereby risk losing outstanding faculty, or it can accommodate faculty and risk that they give the university less and less time and devotion.

This dilemma might be solved by moving faculty determined to engage in major outside activities into a new faculty status. This new status would resemble the position of Professor in Residence in medical schools, which provides for part-time university employment while limiting privileges.

More generally, for the sake of minimizing conflicts of commitment, a policy should be developed, which defines clearly what are unacceptable levels of outside activities and whether, and if so when, university approval is to be obtained. Disseminating this information effectively and broadly is essential.

Curtailment of faculty rights

All too often academics, used to an exclusive right to determine what, when and where to publish, find this freedom impinged upon by corporate sponsors. Corporations are keen on having the right to review manuscripts and to delay their publication. Likewise, they tend to insist on confidentiality and seek ownership of patents and copyrights related to research that they have funded.

There exists no magic formula to solve these opposing interests. Cases differ from one to the next. Still, universities can help themselves by developing contract terms that represent their minimum requirements of faculty rights. Faculty and administration are well advised to closely cooperate in developing these minimum conditions. They should be made known to potential funding sources, which would then know already at the start of contract negotiations what conditions would be deal breakers.

Financial risk of universities

Collaborative arrangements between universities and high-tech industry, while often financially rewarding, can carry with them significant financial risks for the university. One is heightened financial instability. It results from the fact that the sum total of research contracts varies greatly from year to year and requires different faculty specialties. For example, for the first time in UC Berkeley's history, it entered in 1998 into a five-year alliance with a corporation, which signed a $25 million research contract. Tooling up for such a temporary effort can lead to a "boom and bust" cycle.

Moreover, universities often face difficult negotiations about intellectual property rights. It is to be expected that the corporate research sponsor and the university tend to be at odds about general patents and copyrights ownership and royalties. They also tend to differ in their views about rights and background rights—licensing rights a university has gained in connection with earlier research, often using funds from other sponsors (Hasselmo & McKinnel, 2001). While faculty members are considered co-owners of intellectual property, those who produced the rights to an existing license are often not party to the new research agreement under discussion. Thus, awarding background rights to a new sponsor can be highly unfair to select researchers. Moreover, giving away background rights can hamper the ability to continue earlier areas of research and to license new technology to other firms that are contemplating entering new research contracts.

Finally, risk arises when corporate sponsors do not pay the full indirect cost, i.e., the research cost accruing to the university above researchers' salaries and the cost of new materials. For example, federally financed research in universities in the late 1990s covered only 70-90 percent of its full cost, with indirect costs accounting on average for 50 percent of overall cost (Goldman & Williams, 2000). The payment of insufficient indirect cost tends to be aided in negotiations when firms are supported by faculty who are eager to see their research funded.

Paying less than the full indirect cost not only forces the university to subsidize the corporate sponsor, but also disadvantages departments with little or no outside funding. They often end up indirectly subsidizing the best-endowed department. A common result is tension within the university and some unhappy departments.

If, under some circumstances, subsidies are acceptable to the university administration, it is important to be frank about them. To this end, universities should develop transparency in their accounting methods and transactions. Admittedly, such a step will often require lengthy discussion with faculty. However, once agreement is reached, it should be widely publicized.

CONCLUSION

As the walls between academia and the outside world are coming down and research alliances proliferate, universities will increasingly place one foot in the world of commerce, while the other foot remains in the world of academia. Alliances can greatly contribute to the economic growth, employment and income of a region. Participating corporations gain access to great research capabilities and universities gain income and interesting research opportunities. But universities also expose themselves to severe risks. These include inter-departmental and intra-departmental imbalances, faculty conflicts of interest and commitment to the university, curtailment of faculty rights as well as financial risks to the university. Since research alliances promise to continue to be part of the high-tech world for years to come, universities (and their corporate partners) are well advised to develop model contracts. Some could be for single projects, while others could be model master contracts to be used in cases of add-on collaboration. Such contracts, which must be particularly sensitive to issues of profound university concern, can greatly benefit from previous contract negotiations. These model contracts can streamline negotiations. In their form and content they tend to fall between individually drafted and boilerplate contracts.

In conclusion, when forming research alliances, universities should make sure that these alliances will make major contributions to both the university and to high-tech industry. At the same time, the alliances must safeguard the defining values of academia. The latter issue is of paramount importance since, to paraphrase John Maynard Keynes, perhaps the great economist of the 20th century, academia must be, "the trustee...of the possibility of civilization".

REFERENCES

Boyd, E. A. & Bero, Lisa A. (2000). "Assessing Faculty Financial Relationship with Industry", *JAMA*, November, 2209-2214.

Caffrey, J. & Herbert H. I. (1971). *Estimating the Impact of a College or University on the Local Economy*, American Council on Education, Washington, D.C.

The Economist (1999). Issue 71, July 3.

Goldman, C. E. & Williams T. (2000). *Paying for University Research Facilities and Administration*, RAND Corporation, Washington, D.C.

Hall, B.H. & Ziedonis R. H. (1999). "The Patent Paradox Revisited; Determinants of Patenting in the U.S. Semiconductor Industry", *NBER Working Paper* No. E-99-268.

Hasselmo, N. & McKinnel, H. (2001). "Working Together—Creating Knowledge", *Business-Education Forum*, May, pp. 60-61.

Hirsch, W. Z. (2000). "University-High tech Alliances in California: Gains and Losses", in Mitchell, D. J. B. (ed.), *California Policy Options*, UCLA School of Public Policy and Social Research, Los Angeles, December, pp. 45-49.

Jaffe, A. B. (1989). *The Real Effect of Academic Research*, 5 (79), December, pp. 957-970.

Marcus J. (1998). "Universities and Private Firms Cash in on Faculty Research". *The Associated Press*, February 18.

Markoff, J. (2002). "California Sets up Centers for Basic Scientific Research", *New York Times*, December 8, A 20.

National Science Foundation/SRS (1998). *Survey of Research and Development Expenditures at Universities and Colleges, Fiscal Year 1997*. Washington, D.C.

Marshall, A. & Marshall, M. P. (1885). *The Economics of Industry*. Macmillan, London.

Marwick, P. (1990). *UCLA Economic Impact*. January, Los Angeles.

University of Illinois at Urbana Champagne (1998). *Policy on Conflicts of Commitment and Interest*.

University of California, San Diego (1995). *Report of Joint Academic Senate: Administration Committee on University Interaction with Industry*.

CHAPTER 10

Technology Transfer at the Swiss Federal Institute of Technology Zurich (ETHZ)

Ulrich W. Suter and Matthias Erzinger

INTRODUCTION

The Swiss Federal Institute of Technology Zurich (ETHZ) is one of the leading science—oriented universities in the world. Although in the last few years important goals for technology transfer were reached, there is still a lot to be done. In every area—research collaboration, commercialization, spin-off-promotion—substantial progress has been achieved, and ETHZ is certainly a trendsetter for technology transfer in Switzerland. Nevertheless, in the coming years, the basic conditions for technology transfer—such as the public perception, the internal anchorage and legal conditions—will change, and there is an interesting challenge to the university to manage these changes.

DEFINITION AND BASIC CONDITIONS FOR TECHNOLOGY TRANSFER IN SWITZERLAND

Definition

Technology transfer is a term used in a very broad way, but this chapter focuses on three main areas:

- Research Collaboration: The University and the Private Sector as Partners in Research
- Licensing of Intellectual Property to the Private Sector

- Spin-off-Promotion as a motor of innovation.

The first important way for the university to transfer knowledge from its research into society is through its students. Those who graduate from ETHZ are highly skilled and can quickly transfer their knowledge to the companies they join. Their network of contacts—professors, scientific collaborators, colleagues—is one of the decisive factors for efficient technology transfer.

The private sector sometimes see technology transfer as a one-way service: universities are obliged to deliver know-how, technologies or the results of their research for free, to whoever intends to use it. But, successful technology transfer offers a much wider perspective:

- Benefits to society—resulting from innovative products that provide new opportunities to the public.
- Benefits to researchers—resulting from the expansion of know-how and external contact.
- Benefits to research in Switzerland—resulting from exposure to new aspects of a problem.
- Benefits to ETHZ—resulting from a more positive image and additional income.
- Benefits to our partners—resulting from sustainable business opportunities generated by research collaboration.

In the long term, all of these interests should be respected in order to support a sustainable ongoing innovation process. If not, the process is endangered, for instance by public opinion, which will not be willing to finance research, if the benefit for society is not visible.

An Overview of ETHZ

The Federal Institute of Technology Zurich was founded in 1854. Until 1969, it was the only national university in Switzerland. Today, ETHZ comprises 83 institutes and laboratories, 330 professors and about 840 lecturers, who conduct research and fulfill teaching obligations. Research and education fall within the competence of 17 departments. A staff of more than 7'500 work in teaching, research and administration. Current statistics show about 11'700 registered students. Each year, around 1'250 receive a degree and a further 530 complete a doctoral thesis. Annual expenditure has reached 1 billion Swiss francs (approx. 660'000'000 US$).

Based on its research activities, ETHZ is able to offer state-of-the-art knowledge in its teaching and continuing education courses. In its mission statement, the university commits itself to the following principles:

- to promote and maintain quality in teaching and research at a high international level;
- to support a universal and system-oriented approach;
- to preserve specialist and cultural diversity and academic freedom in teaching and research;
- to secure an adequate infrastructure and guarantee its renovation;
- to optimize central scientific services in information and communication systems as well as administrative support covering the needs of teaching and research.

The organization of the university is run along the lines of a presidential system, in which the President chairs the Executive Board and bears responsibility for the management of the university. The President is supported by the Rector, who is responsible for teaching, the Vice-president of research and business relations, and by the Vice-president of planning and logistics.

The technology transfer office at ETHZ is called *ETH transfer* and it is one of three branches within the office of the Vice-president for research and business relations. Four Technology Transfer Managers currently work with ETH transfer; they are supported by a full-time secretary and a part-time communications consultant. These managers are responsible for some of the departments of ETHZ. They can rely on a broad network of freelance-specialist (e.g., lawyers) to solve upcoming problems. One of their experiences is that, in technology transfer, the exception is the rule.

Basic Conditions

Economic Situation: One basic factor influencing the policy on technology transfer at ETHZ is the limited "home-market". In 1995, 99.8 % of private companies had less than 250 full time employees. These companies offered about 75 % of all working places in Switzerland.

The budget for R&D in small companies does not allow for substantial collaboration with universities. This leaves open possibilities in a lot of different areas and for a lot of different clients, but requires a lot of small projects and the building up of cluster-projects, which allow the small companies to participate in technology transfer programs and to achieve real benefit.

Comparison with the USA: One difference is in intellectual property. In the United States, the universities are the exclusive owners of the intellectual property created on their campuses. So they can decide what to do with an invention very fast.

In Switzerland, the situation is unclear and attempts to solve this question at national level have not been successful up to now. At ETHZ, there are presently at least three main players who own the intellectual property:

- ETHZ
- The Institute concerned
- The inventors (all the researchers, from the professor to the students who were involved in the project).

If there is collaboration with other universities, or with the private sector, the respective institutions are part of the ownership as well. And, of course, the more people are involved, the more complex negotiations will be.

A second difference of great influence on technology transfer in the United States and Switzerland is the question of security. In Switzerland, we face a much bigger influence of security-thinking on decisions concerning innovation. This may be illustrated with the following example: in the USA, the spirit of "Let's try" is much stronger; in Switzerland, in the same situation, people will say: "Let's wait and evaluate it once more to be sure..."

In both countries, money—or the lack of it—was one of the major factors that enforced technology transfer in the universities. In the United States, the end of the war in Vietnam, later of the disarmament contracts, and then the end of the cold war resulted in reduced military budgets. Since the Pentagon was the most important financial source for research, a lot of research groups lost this income. So, financial pressure was one major aspect that promoted the development of technology transfer offices at American universities.

In Switzerland, the recession in the early nineteen nineties forced the universities to invest in technology transfer. In addition, public opinion, in a pragmatic way, was asking for more "visible output", more "return on investment" of the public money paid to the universities. Up to now, ETHZ is not allowed to take shares in spin-off-companies, while some universities (like Geneva) can take shares in their spin-offs.

RESEARCH COLLABORATION AND COMMERCIALIZATION OF RESEARCH RESULTS

Up to now, research collaboration is the most important part of the work of our Technology Transfer Managers. Efforts during the last years, both by scientists and by ETH transfer have yielded remarkable results. The sum of money generated increased constantly from CHF 40 million to CHF 45 million. Because only contracts with a volume of at least CHF 20'000 are registered by ETH transfer, the following section is based on that information.

Research Contracts

At ETHZ, two kinds of research collaboration are currently treated in different ways. The most fundamental difference concerns the Intellectual Property (IP). If the IP is dedicated to the partner who also more or less decides on the aims and the direction of the research planned, the collaboration is called « Research-Order » and the private company has to pay an additional fee to ETHZ.

The alternative « Research-Participation » is much more university-determined. For its contribution, the private company is granted the right to use the results, for instance by the possibility to buy a license. The IP questions are normally solved within the respective contract.

Right now, the area of research collaboration at ETHZ is being evaluated. There are ideas for a complete new system in order to create more incentives for the institutes and scientists and to hold the IP in the possession of ETHZ.

The development in this area during the past four years is very positive. The number of research-orders grew from 20 in 1997 to 30 in 2000. During the same period, the research-participations grew from 68 to 90. Each of these contracts concerned a volume of at least CHF 20'000. Collaborations concerning smaller amounts are signed by the professors and are not registered. The experience is that scientists are using the services of ETH transfer more and more in earlier stages of contract negotiation in order to prevent legal conflicts. Even the private companies are interested to have secure legal situations. The strategy of ETHZ is to come to basic agreements with its partners, which deal with the important issues like IP or the right of publications.

Licensing

Rising importance is being put on the concrete commercialization of research results, know-how or software developed within research projects. The policy of ETHZ is not to sell IP, as was sometimes done in earlier years, but to license it. There are different kinds of license agreements: exclusive, non-exclusive, restricted to a certain area, etc. If the commercialization possibilities of a certain result are not evident enough to decide on its value, ETHZ offers options on licenses.

Also in this area, an increase from 8 license contracts in 1997 to 25 in 2000 occurred. The income is divided between ETHZ, the institute and the inventors.

The basis for licensing is of course patents. But, up to now, there was no database of patents filed by ETHZ. It is now one of the most important goals of ETH transfer to elaborate such a database. Since the structure of ETHZ is very diverse, it is not easy to obtain the necessary information in time.

Problems to be solved

One of the common aspects of almost every research collaboration project is the question of publications. ETH transfer tries to fix the right for publications in a basic agreement, to be respected during all the different collaborations with the same company. The private companies have an interest to restrict publication of research results. But, for the scientist it is crucial to have the right to publish. Normally, ETH transfer tries to fix a time range of 3 month after submission of a manuscript to allow the company to examine it. After this time range, the scientists are free to publish. Some scientists have the tendency to forget about the possibility of patenting. So a lot of the commercialization potential of IP is lost. EHT transfer therefore tries to raise awareness of this issue. Crucial to this question is to show to the scientist that publications and patents can easily be combined.

SPIN-OFF PROMOTION

One of the most important areas of technology transfer is the promotion of spin-off companies. Sometimes, existing companies are not interested in new products, because they do not want to endanger their own similar products. Or, nobody really believes in an idea, except its inventor. This is the right time to create a start-up. At ETHZ, the recognition that encouraging start-ups is one of the most important means of applying research to the benefit of society has grown even stronger over the last few years. Not only are new products realized with spin-offs, but also attractive new jobs are created. ETHZ has its own label for companies, which are acknowledged as spin-off-companies. Currently, there are about 120 of them, most of them founded during the last five years. This is the result of a strategy to promote the creation of new companies.

Courses and Competitions

ETHZ created a series of courses on founding a company, which within a few years has become the best attended series of courses on founding a firm in Switzerland: over 12,000 people have participated in the programme until now. The results from the first three years of the course were that hundreds of firms and over 930 jobs were created by participants. The unique speciality of the program is its broad variety of participants—from the highly-skilled doctoral student to the carpenter, who has to take over and relaunch the company of his father. The program itself became a spin-off company under the name of *b-tools* and is operating now for three years with ongoing success.

In 1997, together with the management consulting firm McKinsey & Company Switzerland, ETHZ launched the first country-wide business plan competition *Venture 98—companies for tomorrow* with great success. This led to similar initiatives in several countries. Now, the third generation of this competition, *Venture 2002*, is underway, organized by ETH transfer and McKinsey. It is a mixture of competition, networking opportunities, business events for venture capitalists and high-level seminars. For ETHZ, it is an instrument to detect bright brains with entrepreneurial sprits in our laboratories. Even if most of the participants from ETHZ do not really start their own company, ETH transfer is able to support them in other fields, perhaps in patenting, or in the commercialization of an invention.

The experience of the first business plan competition demonstrates that participation in it contributes significantly to the founding of firms: of 87 business plans submitted, 27 firms were founded, and others are in the process of being founded. The winner of Venture 98, today called Sensirion AG, in Zurich, has 45 employees. Sensirion is active in the sensor technology area. "Our idea was to found a company which should only guarantee a sufficient income for both of us," says Felix Mayer, one of the two founders of Sensirion AG. "But, during the competition, we recognized how much bigger the potential of our ideas was." In 1998, the company was founded under the name of Alpha-Sensors. Today, Sensirion is the technology leader for intelligent digital solutions for relative humidity sensor systems, mass flow, liquid mass flow, air flow, gas flow and differential pressure sensors. Sensiron provides OEM/Business-to-Business customers with high quality, fully-integrated sensor system solutions.

Program to support start-ups

Like others, the founders of Sensirion participated in the spin-off program of ETH transfer. Besides the already mentioned courses and the business plan competition, ETH transfer provides a broad variety of services to start-ups.

In the first phase of the spin-off-process, the scientist (perhaps a doctoral student who wants to make use of the results of a thesis) is supported by coaching in order to concretize an idea, to elaborate a business plan, and to organize the next steps, such as founding or financing. During this period, the scientist is still employed by ETHZ, but with reduced duties.

During the same period, the needs of the new company are also identified. Is there infrastructure at ETHZ, such as laboratories, that can be used? Are there instruments needed to develop a prototype? What about the intellectual property? These questions are discussed by the technology managers of ETH transfer and the scientists and are fixed in contracts. In addition to infrastructure, ETHZ is ready to support the spin-off with loans up to CHF 50'000.

The second phase of the ETHZ spin-off program starts with the first real operations of the new company. The founder can reduce his or her job step by step. All the above-mentioned questions are solved in the spin-off-contract, which normally provides the company with infrastructure for two years. All this is not for free, but the spin-off gets reasonable conditions. After two years, the company has to pay back the loan and to leave the rooms rented from ETHZ. This is to prevent the competition between the ETHZ spin-off and an other company becoming too strained. There are some possibilities to extend this range. But, normally, two years are sufficient to build up companies, if the business idea and the team are optimized.

In the following period, the spin-off becomes increasingly independent of ETHZ. For its founders, there is the possibility to participate in a regular spin-off-event, which is used to widen their network. ETHZ is affiliated with the "Technopark" in Zurich, which was opened in 1993. The Technopark provides facilities for start-ups, as well as for innovative established companies. Located near ETHZ and the Universities of Applied Sciences of Zurich and Winterthur are around 190 companies with around 1400 employees. ETHZ has participated and supported the Technopark from the beginning. The ETHZ section (about 10 % of the total 44000 m^2) is administered by ETH transfer. More applied research oriented groups are located there as well as spin-off companies or special projects. Especially for spin-off companies, the entrepreneurial spirit and the possibilities provided at the Technopark are very fruitful. Therefore, they often stay in the building when they have to leave the ETHZ section after the two years mentioned above.

The results in this area are remarkable. Over 90 percent of the companies founded since 1990 (about 80) are active and some of them are growing fast. They are presented on the website www.spinoff.ethz.ch.

DIFFICULTIES, STRATEGIES AND CONCLUSIONS

Difficulties regarding the private sector

As mentioned above, the diversity of the Swiss economy and the great number of small companies are one of the major problems that ETHZ faces in order to broaden its research collaboration. And although there are constantly voices who urge ETHZ to go for more cooperation, the problem is located also on the side of the companies. A few issues in this area are that:

- CEOs of small and medium size companies are busy with daily business. To establish collaboration between such a company and ETHZ needs some efforts, especially to find the ideal partner.
- The communication between the world of pragmatic business and research is not always very easy. Perhaps moderators are needed.
- We observe a certain shyness towards the university.

Strategies to face these issues have to be long term oriented. ETHZ has to do everything possible that will lead to more real contacts between society and research and to show possibilities of interaction between private companies and our institution. There is thus a strategy to establish ETHZ even more as an institution that is open towards the interests of the private company and society in general.

ETHZ was heavily engaged in organizing the *Zürcher Festival des Wissens* (Zurich Festival of Knowledge) in May 2001 in the hall of the main railway station. During four days, about 100'000 visitors came into contact with research. If we are successful in building bridges between society and research in general, this will promote the perception of ETHZ within the group of economic leaders.

In the same line, there is the engagement of ETHZ in Expo.02, the Swiss national exhibition. *Ada–the intelligent space* was realized in cooperation with the University of Zurich. Already now, after a very short time of operating, it is clear that this exhibition has opened contacts to ETHZ that would not have been possible without the public awareness of Expo.02.

> **Ada—the intelligent space awaits you at Expo.02.**
> Experience how our brain functions. Play and communicate with a space that has its own personality. Gain a sense of what artificial intelligence is all about these days. Think ahead to what this actually means to your life. Take part in one of the most exciting research projects being conducted by the University of Zurich and ETH Zurich and visit *Ada—the intelligent space* at the *arteplage* in Neuchâtel. An exhibition that is highly entertaining and simultaneously opens up entirely new horizons.
>
> **A step into the future**
> *Ada—the intelligent space* is more than just an exhibition. Through various events and commentaries, you'll take a look ahead at our future and the relationship between man, machine and artificial intelligence. Care to join us?

In fact, research and collaboration between universities and private companies has to become just a daily thing.

On the other hand, it is crucial to maintain an independent position for research. If ETHZ does not defend its independence towards the economic interest of the private sector, it may lose its top position in research. To communicate this message to private partners is one of the most important tasks of the technology transfer managers.

Internal difficulties and strategies

ETH transfer also faces some internal conditions that are hindering more efficient technology transfer. First, there is the organizational structure of ETHZ. Since our departments, institutes and especially our professors are very independent, there is no chance to urge them to do something, like perhaps be more aware of intellectual property. "To convince by service" is the strategy chosen. But the efforts have to be communicated. In order to strengthen the internal know-how, ETH transfer organized a series of luncheon seminars. After short introductions in the various fields, prominent professors or other scientists presented case studies and reported their experience with the services of ETH-transfer. More than 300 participants joined this pilot project, which for sure will be followed by a second edition. But, there are still people working at ETHZ who do not know about the existence of ETH transfer and its services. So a lot of work is to be done yet.

Also in the fields of teaching and of research, ETHZ is currently enforcing its efforts. Since about three years, there is a professorship for technology management and entrepreneurship.

On a political level, finally, ETHZ has to urge for clarification of the legal situation in the field of intellectual property and the possibility to take shares in private companies as part of its spin-off promotion.

CONCLUSIONS

- In technology transfer, the exception is the rule. Almost every project has its speciality, and too much generalization endangers success.
- Technology transfer cannot be dictated, but it is important to provide a broad range of opportunities to participate, for both the scientists and the private sector.
- In order to overcome the diverse structure of the Swiss economy, there has to be opportunities to bundle interests of different companies and allow them to be part of the game.
- Technology transfer, even more than any other university administration area, has to be known within the respective institution as the most friendly and service-oriented office.
- The independency of research is more important than single research collaborations. If the collaboration endangers the right to publish, for instance, it is not worth signing.
- Even if the last years have showed a clear improvement and better financial return on investments in technology transfer at ETHZ, a lot remains to be done.

FURTHER INFORMATION

www.ethz.ch
www.transfer.ethz.ch
www.spinoff.ethz.ch
www.ada-ausstellung.ch

CHAPTER 11

Transforming the Walls of Academia into Bridges: Connecting Research Universities and Industry in San Diego, California

Peter Preuss, Charles F. Kennel and Sharon E. R. Franks [1]

INTRODUCTION

When they respond to internal and external stimuli, universities are challenged to broaden and deepen the ways in which they carry out their trilateral mission to educate, encourage the pursuit of unfettered research, and serve as relevant public citizens. In order to attract and retain the best and brightest scientists, support increasingly costly, often interdisciplinary research, train growing numbers of students,

1 We gratefully acknowledge the following people for sharing insights that contributed to the development of this paper: Robert C. Dynes, Chancellor, UCSD; John A. Woods, Vice Chancellor Resource Management and Planning, UCSD; James T. Shea, Director of Constituent Relations, UCSD; Mary L. Walshok, Associate Vice Chancellor for Extended Studies and Public Service, UCSD; Alan S. Paau, Director Technology Transfer and Intellectual Property Services, UCSD; Fred G. Cutler, Director, UCSD CONNECT; Edward Furtek, Associate Vice Chancellor Science, Technology and Policy, UCSD; Julie Meier Wright, President and CEO, San Diego Regional Economic Development Corporation; Irwin M. Jacobs, Chairman and CEO QUALCOMM Inc.; Duane Roth, President and CEO, Alliance Pharmaceutical Corporation; Edward A. Frieman, Senior Vice President, Science & Technology, Science Applications International Corporation, and Chair, San Diego Science and Technology Council.

and take on a greater role with respect to public service, university leaders are questioning how the multifaceted relationships among research institutions, government and industry will evolve.

Alliances between universities and industries support the research, teaching and public service elements of the university's mission. While bolstering research excellence and benefiting students, these collaborations also provide opportunities for the university to play a vital role in an increasingly globalized economy. As generators of new knowledge, research universities—the fundamental building block of economic prosperity in the information age—will play an increasingly important role not only in the generation of new industries but in supplying the educated, entrepreneurial talent required to launch and sustain successful commercial ventures (Porter & van Opstal, 2001; Regents of the University of California, 1997).

In an effort to understand the forces that are re-shaping university-industry relationships and the power these alliances can have economically (Hirsch, this volume) and environmentally (National Research Council, 2001), we begin with a brief discussion of the motivation for building industry-university partnerships. Recognizing that such partnerships carry risks as well as potential rewards, we summarize potential drawbacks to these alliances, and try to put into perspective controversial aspects of university-industry collaboration.

By way of example, we turn to the experiences of the University of California, San Diego (UCSD) in spawning, nurturing and now working to sustain a somewhat unlikely high-technology economic cluster in the lower left corner of the United States (Cohen, 2001; Wilson, 2001). How has UCSD come to play a major role in regional economic development? How can the university sustain the highest levels of innovation, respond to the changing needs of the maturing business community, and rise to the challenge of maintaining the outstanding quality of life that has attracted so many brilliant scientists and entrepreneurs to San Diego?

POTENTIAL BENEFITS AND HAZARDS OF UNIVERSITY-INDUSTRY PARTNERSHIPS

University-industry interactions take a variety of forms that contribute to economic prosperity locally and globally, facilitate more rapid commercialization of the results of university research, enhance the training of future scientists, provide intellectual stimulation to academic researchers, help finance university research and allow the university to be an involved, trusted member of the local community. Corporate partners may provide funding for research, endowment of chairs, student support and technical assistance to individual scientists and departments in exchange for privileges that include attending seminars, interacting with faculty and students, and opportunities to recruit promising graduate students. Industries look to the university for their most important resource: talented, skilled, creative individuals (Regents of the University of California, 1995). In addition to people, the university offers industry a window on the latest research, infusion of new ideas, and access to long-term, basic research that cannot easily be sustained by many private companies.

Not all benefits that result from university-industry partnerships are immediate or even readily quantifiable. Powerfully positive outcomes can be unanticipated, far-reaching and long-term. University leaders at UCSD have observed that commitments from businesses tend to expand the longer these relationships thrive. Businesses with which the university has enjoyed long-term interaction are better positioned to respond positively to unforeseen opportunities, for instance when matching funds are required or capital must be raised for new buildings. Clearly, it is in the university's best interests to cultivate valuable relationships with businesses with the same level of care accorded to nurturing the institution's private donors.

Development of successful relationships between university and industry partners requires that those involved understand and respect cultural differences that are likely to color their interactions (National Academy of Sciences, 1999). One fundamental difference between the business community and the university has to do with time horizons. Business partners are sometimes frustrated by the pace of institutional review and decision-making within the university, particularly when expediency is necessary to ensure competitiveness. The incongruity may be rooted in managerial and philosophical divergence that, if unrecognized or under-appreciated, can thwart progress when businesses and universities try to work together. In the private sector, governance tends to be strongly hierarchical; in academia decisions are more commonly reached by building consensus (Dynes *et al.*, 2001). The corporate world is generally more comfortable taking on risk, whereas the academic culture, when dealing with issues that affect the institution as a whole, tends to be more risk averse.

A situation in which university partners typically move more rapidly than their business associates is in the dissemination of research results. Prompt publication of research findings is essential to academic career success, but it may hinder patent protection of intellectual property. Academic researchers wince at requests to delay publication for weeks or months while companies evaluate the market potential of discoveries, knowing that once in the public domain, if unprotected by patents, they may be no longer attractive to venture capitalists able to support lengthy laboratory and clinical trials.

Much has been written about risks to academic research posed by commercial sponsorship (Press & Washburn, 2000; Atkinson, 2000; Hirsch, this volume). Aware of concerns that certain types of association with industry can, in the absence of appropriate safeguards, represent a threat to academic freedom, the majority of UCSD leaders we interviewed believe that the technical and legal aspects of working with the business community can be handled so as not to compromise academic integrity or adversely affect students. With suitable checks and balances regarding issues of non-exploitation of students, healthy, mutually beneficial relationships can prosper. A 1999 report [2] issued by a UCSD committee composed of faculty and administrators described the many benefits of university interactions with industry and made recommendations about topics ranging from conflicts of interest, to involvement of students and postdoctoral scholars in industry activities, appropriate use of university facilities for industry-related purposes, and an organizational structure for overseeing and managing UCSD interactions with industry.

Another aspect of university-industry collaboration that has garnered considerable criticism involves technology transfer, or more broadly, intellectual property management. In the United States, formal technology transfer policies became necessary to manage intellectual property created by the Bayh-Dole Act. This 1982 legislation gave universities the incentive to move ideas into the marketplace, because it granted to universities, rather than to the government, intellectual property rights for discoveries made in the course of federally funded research. Technology transfer officials work diligently to protect the rights of universities and assist in the application and commercialization of discoveries made within academic institutions. However, legal and institutional constraints on the flow of knowledge and capital sometimes lead to technology transfer programs being viewed – perhaps unfairly – as obstructions rather than facilitators of economic development. Despite well-documented success in maximizing the benefits of innovative research, even the best university technology transfer programs in the United States are targets of internal and external criticism.

While acknowledging the necessity of skillful intellectual property management on behalf of the university, we will not deal further with the complex issues surrounding university technology transfer policies in this paper for two reasons. First, the existence of technology transfer programs is predicated on relationships between higher education and the private sector, and our primary concern here is the initiation, growth and sustenance of these relationships, not their regulation. Our focus is on building an environment in which shared intellectual interests are identified, trust established, and the foundation laid upon which to build strong, long-term, mutually beneficial alliances. Second, graduate students, not technology transfer, are the primary instruments by which the university contributes to economic development.

---

2 http://www-ogsr.ucsd.edu/research/industryreport.htm

At UCSD and elsewhere students are highly effective networking agents, working in the private sector to initiate and sustain fruitful associations with industry, and in some cases, launch new businesses. Hence, in training students, the university supports economic well-being by generating the knowledge to help existing industries grow and providing educated entrepreneurs to launch new commercial endeavors.

EVOLUTION OF THE UNIVERSITY-INDUSTRY RELATIONSHIP IN SAN DIEGO

Robert Conn, Dean of the Jacobs School of Engineering at UCSD (1999), asserts that the mission of the research university "now includes the responsibility to proactively ensure that research discoveries are translated rapidly and effectively for the benefit of society and people." Conn argues that given major shifts in the relationships between the federal government and universities and the federal government and industry over the past three decades, the relationship between universities and industry is at a defining moment and that, at this critical juncture, universities need to maintain flexibility and openness. To prompt a discussion of how universities can develop fruitful interactions with industry, we now describe the development of alliances between UCSD and the surrounding high-tech business community.

In a region previously anchored economically by the presence of the military's naval bases, UCSD, from its establishment in 1960, has played an important role in the area's economic development. In the late 1980s and early 1990s, when national defense budgets were cut and the Navy drastically reduced its presence in San Diego, UCSD provided fertile ground for attracting, promoting and nurturing new, small, high-technology firms that grew out of defense industries, then rapidly adapted to meet the demands of the commercial market.

UCSD, together with The Salk Institute and The Scripps Research Institute, fertilized the blossoming of high-technology industry in San Diego (Ferguson, 1999). Under the leadership of visionary individuals who were not only committed to making UCSD a center of research excellence but also worked diligently to make the university supportive of entrepreneurial endeavors, UCSD became a highly effective agent of regional economic development. Plentiful Southern Californian sunshine, the availability of affordable commercial land close to the research institutions, the region's military legacy, and the timing of advances in the computer industry all played roles in attracting high-technology business to San Diego and transforming the region into a recognized economic cluster in which high-caliber, small companies thrive.

UCSD continues to incubate industries dependent on scientific discovery. Not only does the University train many of the engineers and scientists who later take positions with the region's high-technology firms, it also provides a valuable science and technology base for these businesses.

Over the last decade, small technology firms have led the way in setting new directions for San Diego's economic future. Initially, the growth of these high-technology businesses was practically unlimited by external forces. Connections between industrial entrepreneurs and the University were simple, intimate, direct and based on scientific progress. While young businesses grew into San Diego's empty spaces, today, industrial development no longer fills a vacuum.

San Diegans have begun to experience undesirable side effects of rapid industrial growth: decline in the availability of land, worries about affordable water and power supplies, daunting increases in housing costs, traffic congestion, and concerns that the region's public schools are not preparing children adequately to compete for high-paying jobs (Kupper, 2001). While UCSD remains an intellectual leader in the community, relationships among the University, high-technology businesses and government have become more complicated. Increasingly, the community will look to the University to help identify and ameliorate a wide variety of growing pains that have accompanied regional economic development. The challenge to UCSD, and all modern research universities, will be to fulfill a vital civic and intellectual role in regional development, while continuing to build a global knowledge base across disciplines.

BUILDING BRIDGES BETWEEN UCSD AND INDUSTRY

UCSD Chancellor Robert Dynes characterizes UCSD as a start-up university, in part because the institution has played such an important role in spawning and assisting many high-technology entrepreneurial ventures. UCSD shares certain characteristics with start-up, private-sector businesses. A relatively youthful university, UCSD, has as its fundamental strength talented, motivated people whose ideas and commitment to excellence are the seed corn for innovation, economic success, and potential leadership regionally and globally. As for a young business, opportunities for the university to create, refine and disseminate groundbreaking discoveries are plentiful. UCSD must continue to attract expertise and capital while cultivating the vision and flexibility needed to achieve its goals. The entrepreneurial spirit that thrives at UCSD and in the local business community may be a key ingredient in the success of alliances forged between the university and industry.

Interactions between UCSD and the business community take many
forms. Some were initiated by the university in response to internal stimuli
or external opportunity. Others enjoy affiliation with the university but are
independent of UCSD economically and politically. Below we highlight several programs and organizations that build and reinforce powerful, resilient
bridges between academic and business partners.

UCSD CONNECT

Created as an interactive, community-based organization in 1986, CON-
NECT [3] is an excellent example of a university program that promotes economic development by sponsoring ongoing informal and educational activities supportive of the commercialization of research findings, formation of
new enterprises, and growth of small companies. Through its educational and
networking programs, it leverages the multiple advantages of the San Diego
region—world-class research institutions, an urban business-industrial context, available land, and hospitable geography—to support local high-tech
enterprises that stimulate and maintain the long-term prosperity of the
region.

Entirely self-supporting, CONNECT receives no funding from the University or the State of California. It is supported by membership dues, course
fees, grants, and corporate underwriting for specific programs. This autonomy
positions CONNECT to serve as an honest broker of information and ideas.
CONNECT is not a technology licensing office, nor is it a formal incubator;
rather, it is a deliberately developed network of professional competencies
focused on building shared knowledge and robust entrepreneurial teams that
can build and sustain technology based companies. With its combination of
hands-on mentoring and support for entrepreneurs to create business opportunities built around world class scientific discovery from UCSD, CON-
NECT has succeeded by bringing together people, technology, ideas and
capital. Currently under the direction of an accomplished former software
entrepreneur, CONNECT has served as a model for analogous organizations
at other US and European universities.

Through its programs, events, and forums, CONNECT provides numerous
networking opportunities for both local entrepreneurs and entrepreneurial
campus researchers with venture capitalists and seasoned business advisors.
The product of these interactions frequently result in the formation of new
companies based on scientific discoveries born in UCSD's research labs.
CONNECT's designation as an "incubator without walls" attests to its success in catalyzing the formation of various high tech industry clusters in the

---

3 http://www.connect.org/

San Diego region. Strengthening regional clusters of innovation can have global impact, as Porter and Van Opstal (2001) observe: "Although national boundaries matter less in some respects in a global economy, the clusters of firms and industries concentrated at the regional level matter more."

In its early days, CONNECT focused its resources on helping new high-tech companies launch themselves on a good trajectory and attract the venture capital required to exploit and bring to market intellectual property. While it continues to serve in this capacity, in support of the economic stability mature companies give the region, CONNECT's role has expanded to assist the growing "adolescent" firms that look to the university for human capital and continuing education and training for employees. The organization has also taken on a greater role in evaluating, facilitating and defending local policy and infrastructure developments relevant to the maintenance and establishment of new businesses.

In expressing optimism about the direction UCSD is going in developing industry partnerships, university and community leaders we spoke with emphasized the importance of ongoing, informal dialogue between academic researchers and representatives from the private sector who have the resources to assist in the commercialization of the products of research. Repeatedly, CONNECT was praised for its success in initiating links between UCSD and industry, while providing a mechanism to help the university stay abreast of private sector developments that may have intellectual, educational, and social implications for academia, the region, the nation, and the world. CONNECT has also furthered UCSD's involvement in local public policy, an arena a world-renowned research institution may not have chosen to participate in so earnestly had it not been for this organization.

Despite consensus regarding the value and promise of CONNECT, we noted a modicum of disagreement about how CONNECT and the UCSD Technology Transfer and Intellectual Property Services (TTIPS) should interact. Currently the two operate independently, with the former not representing UCSD's interests as does TTIPS. This is seen as a strength by those who cite the separation as a factor in CONNECT's dialogue-enabling success. CONNECT's credibility with the business community might be compromised if it were perceived as another agent of the university. Others, critical of technology transfer efforts, believe it could simplify industry-university interactions if UCSD's networking organization and the group that oversees intellectual property issues joined forces. Given the related but distinctly separate functions of TTIPS and CONNECT, merging the two would be ill-advised. In the interest of heightened internal awareness of the diversity and depth of industry partnerships, exchange of information between CON-

NECT and TTIPS is highly desirable and actively encouraged by the university administration as well as the directors of both organizations [4].

UCSD Extension

UCSD Extension [5], like CONNECT is part of UCSD's Division of Extended Studies and Public Programs. Serving the lifelong learning needs of nearly 40,000 adult students annually, Extension's departments develop and conduct over 2000 courses and 100 certificate programs each year for working professionals, thereby serving the skill development needs of individuals, organizations, and the community. Extension's effectiveness, based on a blend of instruction by both faculty members and practitioners, contrasts with the more structured, degree-oriented, faculty-taught courses offered by UCSD's traditional academic departments. In responding to the changing needs of the business community, Extension provides multiple pathways by which UCSD can help sustain the regional economic prosperity it has been so instrumental in creating. Will society's rapidly growing need for lifelong learning spur universities to incorporate continuing education into their core missions?

California Institute for Telecommunications and Information Technology [Cal-(IT)^2]

In late 2000, an unprecedented three-way partnership linking state government, industry and the University of California was launched. The Governor of California, convinced of the economic value of long-term research and high-level graduate education, announced his support of four California Institutes for Science and Innovation [6] (Dynes, 2001). The intention of this effort, which originated with business and academic leaders, is to foster an environment that increases opportunities for cooperation between industry and the University to speed delivery of public benefits from research and education. One of these institutes – the California Institute for Telecommunications and Information Technology [7] [Cal-(IT)^2] – will team more than 220 UCSD and the University of California, Irvine (UCI) faculty with professional researchers from 43 leading Californian companies to expand the reach and capacity of the global wireless Internet. It will use the new telecommunications infrastructure to advance applications important to California's economy, including education, environmental monitoring, health care

---

4 For a detailed examination of CONNECT's approach to facilitating economic development in San Diego see: Walshok (1995, pp. 175-191) and Preuss (1999, pp. 93-98).
5 http://extension.ucsd.edu/
6 http://uc-industry.berkeley.edu
7 www.calit2.net.

delivery and transportation (Markoff, 2000). With $100 million in state funds and $200 million in matching funds from industry and private sources Cal-(IT)^2 will support investigations of a scope and scale that could not be undertaken by a single investigator nor supported by the resources of an individual company.

Industry-University Cooperative Research Program

Pre-dating the California Institutes for Science and Innovation, the Industry-University Cooperative Research Program [8] (IUCRP) begun in 1996 is additional evidence of California's ongoing support of university-industry collaboration (Penhoet and Atkinson, 1996). The IUCRP serves the nine-campus University of California (UC) system by providing incentives for California businesses to develop research partnerships with UC scientists and engineers, enabling them to engage in fundamental research that could not be accomplished with the limited resources of entrepreneurial R&D firms. The program now invests $60 million a year ($21.6 million from the State, 3 million from UC, and $35.4 million from industry) to create new knowledge and make California businesses more competitive.

Industrial Affiliates Programs

Programs to foster continuing dialogue between corporate executives and academics thrive at UCSD. Industrial affiliates programs provide an effective vehicle for fostering intellectual exchange among university researchers, students, and industry. In UCSD's Jacobs School of Engineering [9], through the highly successful Corporate Affiliates Program, ideas are exchanged, curricula updated, student internship and professional recruitment opportunities are created, and long-term relationships between the university and private companies are cultivated. By encouraging both formal and informal interaction, the Corporate Affiliates Program provides opportunities for collaboration that lead to enhanced economic prosperity in the private sector, while ensuring the fiscal and intellectual support of the university's research and educational missions.

San Diego Regional Economic Development Corporation

University and business leaders we talked with unanimously asserted that UCSD has a civic responsibility to participate in urban planning and in addressing the social and economic problems that have accompanied the rapid growth of high-tech business in San Diego. As a council member of the

---

8 http://uc-industry.berkeley.edu/
9 www.soe.ucsd.edu

San Diego Regional Economic Development Corporation [10], UCSD Chancellor Robert Dynes meets with leaders of local businesses to discuss concerns about the consequences of regional development (e.g., diminishing land availability, worries about the adequacy of existing water and energy resources, traffic congestion) and debate the merit of potential solutions. Dynes' participation in the council's activities helps to keep him informed about issues affecting the current and future prosperity of the region. Organizations like the Economic Development Corporation, and the San Diego Dialogue, described below, help close the gap between academic and civic knowledge.

San Diego Dialogue

The San Diego Dialogue [11] is a self-funded organization based at UCSD. Its invited membership consists of some 150 civic and community leaders from San Diego and northern Baja California who work to identify and address cross-border and quality-of-life issues, such as transportation, affordable housing, pre-college education, and environmental preservation. The emphasis on cross-border issues stems from the recognition that San Diego is unique among large industrial regions in that there are 2-3 million people on either side of the US-Mexican border, and cultural, linguistic, and economic differences, as well as issues of nationalism, must be confronted in regional planning. Many private companies that have R&D operations in San Diego have manufacturing facilities in Tijuana. San Diego Dialogue's research and public education activities are funded by a combination of foundation and corporate grants, as well as revenues generated from public events and corporate and individual affiliate programs. Though independent of UCSD, its university association provides another effective mechanism for civic exchange.

UCSD's new professional schools

Rapid expansion in San Diego's high-technology business community made it clear to industry leaders that a technology management-oriented MBA program would benefit the local industrial infrastructure. Generously supported and aggressively promoted by industry, UCSD's new School of Management is now in the development stages. A parallel development took the form of a call by local biotechnology industries to establish a School of Pharmaceutical Sciences at UCSD. These developments illustrate UCSD's responsiveness not only to the needs of the business community, but also to opportunities created by the strong life sciences research community at

10 www.sandiegobusiness.org
11 http://www.sddialogue.org/

UCSD. Balancing the long-term interests of the university and the needs of the maturing business community will be an ongoing challenge to university leaders.

CHALLENGES FACING UCSD

What will be UCSD's contribution in the next chapter of industrial development in San Diego? Will the increasing globalization of the economy force UCSD to adopt a more global approach to university-industry relations? The university will continue to be an intellectual wellspring, but it has the potential to do so much more in working with the business community to achieve economic prosperity and sustain the high quality of life that has attracted brilliant scientists and entrepreneurs. The heightened interest of large corporations from outside the region in the work of UCSD scientists and in the entrepreneurial activities of local start-up companies will afford new opportunities for university researchers to have global impact.

UCSD's Mary Walshok in a discussion of knowledge linkages needed for new forms of economic development asserts that research universities need more "responsive institutional mechanisms and resources committed to the dissemination and application of knowledge useful to economic development as well as continued support for basic research." She observes: "Economic development in knowledge-driven economies arises out of a confluence of technological, sociological, economic, and political forces." How can UCSD maximize the value of its partnerships with industry, which are focused on addressing technical and engineering issues? Walshok asserts that the university must build a "reinforcing set of knowledge linkages, which assure a policy environment supportive of economic growth, a regional infrastructure ready to support new and renewing industries, and an appropriately competent, informed technical labor force." (Walshok, 1995).

How can UCSD lead or participate in building and maintaining a network of social and infrastructure supports? It must recognise that adaptability and flexibility in the face of uncertainty are essential. Readiness rather than planning is the key to high-tech economic development, because it is difficult to predict which research programs will yield results or implications that can be adapted for useful, profitable individual, social or industrial purposes.

Projections of growth in the regional population and anticipated increases in the number of undergraduate students at UCSD (a staggering 60,000 in the next 10 years) will require the University to participate in urban planning and resource management. Known for excellence in scientific and technological research, UCSD is not commensurately recognized for its expertise in fields that bear upon current regional economic and social issues. Rather than attempting to serve as an authoritative voice in solving urban problems,

UCSD can strive to be an impartial but caring convenor of experts and stakeholders for the purpose of addressing quality-of-life issues. The University can do what it is good at: accessing, sorting, interpreting, validating and packaging knowledge. If UCSD desires to take on the role of leader rather than integrator, it will need to build expertise in fields for which the campus is not now known to excel on a national level. Should the university aspire to make more of its departments world-class? Should UCSD aspire to preeminence in all fields, or is it more sensible to choose to shine in some areas while contributing in others?

At the heart of many decisions UCSD will make is the question: To what extent should direction be influenced by internal and external stimuli? Pressures to form, define, promote, limit interactions with private enterprise stem from internal motivation—for example, the ongoing quest to support the highest caliber research—as well as external forces—for example, the call to provide lifelong learning opportunities and respond to environmental and social problems that have accompanied regional economic growth. Distinction between internal and external incentives reflects the university's dual intellectual and civic mandates. It also highlights the institution's role in both the global and regional economy. What approach should the university take in balancing its multiple commitments?

For businesses and universities alike, having a vision of organizational goals can serve as a good foundation for decision-making. Difficulty in predicting technological developments that will revolutionize the way we think, live, and work suggests that readiness rather than planning may be the best strategy any organization can take. How can research institutions ensure the level of adaptability and flexibility that are essential in the face of uncertainty? Gordon Moore, co-founder of Intel, put it simply: "First, surround yourself with the best people you can possibly find." (*Technology Review*, 2001). Acknowledged intellectual leadership positions the university to achieve political leadership.

CONCLUSIONS: WHAT CAN BE LEARNED FROM UCSD'S EXPERIENCE?

From the university's perspective, forging and nurturing relationships with industry can enhance academic research, add value to the educational experience of students, create diverse opportunities for the institution to participate in civic affairs, and support regional economic development. Formulating policy to guide university-industry interaction is a multi-dimensional task intended to safeguard academic freedom, ensure that university resources are not misused, and, more generally, maximize the benefits of corporate-academic alliances. Building on common interests and goals while acknowledging cultural differences, academic institutions and private sector partners can rise to the challenge of framing highly successful collaborations. By continuing to provide opportunities for open dialogue with the business community, supporting research excellence, and embracing an attitude conducive to collaboration (i.e., serving as a hub of knowledge rather than the master architect; striving for flexibility and adaptability), the university can pave the way for the development of synergistic links with the private sector.

The types of relationships that are desirable are likely to differ among industries and academic disciplines. There have been and are likely to be more mis-steps taken as universities and businesses try to get it right, but the potential rewards are great enough that universities and the private enterprise should not let these fumbles dissuade them from cooperation. Instead, these growing pains should be viewed as opportunities to be more careful, creative and visionary in conceiving and implementing future interactions.

UCSD has done very well in initiating and sustaining healthy relationships with the surrounding high tech business community. In that so many entrepreneurial ventures in San Diego have roots in the university, UCSD's relationship with these young businesses has been somewhat parental. Now that many of these companies have matured into "adolescence" and have more complex needs, their relationships with the university are changing. They turn less to the university for help in finding venture capital, but seek more in terms of human capital. Much like teenagers who, despite increasing independence, benefit from parental ties, maturing businesses look to the university for enhanced collegial relationships. How can UCSD amplify its permeability, expand its engagement in the service of its "offspring", and prepare to spawn new "fry"?

Drawing on our own observations and those of others, we have discussed a number of ways the university, by way of interaction with industry, can add value to the regional economy. The university has much to contribute by:

- generating new knowledge through research,
- building an educated workforce through teaching and graduate education,
- serving as an honest broker, integrator, convenor and dialogue enabler,
- expanding institutional engagement and permeability of the university,
- responding to community needs and participating in urban planning,
- working with industry to overcome obstacles to collaboration,
- bringing to bear global expertise on the local agenda.

In the interest of summarizing the most vital themes of our discussion and providing a starting point for discourse, we suggest that in building resilient, fruitful liaisons with industry, universities would do well to consider the following strategies:

1) Recruit and hold on to the very brightest people.
2) Emphasize readiness rather than planning.
3) Deliberate on the balance to be struck between:
   a. local and global aspirations.
   b. quantity and quality (e.g., number of students versus quality of education).
   c. requirements to respond and lead, sustain and innovate.
   d. seeking benefits and tolerating or avoiding risks.
   e. long-term benefits and short-term gains.
4) Support programs like CONNECT and corporate affiliates programs that increase the permeability of the institution, track and nurture university-industry interactions, and provide a forum for dialogue with industry leaders to better understand the interests, culture, current and future needs of the ambient economic cluster.
5) Support the highest-quality graduate education to equip students preparing to enter the workforce with the broadest knowledge base and skills to join existing businesses or start new companies.
6) Embrace the role of honest broker in gathering, synthesizing and disseminating knowledge.
7) Maintain awareness of local economic, political and environmental issues and work with the community to solve problems.
8) Craft sensible, flexible guidelines for university-industry interaction, but evaluate the justification, merits and potential risks of collaborations on a case-by-case basis.

REFERENCES

Atkinson, R. A. (2000). Response to suggestions about university-industry relationships in "The Kept University", *The Atlantic Monthly*, March.

Cohen, W. (2001). "The New Boomtowns", *Prism*, American Society of Engineering Education, January.

Conn, R. W. (1999). "The Research University Complex in a New Era: An Inquiry and Implications for Its Relationship with Industry", August.

Dynes, R. C., Franks, S. E. R. & Kennel, C. F. (2001). "Three successful modes of research governance: Lessons from the past, issues of the present, implications for the future", in *Governance in Higher Education: The University in a State of Flux*, Hirsch, W. Z. & Weber, L. E. (eds.), Economica, London, pp. 167-181.

Dynes, R. C. (2001). *$300 million UC San Diego-UC Irvine Research Initiative to Guide Innovation in Telecommunications and Information Technology*, UCSD News Release, December 7.

Dynes, R. C. (2001). *Chancellor's Report*, University of California, San Diego, Issue No. 15, Winter.

Ferguson, T. W. (1999). "Sun, fun and Ph.D.s, too", *Forbes*, May 31.

Hirsch, W. Z. (2001). "University-high tech alliances–Alluring economic opportunities and challenging threats", Paper prepared for the *Third Glion Colloquium*.

Kupper, T. (2001). "The Price of Success", *The San Diego Union-Tribune*, March 11.

Markoff, J. (2000). "The soul of the ultimate machine", *The New York Times*, December 10.

National Academy of Sciences, Government-University-Industry Research Roundtable workshop report (1999). "Overcoming Barriers to Collaborative Research", March 23-24, 1998, Irvine California.

National Research Council, Committee on Global Change Research chaired by Kennel, C. F. (2001). *The Science of Regional and Global Change: Putting Knowledge to Work*.

Penhoet, E. E. and Atkinson, R. C. (1996). "Town and Gown Join Forces to Boost State", *Los Angeles Times*, December 31.

Porter, M. E. and van Opstal, D. (2001). *U.S. Competitiveness 2001: Strengths, Vulnerabilities and Long-Term Priorities*, Council on Competitiveness.

Press, E. and Washburn, J. (2000). "The Kept University", *The Atlantic Monthly*, March.

Preuss, P. (1999). "The Research University's Potential as an Area's Growth and Prosperity Stimulant", in *Challenges Facing Higher Education at the Millennium*, Hirsch, W. Z. & Weber, L. E. (eds.), The Oryx Press, Phoenix, pp. 93-98.

Regents of the University of California, Kumar P. C. (ed.) (1995). *Reinventing the Research University*: Proceedings of a Symposium Held at UCLA on June 22-23, 1994.

Regents of the University of California, (1997). *The University of California's Relationships with Industry in Research and Technology Transfer*, Proceedings of the President's Retreat Held at UCLA on January 30-31.

Technology Review, (2001).

Walshok, M. L. (1995). *Knowledge without Boundaries*. Jossey-Bass Publishers, San Francisco.

Wilson, E. K. (2001). "Biotech Eden" *Chemical & Engineering News*, March 5. http://pubs.acs.org/cen/index.html

CHAPTER 12

Facilitating Lifelong Learning in a Research University Context

Mary L. Walshok

INTRODUCTION

The paradox of the modern research university is that it is not changing fast enough and it is changing too fast. Where it is changing is in the speed, the quality, the diversity and the expanding potential value to society of the knowledge it is creating. Where it is not changing is in how it organizes, disseminates and integrates the rapidly changing substance and forms of knowledge within the society it ostensibly serves. The greatness of the modern research university resides in its extraordinary knowledge development capabilities and in the preparation and certification of young adults' mastery of that core knowledge. The weakness of the modern research university lies in its failure to integrate into its core culture and practices lifelong knowledge dissemination and integration capabilities equal to its knowledge creation activities.

Such capabilities are essential today because of the increasingly significant role academic knowledge plays in economic, organizational and civic spheres and because of the increasingly significant value that access to these spheres represents for knowledge development activities within research universities themselves. These dissemination and integration capabilities are also essential because professionals, practitioners and citizens from all walks of life can no longer be effective when the half-life of basic knowledge in increasing numbers of arenas is five years or less. They need access to learning opportunities lifelong so that they can continuously acquire and integrate "new" concepts, principles and practices as well as shed no longer valid "old" concepts, principles and practices. Finally, the need for a culture and organizational capacity as attune to knowledge integration lifelong as it is to knowledge creation has a political and resource dimension. As the challenges of living, working and assuring prosperity become ever more complex and multi-dimensional, the growing disconnect between the highly specialized disciplines within the university and it's attendant inability to constructively engage very real societal needs for information, analysis and interpretation could erode public and leadership confidence in the research–knowledge development process.

It is the premise of this chapter that the modern research university has a unique and essential role to play in lifelong learning activities, which enable continuous interaction between the academy and the society in support of a number of individual, organizational and civic needs. This role is one which is grounded in the key differentiating features of research universities. These include habits, as well as rules, of discourse, analysis and documentation of scholarship and systematic research, which in turn inform generalization, interpretation and, ultimately, action. At its core, the research university represents a set of values and disciplined practices with regard to gathering information, organizing principles and knowledge development. These are the essential "tools" or "skills" of the academy and they are, in turn, those required for lifelong learning, particularly in advanced, rapidly-changing conditions.

The disconnect between the central knowledge activities of the university and the needs of society arises, because the culture and organization of knowledge work within the university is based on increasing levels of special-ization, whereas the integration of knowledge—whether it be in a product, a social problem, an organizational practice or a cultural trend—requires inter-disciplinary and cross professional knowledge. The central lifelong learning challenge confronting research universities today is how to "bridge the gap" between cultural values and organizational practices that reinforce specializa-tion and the fragmentation of knowledge within the academy and the grow-ing need for the integration of multiple knowledge resources throughout society.

The lifelong learning challenge facing the modern research university is not about abandoning a commitment to "free" inquiry in favor of currently "useful" knowledge. Nor is the challenge one of abandoning "useless" theory in the service of more "applied" objectives. The challenge to research univer-sities is also about more than the need for increased "public service" or responsiveness to "new markets." The challenge is fundamentally about the changing role of knowledge in society and the need for integrative and bridg-ing mechanisms suitable to the modern requirements for knowledge in light of its diverse and rapidly changing forms. This chapter therefore addresses that challenge by focusing on three spheres of activity for which research university knowledge is continuously essential: economic growth and transformation; professional and workplace competencies; and civic capacity. It also suggests a variety of ways in which universities can and are creating mechanisms that "bridge" the work of the academy and the knowledge needs of society in cross-disciplinary and integrative ways, thereby addressing life-long learning needs simultaneous with retaining research excellence.

THE CHALLENGE

In a collection of essays entitled A *Digital Gift to the Nation* (2001), the dis-tinguished co-editors Newton Minnow and Larry Grossman remind the reader of a series of "farsighted investments" in higher education made by the United States over three centuries without which the country would not have achieved it's greatness in both economic and civic affairs. They cite in particular three public investments that assured an educated citizenry and productive economy: the 1787 Northwest Ordinance setting aside public land to support public schools in every state, thereby building literacy throughout a new nation; the 1862 Morrill Act which led to the establish-ment of one hundred and five land-grant colleges, which today represent the backbone of America's global preeminence in research and higher education; and the 1944 GI Bill, which provided access to higher education (previously primarily available to elites) to over twenty million everyday American citi-zens, men and women who fought in World War II.

Minnow and Grossman are advocating a fourth such 21st century invest-ment, which would "open the door to a knowledge based future" for all Americans. They are recommending the creation of a multi-billion dollar Digital Opportunity Investment Trust to be derived from revenues the United States federal government will earn from it's auctions to telecommu-nications providers of "the publicly owned electro-magnetic spectrum, the twenty first century equivalent of the nation's public lands of an earlier time." In their introduction to the collection Minnow and Grossman open with a powerful assertion: "In the age of information, the nation's prosperity, its democracy, its culture and its future will depend as never before on the training, skills, ideas and abilities of its citizens. The people's access to knowledge and learning across a lifetime in the sciences and humanities must become a national imperative in the emerging knowledge-based economy".

I begin this essay on lifelong learning and the future of the research uni-versity with this reference to underscore how central this issue has become to leadership in the U.S. and to suggest how broadly we need to think about the challenge as we more thoughtfully and systematically conceptualize and implement comprehensive lifelong learning strategies within the great public research universities of Europe and America.

Without a guiding conceptual framework which addresses: a) the role of knowledge across the full range of human activity; b) the various types and forms of knowledge to which citizens need lifelong access; as well as c) the unique capabilities of research universities to relate to a) and to b), we cannot arrive at a thoughtful and comprehensive strategy. There are growing numbers of "apologists" for specific forms of continuing education and existing programs of "outreach", "service" and "extension." What is lacking, however, is a framework for thinking about these activities, one which integrates lifelong learning into the central mission of research universities in light of the national "imperative" articulated by leaders such as Minnow and Grossman in the United States.

The challenge is conceptual and practical. It requires thinking about three distinct issues:

- Better Understanding the New Imperatives for Lifelong Learning.
- Developing Concepts and Metaphors Useful to Thinking About Lifelong Learning in a New Age
- Building Institutional Capacity for Lifelong Learning Within Research Universities.

BETTER UNDERSTANDING THE NEW IMPERATIVES FOR LIFELONG LEARNING

Our post-modern world is characterized by perpetual change and uncertainty. Individuals, organizations and communities must continually adapt, shed old practices and structures, integrate new information, skills and systems for accomplishing desired ends at home, at work and in the community. That is why we live in a knowledge age. We have come to recognize that learning throughout life is the only way to manage or adapt to change.

This continuous change is driven by many factors, but it can be broadly understood in terms of three macro-phenomena which touch all communities: the speed of technological change; massive demographic shifts; and globalization.

The forces of technology are everywhere, not just in the putative "new economy" of dot coms, biosciences, composite materials and bioinformatics. Advances in science and technology result not only in new products and industries, they transform traditional ones: agricultural food processing becomes as important as food production; computer design and cutting equipment changes clothing and furniture manufacturing; super-computer simulated earthquakes, drug testing, prosthetic device assessments change how we research complex questions previously requiring natural settings.

And so, regardless of our level of educational attainment, the content of our lives and work is continuously shifting and we must learn new things.

The forces of demographic change go far beyond the usual indicators of population concentration in urban centers throughout Europe and America, or the growing numbers of elderly as a particular percentage of our population. The challenging implications lie in facts such as that 11 % of the 2 million population of the City of San Diego is Filipino and 6 % is African American; or, that, today, in the United States, there are more Muslims than Jews and more Buddhists than Episcopalians. Also, more Americans work for companies owned by women than Fortune 500 companies. Ninety-five percent of the new jobs in the United States (33 % of jobs available are new, while another 33 % are becoming obsolete) are being created by small entrepreneurial companies. These demographic trends speak volumes about what one has to "know"—sometimes unlearn, always relearn—in order to effectively develop management and leadership skills; design, manufacture and sell products; teach children; treat patients; run successful cinemas, bookstores or arts and cultural organizations.

Finally, globalization—the fact that ideas, investment capital, manufacturing and distribution centers, suppliers and markets are no longer concentrated exclusively in a few major cities but are present, accessible and mobile across the globe—means that local communities, regional suppliers and producers, consumers everywhere are as affected by developments in London or Hong Kong as they are by Washington or Sacramento. It also means that universal human questions, such as environmental sustainability, health and disease, war and peace are affected by many more places and at much faster rates, so that global intelligence becomes as vital a requirement of citizenship in Des Moines, Iowa or in Bergen, Norway as it is in New York, Paris or Berlin.

The force of these factors—technology, demography and globalization—also gives rise to a paradox of modern times which it is essential to grasp when thinking about lifelong learning and research universities. Everything local is affected by macro trends, often driven by developments outside one's region, and yet the only way to understand, harness, shape and integrate these forces into our civic and work lives is through local and regional initiatives. These initiatives must support continuous learning and facilitate the integration of new knowledge and skills into the daily activities of individuals, organizations and communities in their regions. That is why citizens, industry leaders, politicians and "do gooders" everywhere are calling upon universities to become more engaged. Today, university engagement means not just producing the research and scholarship that is shaping the macro drivers of economies or the initial credentialing of the intellectual and human capital contributing to the economy and society. A new form of engagement is essential. This form of engagement acknowledges that increasingly the key users of knowledge are regionally based. Thus, it requires a distinctively regional approach to meeting the lifelong learning needs of communities, organizations and individuals in the university's locale.

This regional focus does not conflict with traditional research and teaching roles serving global knowledge development. Rather, it can add a new dimension to the work of the modern research university, a dimension with which, however, the university's current culture, organization and leadership are ill-equipped to deal. What is required is added capacity, rather than a transformation of mission. Research, scholarship, residential degree programs are all respected and valued hallmarks of the modern university. However, in this new age of regionalism, the university must also embrace a commitment to local engagement, knowledge integration and the need for lifelong learning, if it is to sustain its social value and political support as well as its intellectual integrity.

DEVELOPING CONCEPTS AND METAPHORS USEFUL TO THINKING ABOUT LIFELONG LEARNING IN A NEW AGE

The lifelong knowledge needs that must be addressed regionally are of at least three distinct types, based on the sort of forces that continuously challenge and shift the contours of regional economies, critical social institutions such as schools, health care systems and local government, and the competencies of the regional professional and managerial workforce. Research universities are the logical centers of new knowledge for these challenges. This is because of 1) the potential contributions of science and technology research to the development of high wage jobs through the growth of new globally competitive technology based industries drawing on the unique intellectual capital in and around the university; 2) their cutting-edge degree programs, which prepare and credential a cadre of potential workers and professionals, as well as their capacity to organize and authenticate emergent and cross disciplinary knowledge essential to advanced forms of continuing education and practitioner credentialing and 3) their long traditions of scholarship and discourse in the arts, humanities and social sciences, which link them to global conversations and perspectives representing valuable resources to community problem-solving and citizen education. Universities need to think about their connections to community learning needs in ways that address all three roles.

Universities rarely think this comprehensively however. They tend instead to point to individual initiatives, which often arise out of self referential needs and interests—an industrial affiliates program in engineering; high fee professional and management part-time degree programs; associates and

friends of this gallery or that theater program. Rarely do the research universities in the United States develop comprehensive lifelong learning strategies
that serve the many corners of their communities who want to learn and
grow. Too often, they focus only on those sectors with the wherewithal to
fund the more specialized interests of the faculty or particular learning constituencies.

To build capacity for genuine engagement with the region requires a corporate sense of mission vis-à-vis the region, one that addresses at least three
types of distinct but over-lapping knowledge needs:

- The need for innovation through science and technology, which supports regional economic renewal through globally competitive industrial applications of technology as well as entrepreneurial enterprises.
- The need for education and credentialing programs, which not only
  launch people into careers and professions but address their lifelong
  needs for retooling, up-grading, inter-disciplinary and cross professional education and training.
- The need among citizens and vital social institutions to understand
  the forces shaping their effectiveness, as well as forums and settings
  which develop and integrate regionally relevant knowledge to help
  them adapt and change in ways that assure continued well being in a
  democratic community.

In other words, the university leadership—faculty, administrators and
trustees—has to be thoughtful and strategic about where it can add the most
regional value vis-à-vis:

- Economic renewal and development
- Workforce training and continuing professional education
- Community problem solving and citizen education.

A broader conceptual framework for thinking about lifelong learning will
result in different kinds of activities and collaborations campus-by-campus
depending on regional differences. However, in any context, the knowledge
resources of research universities can be responsively and appropriately mobi-
lized around these three imperatives.

In addition to a broader framework for defining the mission and purposes
of lifelong learning, universities need to become a) listeners not just teachers; and b) present themselves as "hubs" of knowledge rather than the exclusive sources of knowledge. To be regionally effective and professionally relevant requires a commitment to listening and learning about and from
diverse regional constituencies as well as high levels of expertise in a field.
Listening is essential to assessing what aspects of the university's knowledge

capabilities are most relevant and can be most useful to the community, as well as what parts of the university's intellectual work can be positively enhanced by the knowledge and concerns residing in the region. To achieve this requires genuine dialogue and collaboration between the higher education institution and the community. The traditional knowledge work of the academy—basic research, scholarship, and degree granting—is shaped primarily by national and international communities of discourse, evaluation and authentication. Today, university knowledge also needs to be informed by the peculiarities of local factors and concrete experience in order to be regionally relevant. Thus, the lifelong learning agenda needs to be informed and validated by a regional constituency, as well as by principles and expertise anchored in more national systems. The idea of "shared agenda setting" is the critical concept here.

A third concept for thinking about developing an institution-wide lifelong learning capacity is the notion of the university as a "hub" of knowledge rather than as the exclusive source of knowledge. The mandarin culture of too many research universities presumes scientific and academic forms of knowledge and discourse are superior to less well developed forms of knowledge evolving out of lived experience and the practical uses and applications of information. However, the methodological rigor of much scientific and scholarly work requires "screening out" contaminating variables, developing a precise and often esoteric language, separating facts from values and timeframes that rarely include a sense of "urgency" about coming to closure or solving a problem. The successful application of knowledge requires integrating these "messier" forms of knowledge with "purer" forms of academic knowledge. Successful lifelong learning initiatives—be they focused on economic development, continuing education, community problems or civic education—cannot succeed without the university seeing itself as a convener, a broker, an integrator, an authenticator and interpreter of knowledge across many communities—lay and academic—and across many disciplines. If the university persists in asserting that its specific forms of knowledge are more valid and that its forms of expertise are superior, it cannot build the sorts of robust lifelong learning connections that will enrich the work of both the academy and the community.

Thus, three key ideas need to conceptually frame strategic thinking about lifelong learning in a research university context.

- Lifelong learning needs to be an institutional mission and broadly understood in terms of its form and content. At a minimum, it should include initiatives that can support a) the continuous renewal and development of regional economies; b) the continuous learning needs of regional labor pools, executive and professionals across a variety of fields and institutions; c) community and organizational learning and problem solving in times of continuous change; and d) civic education and enrichment relevant to understanding the forces shaping the quality of life and democratic processes in the region.

- Because most lifelong learning initiatives are regionally anchored, regional knowledge, experience and voices need to be integrated with the global academic knowledge base and resources the university represents. This means collaboration and shared agenda setting must shape most lifelong learning initiatives.

- The university's position at a regional level cannot be that of an intellectually superior source of indisputable expertise. Rather, it is a "hub" of knowledge resources, equally adept at harvesting and integrating community and academic knowledge. It needs to be an "honest broker" in arenas typically fraught with special interests, incomplete facts and an absence of trans-regional perspectives. The university's knowledge gathering, authenticating and interpretive capacity is as important regionally as the distinctive areas of expertise within the faculty.

BUILDING THE CAPACITY FOR LIFELONG LEARNING WITHIN RESEARCH UNIVERSITIES

If these three broad conceptual frames are correct, then the institutional capacity to play convening, listening, agenda setting, authenticating, interpretative and translational roles needs to be an integral part of the university's culture and organization. It requires academic professionals who are good facilitators and interlocutors. This means offices, which can organize, document and record community input and conversations. It requires specialized staff and facilities to implement events, roundtables, forums, courses and seminars based on consultative meetings and wide inputs. This means resources—line items in campus budgets, grants and underwriting, fees for services—to support the delivery of programs and learning, as well as to give incentives to new forms of faculty engagement and new approaches to gathering and developing regionally-relevant knowledge. Finally, it requires credible, strong leadership in the highest administrative and academic councils of the university in order to assure its integration with traditional research and teaching activities.

The most critical organizational issues may not be such things as new tenure policies, new rewards for individual faculty or for activities, which are primarily led and defined by faculty experts. More critical may be the integration of faculty professionals and community expertise through a collaborative process which assures programs and educational initiatives which draw upon the intellectual standards, expertise, and knowledge resources of the university and the community. The challenge is an institutional one, not a problem of individual faculty on their own, without proper support, getting involved in individual public service. Universities need to have an academic and administrative infrastructure in place that allows them to serve lifelong learning needs in a highly interactive way. Campuses need offices and professional staff who can work with faculty to develop academic programs that build vital social and economic partnerships with their communities. This new infrastructure of support should also provide places for meetings, dialogues, instruction regional research capabilities and a complement of skilled professional and ongoing programs essential to building continuing relationships with community constituencies.

All of this requires professionals and processes that contribute to the capacity of the campus and its constituencies to engage in problem solving. This could be through such things as continuing professional education; technical assistance to schools, hospitals and companies in transition; or the commercialization of research that can be used in enterprise development or job creation. There need to be institutional mechanisms that facilitate ongoing community dialogues, which engage the full range of campus disciplines and the diverse needs of changing communities. This requires a new kind of knowledge professional, who can work with faculty and the community to develop intellectually enriching activities as well as programs of community value.

The research university's lifelong learning agenda goes well beyond the provision in specific schools of support staff to implement existing degrees on a part-time basis or instructionally focused continuing education programs in classrooms for professional credit taught by practitioners. These are essential, but not enough. If the agenda includes assistance in regional economic development, learning partnerships around organizational and community renewal and change, civic education and community knowledge, as well as regionally focused research and technical assistance programs, then universities will need to develop institutional mechanisms and academic teams with distinctive characteristics. This includes intellectual bridging skills, convening capabilities, local knowledge development capabilities and academic program delivery capabilities (Ehrlich, 2000).

The University as Convener

It is imperative that campuses invest in offices and people with the authority, skill, time and resources to organize conversations across academic fields and special interest communities. This is not an easy task. To be a convener requires a number of characteristics that many campuses do not possess among existing faculty, staff, or administrators. Community links through which issues and concerns can be fed into the campus are essential; this means people on campus committed to and charged with listening. To know to whom the campus needs to listen and what constituencies should be convened also requires an accurate map of the social and economic world in which the campus is located. Who is responsible for developing and updating these maps and what competencies do they need to do this?

Convening requires a network of active relationships both on campus and in the community to mobilize appropriate expertise and leadership to address the varied dimensions of the civic agenda. Research universities, in particular, are typically not good at this, because of the highly specialized and self-referential character of so many academic fields and the narrowly defined missions of offices charged with community outreach and public service. Nonetheless, there are knowledge professionals or public intellectuals in many cases who, if integrated into the academy, could be catalytic agents in brokering the highly specialized programs and departments within the academy that are potentially relevant to a knowledge problem in the larger society. For example, assuring a responsive community healthcare system requires knowledge not only of up-to-date medical practices, but of culture, religion and gender in communities with new immigrants; of citizen attitudes and public policy if systems need changing; of local history and religious values in the face of changing social dynamics and new ethical dilemmas. Engaging diverse forms of knowledge in sensitive and integrative ways is something research universities could do exceptionally well if they have proper people to play these "knowledge bridging" roles.

New Kinds of Knowledge Professionals

Coalescing academic expertise, community know-how and research and development resources to fill regional knowledge gaps, organize information and elucidate issues is a formidable challenge. This is because, at least in the United States, higher education since World War II has been focused on developing deeper (and narrower) academic disciplines and increasingly specialized expertise. The ability to operate simultaneously in the world of the esoteric academy and that of the everyday layperson is a capacity fewer and fewer people have. Thoughtful journalists, specialty magazine writers and editors, research librarians, documentary filmmakers, art and culture curators and community and extension educators typically are very good at this. They represent professionals who have chosen to be interlocutors and interpreters of ideas, values, and cultural forms to selected publics. As such, they represent bridges between specialists and generalists and, most importantly, they are able to translate the central concerns and ideas of each community to the other.

It is this sort of quality of mind and communication skill that is essential to developing shared agendas and harvesting the diverse knowledge resources needed to address complex lifelong learning needs. Universities need to draw people with these qualities into partnerships with faculty and community representatives to build knowledge and understanding. These partnerships can yield research projects, educational initiatives of value to the region, as well as traditional students and community forums of regional significance.

Program Delivery Capabilities

The prior two capabilities relate to forms of interaction, styles of agenda setting, and qualities of people essential to building partnerships that can simultaneously serve academic and community knowledge needs. Program delivery relates to the nuts and bolts of turning a well-developed academic community plan into activities such as a community forum, an applied research project, a publication for a community readership, or a professional development seminar. There is a significant component of management, marketing, and financial expertise that goes into effectively implementing these hybrid programs. As such, they represent significant investments. However, if properly designed and administered, they can also attract private funders, qualify for grants and contracts, secure corporate sponsorships and underwriting, and charge tuition or fees.

There is much to be said for some sort of centralized coordination function to handle such a full range of lifelong learning programs and services. The capacity to support such a wide range of lifelong learning activities is at a minimum linked to six essential organizational characteristics:

- Support from Senior Administration and key academic leadership at the university, especially the Chancellor and Provost. The leader of the life-long learning unit needs to be a member of the Leadership Councils, participate in senior Deans meetings and interact regularly with the Provost and Faculty Senate.
- Highly qualified professionals leading all of the lifelong learning initiatives. There have to be competent and credible people, who articulate and advocate the mission as well as facilitate partnerships and program development. Such persons need to be full-time, academically qualified, and intellectually engaged as well as community focused. They are the champions, the visionaries, and the catalytic agents in the academic/civic partnership. Typically these professionals are PhD's, MBA's and attorneys, and similarly prepared individuals.

- Space and Support Staff. There need to be places where people can meet, converse, learn, research, create and, even, park. There need to be people who answer phones warmly, who schedule events, set up meetings, keep notes and records, follow up on promises made, supervise students, attend events, and are involved in the community.
- Communications. There need to be mechanisms and staffing to facilitate regular communication about opportunities, aspirations, needs, achievements, and findings. These include newsletters; occasional papers; reports; journals; issue and research briefings for the media, decision makers, and elected officials; information-rich radio, television, and internet series. They also include marketing and PR expertise. These skills are not typically located in university public information offices.
- Business Functions. Managing budgets, developing contract and grant proposals, acknowledging donors, and forming strategic partnerships on and off campus require administrative, legal, and financial expertise. Once again, student enrollment and grants administration systems in research universities are not well suited to lifelong learning financial and administrative services.
- Diverse Sources of Funding and Political Support. Finally, comprehensive lifelong learning strategies require cash and political support.

Lifelong learning cannot be the pet project of a single department, function, or dean. It cannot be exclusively financed by a short-lived foundation grant or special legislative allocation. It cannot be wholly dependent on fees for services or market needs that often overshadow an intellectual agenda. It must represent many stakeholders, many advocates and many sources of financial support just like other campus programs in research universities. Even if implemented through a single centralized campus unit, lifelong learning must reflect diverse campus and community interests.

CONCLUSION

In conclusion, it may be useful to share the experiences of one of the more dynamic, young research universities in the United States, the University of California, San Diego. Our experience is interesting because we have been able to develop a campus culture and an approach to academic program initiatives which is highly innovative, in part because the campus has not had to deal with decades, much less centuries of traditions and established interests. The campus has therefore developed a number of interdisciplinary research programs and pioneered a variety of academic fields such as cognitive psychology in a manner that has brought significant national and international attention to the faculty. Currently UCSD is ranked number seven in the United States in annual research funding. Nineteen of its graduate programs are ranked in the top ten nationally. In addition, a disproportionate number of faculty (based on size) are members of the national academies of science, engineering and medicine. This is true as well for awards such as Nobel Prizes, Macarthur Fellowships and Guggenheims.

In the context of a young prestigious university, UCSD, the development of a robust lifelong learning activity has honored many of the principles described throughout this article. Over a twenty-year period, with significant support from the office of the Chancellor and senior academic officers, the university's linkages to the San Diego region have grown in complex and meaningful ways. For example, an important emphasis has been placed on helping assure that the presence of a research university and related research institutions in San Diego benefit the regional economy. To this end, the university developed an Executive Program for Scientists and Engineers emphasizing the sorts of leadership and management skills required in science based companies. It has been operating very successfully for more than seventeen years. Over the last fifteen years, the university has also been home to UCSD CONNECT, a program focused on networking the competencies needed to start and grow science based companies, which create high wage jobs and new forms of regional wealth. The CONNECT program, through more than eighty events annually, has helped develop a community of entrepreneurship that is unparalleled. Scientists and engineers interact on a regular basis with attorneys, accountants, management consultants and venture capitalists, in a manner which enhances the science knowledge in the business service and management communities as it builds entrepreneurial "know how" and business development skills among leaders of promising science based companies.

With regard to relating to the ever-changing needs of a regional professional and managerial workforce, the university has developed over the last twenty years an imaginative array of continuing education and executive education programs focused on key technology sectors such as IT, life sciences, environmental sciences and software. More than forty thousand adults, eighty percent of whom are college graduates, participate in these evening and weekend programs, which enhance their workplace skills or prepare them for new opportunities and requirements emerging in science based companies. More than eighty certificate programs (four to eight course sequences designed to ensure workplace competency) are offered through the university's Extension division. They include such things as CDMA technology, teaching English as a second language, clinical trials management, biotechnology manufacturing or the design and construction of research facilities. In addition, the division offers a number of advanced institutes and seminars on topics especially pertinent to professionals in the regional economy such as medicinal chemistry, math and science education in the public schools or doing business in a cross border environment.

With regard to public policy issues and community change, the university has also supported the development of a variety of programs that are designed to fill regional knowledge gaps through research on topics of regional significance, newsletters, forums and roundtables which bring academic and community expertise together. The San Diego Dialogue is a cross-border, regional, public policy initiative, which focuses on issues of community value and plays a interlocutory role between the expertise in the academy and the needs of the community. It gathers data, sponsors public forums and seminars countywide, as well as publishing a newsletter and occasional reports. Fully funded by foundations, memberships and corporate underwriting, the Dialogue has a distinctly regional focus, but benefits from the intellectual resources of a great research university. A new initiative funded by the PEW Charitable Trusts at UCSD is the UCSD Civic Collaborative. It is a program that provides professional support as well as financial resources to link faculty interested in research and teaching on topics of regional significance. Particular emphasis has been placed on such things as local history, recent demographic trends and cultural shifts, The Collaborative is helping to build a significant regional knowledge base that has both academic and public value.

Finally, with regard to civic knowledge, the university has initiated a broadcast television station, which is unique in its focus. The purpose of UCSD-TV is neither to provide distance learning courses nor to be a conduit through which programming produced by networks such as the Public Broadcasting Service are delivered to the San Diego region. Rather, the mission of UCSD-TV is to capture for broadcast and web casting important cultural, political and scientific events and programs of community value. The university's commitment to growing civic knowledge is further supported by a variety of endowed public lectures and distinguished visitor programs, which have been set-up for the explicit purpose of bringing intellectual resources from around the country and around the globe to the San Diego region for public programs. Many universities have endowed lecture programs that focus primarily on faculty interests or undergraduate students. UCSD has been fortunate to secure endowments which support programs that benefit both the academy and the community simultaneously.

The purpose of sharing these examples from the University of California, San Diego is not to suggest that the campus is a model for what ought to be done. Rather, it is to demonstrate that it is possible to develop a very rich multifaceted approach to lifelong learning initiatives in a research university context. A common theme in all of the initiatives at UCSD is a focus on spheres of activity and forms of knowledge that articulate well with a character of a research university. This means focusing on support for science and technology based companies (as opposed to local retail or tourism) as a way to assist the regional economy. It means emphasizing continuing professional and executive education for post-baccalaureate adults working in enterprises and professional fields that reflect the character of the UCSD campus such as research and development, high school and college teaching, medicine and healthcare management. It means approaching community forums and civic education in a manner that also takes advantage of the unique characteristics of a research university. By having national and global links for example, the campus is uniquely positioned to bring expertise from other communities and other regions to San Diego in a way that can inform local discourse about important issues, be they transportation planning, strategies for sustaining the natural environment, or innovative approaches to serving the needs of low-income children in urban school districts. In all of these cases, the fact that UCSD is a research university is an essential reason for the success of the programs.

These programs are supported by fees, grants and contracts. They are highly valued in the region, because they make a unique contribution that is not replicated by other colleges and universities, much less other lifelong learning programs. Attracting more than $30 million dollars annually in fees and support, and employing more than 200 of the sorts of new knowledge "professionals" described in the earlier section of this chapter, UCSD's initiatives in public programs and through University Extension reflect many of the principles suggested in this paper.

Research universities across the United States and Europe have a distinctive regional role to play in the provision of lifelong learning initiatives that address an increasing number of professional groups, community issues and regional economic challenges. They are uniquely positioned to be a resource and it is essential that leadership in higher education institutions of this character begin a more serious dialogue about the role they have to play in lifelong learning. Out of that dialogue, an institution-wide strategy needs to emerge, in which campus leadership, faculty leadership and community stakeholders are invested equally. Such a shared investment will make it possible to build the financial and political support needed for a comprehensive institutional strategy, which includes a variety of highly interactive programs, a highly skilled professional academic staff and the needed support for program implementation. The research university intellectually is one of the most dynamic institutions in society today. It needs to be similarly dynamic in its approaches to organizing, disseminating and integrating knowledge in society.

REFERENCES

Ehrlich, T. (2000). *Civic Responsibility and Higher Education*, The American Council on Education and the Oryx Press, Phoenix.

Grossman, L. K. & Minow Newton, N. (2001). *A Digital Gift to the Nation: Fulfilling the Promise of the Digital and Internet Age*, The Century Foundation Press, New York.

CHAPTER 13

Facilitating Lifelong Education

Leslie Wagner

CHANGING DEMAND

L ifelong education has become an increasing feature of the work of universities over the past decade. The reasons for the increased demand for lifelong education have been well documented. They are essentially the interlinked forces of technological and other change, increasing professional standards, globalization and growing personal responsibility for career development (Fryer, 1997; CIHE, 1998; Salmi, 2001).

Scientific and technological change seems to be increasing at an exponential rate. It is being created both in university research departments and through government and corporate research and development. Changes in information and communication technology (ICT) are the most prominent, but there are significant breakthroughs in many other areas, such as biosciences, biotechnology, pharmaceuticals, and medicine. The postgraduate and even the undergraduate curriculum in these subjects is seriously out-of-date within a few years. Those researching in these areas, even if they themselves are contributing to the change, must keep abreast of what others are doing. Companies also need to maintain the understanding of leading-edge developments by their scientific and technological and managerial staff in areas in which they operate.

An often neglected driver of lifelong learning is legislative change. This is sometimes stimulated by technological change (e.g., data protection or the use of embryos), but also by changing norms in society (e.g., health and safety or pollution issues). Clearly, lawyers need regular updating of their knowledge, but so do many other professionals and managers. There is hardly any area of professional or commercial activity which is not affected by regular legislative change. In addition, notions of professional competence change and standards that were accepted previously are more regularly challenged. As a result of all these factors, continuing professional development (CPD) has become an integral part of professional activity and many professions now require a minimum annual level of CPD activity from their members to enable them to maintain their license to continue professional practice.

This concern to achieve higher standards and remain up-to-date goes beyond the professions to the general area of management. Legislative change impacts broadly across this area, most notably on health and safety issues and employee relations. More generally, the competence of managers at all levels in an increasingly competitive environment puts performance under greater scrutiny and updating of skills, attitudes and competencies at a premium.

Increasing globalization of economic activity is fuelled not just by technological change, but also by other forces, and this in turn has an impact on the need for greater lifelong learning. The huge investments in research and development needed to create major technological change in pharmaceuticals, for example, require world markets for commercial exploitation and thereby reduce the number of firms able to compete in those markets. Capital is mobile, labor less so, and large groups of the population can find themselves without employment by corporate decisions to move manufacturing or headquarter activities across the globe. Increased globalization can mean that when a company is in commercial difficulties the impact across many communities is much larger. For all these reasons, people pursue lifelong learning not just to update their knowledge and skills but to re-orient their careers through new skills and qualifications. This more radical re-direction of careers is also fuelled by technological change making previous skills and qualifications obsolete and redundant.

All these forces are making the notion of the lifelong loyal company employee a thing of the past—even in Japan. A job is no longer for life. It may not even be for this year! One of the consequences is that employees are increasingly taking responsibility for their own career development and not relying entirely on their employer. They may seek employer support for their program of learning, and enlightened and far-sighted employers will provide it. But the drive for identifying the program comes from individuals anticipating their future career needs.

CHALLENGE AND RESPONSE

This wide range of forces has resulted in large and varied demand for lifelong learning provision ranging from three or more years of PhD study to a one-day updating course on recent legislation. The first example is most obviously provided by a university. Indeed in most countries it cannot be provided in any other way and it offers no challenge or threat to university tradition. At the other end of the spectrum, there will be many private organizations better able than a university to offer cost-effective one-day updating courses. It is between these two extremes that the battleground between universities and other providers lies. The greater challenge, however, is within universities themselves and it is one of culture and values. Only when that is resolved will universities be able successfully to meet the challenge from other providers. Or, more precisely, only then will they be able to decide which challenges from other providers they wish to meet.

The traditional university through the 20th century saw itself, and continues to see itself, essentially as a place of scholarship, research and the development of the highest possible intellectual standards. Certainly these are the norms and values of the individual academic. Students, it is argued, need to be exposed to this culture if they are to develop their intellectual potential and proceed on graduation to contribute most usefully to research, the economy and wider society. Students are important for all sorts of reasons (not least financial), but the needs of the subject and the discipline come before the needs of the student.

Even for the purists, however, continuing education has a legitimate place in higher education where it is related to the core value of research. Indeed the university is often the only place where exposure to leading-edge technological change can be experienced. Moreover, the purist approach has long been diluted by higher education's central role in preparing people for the leading professions, such as medicine and law. Over time, many other professions from architecture to teaching have become subjects of study in universities. It follows naturally that continuing education and development in these professions is also seen as a function of universities.

There is also the curious case of business education, largely neglected for much of the 20th century at undergraduate level in the traditional universities but increasingly sought as a mark of excellence at postgraduate and specifically post experience level. In the most traditional of universities, business education is seen exclusively as a form of continuing education linked to research.

The picture would not be complete without reference to another form of continuing education which has typified the traditional universities, certainly in the United Kingdom, and whose objectives are in complete contrast to technological and professional updating: extra-mural or adult education. Its focus is largely the humanities and social sciences and its purpose is to educate and stimulate the general population. Often uncertificated, its values are those of liberal humanitarianism, of making the scholarly resources in the university available to the wider population.

All these well-established forms of continuing or lifelong education have been increasingly challenged from a variety of sources in recent years. Universities are not the only source of scientific and technological discovery and leading-edge activity. Indeed, the closer the discovery is to the market place the more likely it is to be found in the laboratories of the corporate sector. And the more likely it is that commercial confidentiality will lead to corporations organizing their own updating for their staff. Increasing research partnerships between universities and corporations does not change this drive for technological updating to be more Individual Corporation focused.

The challenge to universities on professional updating comes both from the professions themselves and from private providers. And the issues here are ones of competence and attitude. A professional body may believe it is more in touch with the issues of professional updating than a university department and thus better able to provide what the individual professional is seeking. A private provider dedicated to updating courses and depending for its livelihood on performing well is likely to be more alert, flexible and focused than a university department for which this is not its central activity.

Business education is a more complex area. On the one hand, the most prestigious of the traditional universities are able to flourish in the MBA and other post-experience areas relying on their research expertise and elite status. On the other hand, the price insensitivity of the market allows a high-quality, private, non-university based sector to flourish in competition with the elite universities. And, below this level, much rougher forms of competition exist with a range of providers, including universities, colleges, corporations and private entities.

In the U.K., even the liberal humanitarianism activity of continuing education is under challenge, but less from competitive predators and more from the difficulties of funding. In the current instrumentalist culture, in which higher education and certainly continuing education is expected to lead to economic return, the utility of spending public money on learning for pleasure is increasingly questioned.

The Role of Technology

Much has been made of the increasing role of information and communication technology in challenging the role of higher education in lifelong learning. The discussion is much confused and some clarity is required.

As has been argued, higher education's role in lifelong learning is under challenge, without any influence from technology. The challenge has arisen from questions about higher education's competence in and attitude towards lifelong learning and ambivalence about whether it is a legitimate function of the academy.

The use of information and communication technology in learning has existed for a long time. Audio and visual technology has been available for over forty years and computer-managed instruction almost as long. The introduction of web-based technology has created a step change in the opportunities available. But the key point is that technology only provides the opportunity. It does not by itself provide the change. That is stimulated by educational and market opportunity. The best example of this is perhaps the UK Open University.

The Open University was established over thirty years ago and has gained a worldwide reputation for its use of information and communication technology. It began in 1971 entirely with an undergraduate program, widened this to post-graduate, and now has one of the most extensive post-experience programs in the country, if not wider afield. It is the lifelong learning university *par excellence*. Most observers praise its technological innovation, but in doing so they miss the point.

When the Open University was being established in the late 1960's, its founders did not survey the most advanced technology available and ask themselves how they should use it. They began with their educational objectives and asked how they could best achieve them. The cornerstone of the Open University's work is not technology, but access. Its core initial objective was to offer the opportunity of a second chance for undergraduate education to adults who had not been able for a variety of reasons—educational, personal, financial—to go to university at the traditional age of 18 or 19. Contemplating how that opportunity might be provided across the country to people who had many other commitments, the obvious answer was distance education.

When the components of this distance education were considered, educational and cost effectiveness were the overriding factors rather than technology. So the printed word, a technology first invented in the 15th century became the dominant feature of the Open University's instructional package, and remains so to this day. Of course, other more advanced technologies are also used, including radio, television, cd-rom, web and email, but the criteria remain the same: educational and cost-effectiveness, not technological determinism.

This simple but powerful lesson of the Open University's experience is vitally important for understanding how technology may shape the role of lifelong learning in the universities. There are too many examples of technological solutions searching for an educational problem rather than the other way round. Yet the lifelong learning challenge today is the same as that faced by the Open University over thirty years ago. How can educational opportunities for continuing learning best be provided to people who are time, locationally and possibly financially constrained and whose needs are likely to be highly focused? In many cases, advanced technology may be the answer through, for example, the Internet, use of email and other electronic media. In other cases, it might be distance education using the postal service or radio. And in yet others, it might be a network of real not virtual study centers based on existing educational facilities in a range of locations. The Open University uses all these approaches. For its core undergraduate provision, the most used and popular forms of instruction are the written text distributed through the postal system and face-to-face tutoring in real study centers! (Wagner, 1982).

LIFELONG LEARNING AND THE UNIVERSITIES

The key question is not how best universities can meet the outside challenges to their role in lifelong learning but whether they wish to do so. The challenges are ones of culture and values not technology. And language is also important. So far the words continuing education and lifelong education or learning have been interchanged as if they mean the same thing. It is time to question this assumption and to ask "What's in a name?".

"Lifelong Education" is an elastic phrase capable of being stretched to cover a variety of meanings. It is the latest in a long line of expressions covering broadly the same activity. Veteran students of higher education policy will remember the arcane debates of the 1970s about the differences between recurrent education, continuing education and "éducation permanente" (OECD, 1973). In that sense, lifelong education, or lifelong learning as it is increasingly called in the UK, is just the latest variant on the same theme.

Or perhaps not, for different words should imply different meanings. The word "continuing" implies a continuation of something which has already started. Its conceptual framework is of an initial phase of full-time study to bachelor, masters or doctoral level. Continuing education is then what follows, after a break from study. It can involve, for some students, following courses from the "initial" phase, but for most students it involves shorter more ad hoc more flexible study leading to non-traditional qualifications, or even to no qualifications. The motive for such study is usually occupational or professional need, but it can occasionally be driven by personal needs.

This typical model of continuing education does not challenge the basic values and structure of the traditional system. It accepts its essential foundations of an initial phase of full-time study which changes slowly according to traditional academic norms. Whilst some "continuing education" students will study these "initial" courses, they will be a minority alongside those pursuing "initial" higher education and the courses will not be changed nor adapted to their special needs. The majority of continuing education students will be taking different shorter courses outside the core provision.

However large such continuing education might be in volume, it is, in cultural terms, peripheral to the life of the universities and makes little impact on the lowering, let alone the tumbling, of the walls of academia.

For some, the word "lifelong" means the same as "continuing". Its difference, if any, is to inject freshness into an old concept amounting to nothing more than old wine in new bottles. It implies no change in the traditional model of initial and continuing higher education as two distinct and separate phases and therefore poses no serious challenge to the walls of academia.

For others, "lifelong" means something very different to "continuing". It offers the opportunity for radical change. Lifelong is an all embracing concept. It does not follow anything. Lifelong covers the beginning, middle and end of the higher education experience. There may be still different phases or stages, but no one phase inherently has hegemony over the others. More fundamentally, the phases must be integrated and a holistic approach to the process adopted. The lifelong higher education needs of students require all phases to be subject to interrogation and the initial phase perhaps most of all. Here, embracing the concept of lifelong education creates fundamental challenges to the walls of academia.

An even more radical challenge is created by the use of the word "learning" rather than "education". Both are nouns, but one views the process from the provider's perspective and the other from the student's perspective. Education is what universities provide. Learning is what students experience. Using the word education from the student's perspective requires the use of the phrase "being educated". Using the word learning from the university's perspective requires the use of the phrase "providing learning opportunities". The words "education" and "learning" on their own fall naturally on either side of the divide. Education is a supplier's word—it is what is provided. Learning is a consumer's word—it is what is experienced.

So the terms higher education or continuing education or even lifelong education betray a, perhaps, sub-conscious, value system focused on a provider's perspective. However sincere the claim to be responsive to students, the value assumption in such a phrase is that provider's needs and judgments come first. The walls of academia take precedence. The term learning, on the other hand, heralds a radically different approach. Learning means that student needs are paramount. So the phrase "lifelong learning" provides a double challenge to the walls of academia. It means changing continuing to lifelong and education to learning. This implies abandoning the notion of an initial higher education experience largely unchallenged in its core structures and processes, followed by a spasmodic continuing experience in a system organised from the provider's perspective and to their convenience. In its place comes a holistic approach to higher education, responsive to student needs (Wagner, 1998).

If continuing education, as defined above, is to be the underlying value, then the walls of academia will barely shudder, let alone be lowered. Research and associated teaching focused on traditional undergraduate and postgraduate work will remain the core activity and source of funding. If this is undertaken successfully, there will be few financial pressures for change to create other sources of income. Continuing education will exist as an adjunct to the core activity and will continue to be regarded by the guardians of tradition as a pimple or abscess on the smooth face of academia. The most telling proof of this is that, in many universities, continuing education is provided in a separate department and the academics involved are not regarded as members of the department that covers their discipline. Even where continuing education and updating are provided in the same department as the core research and teaching activity, they are often undertaken by different staff and have a lower status.

It is one of the great paradoxes of innovation, particularly in higher education, that, in order to enable innovation to occur, it often has to be nurtured in a separate organizational entity. With careful tending the innovation will take root, blossom and be successful. In its own terms, it will have achieved its objectives. However, the very fact that it is separate prevents its lessons being disseminated to the wider organization or system. Indeed, its very separation legitimises the traditional activity. The forces of inertia and conservatism, which required the creation of a separate organization or structure to produce reform in the first place, in due course, prevent that reform from permeating the rest of the organization. This is one of the lessons of the Open University's impact on the rest of the UK higher education system and it applies also to how continuing education is organized inside an individual university. Separation may be the only way success can be achieved but its very introduction is itself an admission of failure (Wagner, 1985).

An important cultural issue at the heart of continuing education or lifelong learning for the traditional university is the supposed distinction between education and training. The term continuing education not only implies a restrictive attitude to what is included in that term, but very specifically excludes "training". This supposedly lower-level activity, traditionalists argue, is not for universities and should be left to others such as colleges or private providers. It ignores of, course, instruction in for example, medicine, law or architecture, which explicitly requires "training" to ensure competence for professional practice. The lifelong learning university has no such pretensions. It recognizes that learning is not only student centered but embodies a wide variety of learning, including skills learning which is the function of training.

A comprehensive lifelong learning approach will shake the academic walls. Lifelong learning requires scrutiny of the initial phase of higher education as well as the continuing phase. It requires scrutiny of curriculum and pedagogy from the student's perspective as well as the tutor's. It requires flexibility as to entry requirements, mode and method of instruction, and to the structure of qualifications. The lifelong learning university still values research and the highest intellectual standards, but balances these objectives with those of meeting student needs. Moreover, its definition of students is much wider than simply undergraduate and postgraduate. It encompasses all those seeking updating, upskilling, retraining and the attainment of the qualifications needed for career change. In the lifelong learning university, the relationship between the initial and the continuing phases of higher learning is seamless, both culturally and organizationally. In such a university, the academic walls certainly come tumbling down, but they are rebuilt with more transparent and user-friendly materials.

REFERENCES

Council for Industry and Higher Education (1998). *Partnership for the Professions: Supporting Individual Development*, CIHE, London.

Fryer R. H. (1997). *Learning for the 21st Century: First Report of the National Advisory Group for Continuing Education and Lifelong Learning*, Department for Education and Employment, London.

OECD (1973). *Recurrent Education: A Strategy for Lifelong Learning*, Paris.

Salmi, J. (2001). "Tertiary Education in the 21st Century: Challenges and Opportunities", *Higher Education Management*, 2 (13).

Wagner L. (1982). *The Economics of Educational Media*, MacMillian, London.

Wagner, L. (1985). *What are the main innovative features of new (reform) universities and other new institutions of higher education and what is their impact, if any, on traditional institutions? The Changing Functions of Higher Education*, Research Institute of Higher Education, Hiroshima University, Hiroshima.

Wagner, L. (1998). "The Radical Implications of Lifelong Learning", Philip Jones Memorial Lecture, NIACE, Leicester.

PART IV

● ● ● ● ● ● ● ● ● ● ● ●

To Conclude:
The Future of University
Partnerships

CHAPTER 14

The Industry View of Collaborative Research

Peter Lorange

INTRODUCTION

C ollaborative research is becoming increasingly important. It can lead to more effective generation of new knowledge, based on a complementary division of labor between industry and academia. However, the benefits to industry and academia alike depend on how well this network relationship works. In this chapter, I first suggest a conceptual framework for the accumulation of strategic know-how and, also, for how to conceptualize a network organization for new discovery. How can collaboration between academia and industry enhance this? I then address six specific challenges regarding this collaborative task. Lack of attention to any or all of these issues can lead to potential dysfunctionalities. First, I attempt to identify potential practical problem areas when it comes to collaborative research. Then, I discuss the question of how negative scientific results might be reported or dealt with. This then leads me to examine the question of publication policies more generally. It is logical that general ethical concerns are then reviewed. This is followed by a discussion of the key economic constraints and challenges of financing this research. It is essential to be clear about what the various parties are paying for—and what patterns of obligation this might create.

I have had a chance to discuss the above issues with seven practitioners—who shall remain anonymous—representing leading corporations active in collaborative research. Three of these corporations are from the pharmaceutical area; one is from the software development area; two are from the food and nutrients area; and one represents a chemicals corporation. I am most grateful for the inputs from these cutting-edge practitioners. However, the conclusions in this chapter are my own.

A CONCEPTUAL SCHEME FOR KNOWLEDGE GENERATION IN COLLABORATIVE RESEARCH

The modern corporation is typically driven by a knowledge-based strategic approach (Von Krogh *et al.*, 2001). Its success largely depends on whether it has the relevant knowledge to pursue meaningful strategies, above all, based on "seeing" and pursuing new business opportunities before they are obvious to its major competitors.

To push for new knowledge that can expand a firm's strategy is therefore critical. This can perhaps be thought of as taking two directions. One would be to go after new interfaces with customers, through pursuing new market opportunities. Established strengths and proven bases for success could perhaps be "exported" into new markets. The other would be to add new competencies to one's established business bases, thereby further strengthening one's business. These two approaches both build on what already works, either through a *leveraging* of one's present business or a *build-on* to one's present business. Exhibit 1 illustrates this.

Exhibit 1: Build on Established Strengths: Basic Competence-Based Framework for Internally Generated Growth

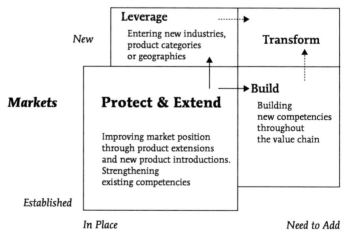

For executives and scientists heavily committed to scientific discovery, a tempting view might perhaps be that one should look for entirely new competencies, to be applied to entirely new market situations—what we call *transform* in Exhibit 1. Research indicates, however, that this is typically a less realistic way of strategically building business success for the future. In contrast, it tends to be more effective to build incrementally on one's present strengths by finding new distinctive add-on competencies (a build strategy) and/or by finding new market applications to utilize what already works (leverage strategies). Interestingly, then, when a build—or alternatively a leverage—strategy has been established, one can *subsequently* add a leverage—or build—dimension, so that one might eventually achieve a transform strategy, but through a longer evolutionary path. Thus, this is done via an indirect route, not through direct pursuit of new "cloud nine" ideas based on entirely new competencies and entirely novel market applications.

Collaborative research can of course play an important role in all of this. Most of all, perhaps, it might be effective when it comes to adding new distinctive competencies. The key here is to make sure that the distinctive competencies are such that they lead to a build strategy, and, further, that there is enough of a link with the present strategy of the firm. The collaborative research must lead to value-add-on capabilities to what is already working. At times, however, the collaborative research may be too unguided, perhaps attempting to achieve a transform-type strategy which, as already noted, tends to be less effective. A safe general conclusion can now be made: collaborative research must be based on a clear strategic positioning of what is to be achieved within the firm's growth strategy.

Before discussing the six more specific challenge areas identified, let us observe that the very context for collaborative research has changed due to the emergence of new web-based communications technology. Cooperation today must thus be seen in this new light. The new communications technology embedded in the web is enabling corporations and outside entities, including academic institutions, to collaborate in radically new ways. Virtual networks for research can be established between a firm and others. One can describe this as going from Research and Development to Connect and Develop. Exhibit 2 illustrates this.

Day (2002) reports on this type of cooperative pattern at Procter & Gamble. It involves a lot of outsourcing—reaching out for innovation through a web of connections. Specifically, Procter & Gamble is reported to have 600 websites readily available for access by its researchers and new product developers, all linked up with outside sources containing the latest relevant thinking. Kimberly-Clark, IBM and Eli Lilly are reputed to follow this type of approach too. At Intel these networks are called *lablets*. This trend towards web-based cooperative networks in R & D will certainly become even more common; it will reshape the role(s) of collaborative research.

Exhibit 2: From R & D to Connect & Develop

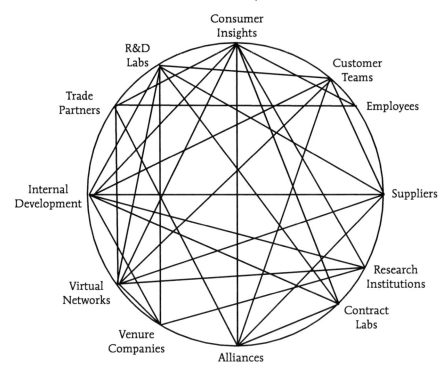

At this stage, a general caveat should be raised. Most corporations will, of course, primarily make available on the web the type of information that they *wish* to communicate. This could, however, create an information-flow bias, in the sense that the more euphoric, positive tidbits about one's recent projects may set the norm to be communicated. On the other hand, realistic, balanced research inputs may be lacking. This potential source of bias may thus in the end hamper network-based collaborative research between industry and academia.

Practical problems of cooperation

Several key areas can be identified. First, the question of intellectual property may be a central source of conflict. It is thus particularly important that this issue is well understood. The expectation equation between the two sides needs to be clear in terms of who finally owns the results of the common research efforts. It further has to do with a clear understanding of the costs of the project, meeting deadlines and ensuring correct reporting. A clear understanding when it comes to reconciling possible time scale differences is also key. Academia, for instance, may take a longer-term viewpoint, with a more basic research focus, whereas the business side may take a shorter view and be more application oriented. This may have profound effects on how to interpret the intellectual property rights. Thus, who will finally own the results of the common research effort? The answer to this should, however, be absolutely clear, stemming from comprehensive contract documentation that takes all the above issues into account.

Second, as already touched on, the time horizon for this research typically differs. The opposite argument to the one outlined above can, however, also be made, in the sense that academia, faced with a "publish or perish" pressure, might indeed have a more short-term focus, whereas business might take a longer-term view. Business might have the resources to take such a long-term viewpoint, which may no longer be the case in academia, one might argue. The "right" answer to this controversy will of course depend on the specific situation. It will therefore be important to establish a good understanding of what the time horizon differences actually are in each case.

A third area of potential conflict may be whether academia will in fact be able to be truly independent, doing *bona fide* freestanding research, and being fully accountable for its research output in a scientific sense. There is controversy here. Take, for example, the pharmaceutical industry. Several people have argued that there is "growing interference by pharmaceutical companies in the conduct of clinical trials and the publication of their results ... The reliability of clinical trials, essential for the development of new drugs, is increasingly imperiled by conflicts of interest, inappropriate involvement of sponsors in trial design and management, and biased in publishing the results. In a highly competitive world, the pressures may be simply too great for individual researchers, universities, medical journals or public agencies to stem the tide of commercial influence." (*Financial Times*, 2001). Thus, the whole area of academic independence is at the heart of a healthy cooperative equation. Premature dissemination of results, for instance, without the full academic rigor behind them, may be part of this problem, since such results may not then stand up to scientific quality principles. The toxicity issue in the pharmaceutical area, for example, absolutely must be addressed when it comes to defining quality. It is the patient's safety that should unquestionably be at the center when defining quality, not the urge to publish "interesting findings" before scientific results are absolutely clear.

A fourth issue may have to do with the "silo cultures" in academic and industry-based organizations alike. It may be hard to work collaboratively across such kingdoms. The resulting fragmentation—leading to isolated atmospheres and non-eclectic realities—can clearly hamper the quality of collaborative research. This implies that a certain level of maturity is required when it comes to organizational culture. There must be a minimum degree of openness. The "not invented here" attitude must be substituted by a "now improved here" approach. The key is "to borrow with pride," as said at one of the firms interviewed.

A final source of potential conflict may have to do with changes in the portfolio strategy of the firm and adjustments in overall risk taking, with the implications that these will have for various academic research projects. At the heart of this is a realization that risk must be balanced—this is critical for all scientific work. The firm must manage its portfolio of research projects from a risk-taking perspective. This means that academic work on specific projects in the portfolio will have different risk profiles—some will be more risky and some less risky. If the direction of the overall portfolio changes, this might lead to shifts in specific projects, redefining specific risk profiles. Similarly, the geographical mix of the firm's overall portfolio strategy may change, so that relatively more projects are run in the United States, for instance, while relatively fewer are run in Europe. The split between basic scientific approaches to be pursued may also be adjusted—relatively more emphasis on chemical components research versus biochemistry research for the portfolio strategy of pharmaceutical firms, for instance.

The key is to come up with an overall *balance*, which is meaningful when it comes to risk exposure, geographic split, types of focus areas, such as biochemistry versus chemical components, etc. To manage this portfolio when it comes to risk, geography, scientific component focus, etc. is critical, particularly if one is going after major innovations. In one of the pharmaceutical companies we examined, it was argued that biochemistry had been relatively too dominant in the portfolio relative to chemicals, and that too much of the research had been focused on the U.S. versus Europe. Further there was a silo mentality issue in the organization of this firm which tended to contribute to an imbalance in the reality of its portfolio. Top management clearly needs to drive all of this. It is when this portfolio balance is being shifted—a key prerogative of top management in any science-driven firm—that potential problems might arise when it comes to cooperation with academia. Specific collaboration projects may have to be dramatically adjusted—and it may be hard for the academic research teams involved to understand this without having access to the firm's (now revised) portfolio strategy.

Disappointing research results?

On the question of negative results, one could perhaps say that there might be two fundamentally different reasons for this: bad craftsmanship of the researcher, based on a sloppy design; or a well-prepared scientific design, which turns out to give a disappointing result.

There was a clear consensus from industry that the latter case represents no problem when it comes to publishing. This is, after all, central to the nature of research. The issue of sloppy research design is more troublesome, however. A quality culture is therefore important when it comes to cooperative research. Good science leads to good quality output—and there is no problem in publishing it then, whether it is positive or negative. Quality must drive the process.

To ensure such quality, perhaps sponsors should be contractually bound to respect the intellectual independence of researchers. This could be done by establishing a registry for "filing" details of all trials, by prohibiting sponsors from taking legal action against researchers except in the case of fraud, and by protecting whistle-blowers who report unscientific and unethical research practices. Dealing with disappointing results thus may have a lot to do with developing a healthy organizational culture with a minimum of organizational politics, allowing truth to be the ruling principle.

Negative results typically need to lead to "stop decisions" on particular research programs. Again, when human lives are involved, the patient's needs have to be key; safety is everything. Beyond this, however, there can clearly be differences of judgment regarding when to stop a project. Here, the organizational culture and reality should be strong enough to counteract any tendency for wishful thinking and entrapment (Brockner et al., 1981).

Should all experiments be hypothesis-driven, the way we have learned to know about it from Popper (1963)? Some argue that we need both hypothesis testing-driven research and more open-ended experimental research design. Trying the latter is important to arrive at unexpected answers, which one would rarely reach via classical hypothesis testing. Hypothesis testing is typically associated with quantitative research based on precise measurements. It could be that more anecdotal research might be more effective in some settings, however (Brunner, 1986). In the area of human genetics, for instance, some felt that a Popperian approach would be relatively less effective.

Publication of scientific results

One key approach seems to be that there might be a *coordinated* process of granting patents and releasing publications, ensuring that both are generated in parallel. This is meant to ensure good protection of each project and research platform. At the same time, one would be able to keep a current date for publication without having to insist on delays for this. The issue is thus *both* to get adequate patent protection *and* have the data disseminated fast. Still, it seems to be generally acknowledged that the publication process needs to recognize the strong sensitivity for protecting proprietary findings, at least until the research is fully ready. Academia may want to report on short-term results through early publications, whereas industry may want longer-term protection through a thorough patent application process. A well thought out procedure of parallel patent and publication coordination is therefore key.

The issue of too early publication may still be significant. A sign-off procedure, whereby the parties would agree on any article *before* publication and be sure that no trade secrets were revealed, may be normal to avoid too early publication. This "right to agree" on any article's content before publication may thus be critical. Although industry seems to appreciate publication, they may still want to make sure that potential trade secrets are being protected (Stern & Simes, 1997). Obviously, there is a fundamental disconnect here between the interests of the two sides—only good faith and mutual trust can resolve this.

The issue of competitiveness will thus of course play a major role when it comes to the publication side of collaborative research. On the one hand, a given corporation will typically not want to engage in a cooperative research project with an academic institution if the knowledge generated might freely benefit other firms, particularly its competitors; hence, the importance of intellectual property rights and delayed publishing. Still, a firm may want to cooperate on more basic research, in which other corporations might also be involved, to enhance the general boundary of useful knowledge within a more basic field. This sharing of resources among several players—to pursue the basics—can clearly be beneficial. We can perhaps label this pre-competitive research. Cooperation between industry and academia might be particularly fruitful here. But this assumes that participating firms will not impose stringent patent protection requirements or publication constraints. The patent policy—and publication policy as well—will thus have to be more flexible and applied differently in the case of pre-competitive research than in cases where there will be a clear threat of competition. Within the pharmaceutical field, the area of genomics is now generally treated as pre-competitive, with no patents and few publication constraints. Similarly, in chemicals, consumer electronics and in several other industries, one can find significant areas of pre-competitive research. Particularly, with the emergence of web-based research networks for Connect and Develop (see Exhibit 2), a key challenge for the participating entities will perhaps be to "move up the barriers" for pre-competitive research, to allow more "space" for this. This should significantly open up for a more straightforward approach to the publishing of results in these areas.

It has been suggested that a *code of practice* governing the relationship between researchers and sponsors should be established, to guide publishing practices, safeguard scientific independence and ensure impartial handling and assessment of the results. For instance, "the editors of thirteen leading medical journals made an unprecedented joint statement saying they would refuse to publish studies where researchers did not appear to have professional independence." (*Financial Times*, 2001). It was further pointed out that often editors of scientific journals might be biased towards publishing primarily hypothesis-driven experiments, in the Popperian tradition. But, what about publications involving the more pre-paradigmatic type of studies? These should of course also be expected to appear. Will industry allow this type of research to be published—perhaps revealing what might be closer to their strategic thinking, and will the scientific community open up for this? Obviously there might be biases here. And what about publication of negative results? These clearly need to be published as well. Here, several have pointed out that there might be an editorial bias against this—such findings are less "catchy!" Some say that it may primarily be the less prestigious journals that in the end might publish negative results (Easterbrook *et al.*, 1991).

Issues of potential ethical concern

These issues of potential publication biases raise ethical concerns too. The implementation of a good collaborative research project might be seen to have at least four ethical aspects. How might these be handled? There seems to be a rather common practice to have an ethical board, both at the university and the corporation level. Key issues regarding potential ethical conflicts seem to be handled through interactions between such boards.

- First, there is the issue of premature publication. It may be particularly important that the so-called Helsinki agreement is not violated here (*World Medical Association*, 2000). Again, a well laid out contract should safeguard the practice of good ethics when it comes to concluding research with adequate scientific design, worthy of publication. An ethics board may also play a constructive role in the timing of publication decisions.
- Second, the documentation around a project raises ethical questions. The issue of having accessible protocols so that other researchers can verify the results, clear guidelines regarding how to collect, analyze and store data, etc. are all aspects of good research practice. As already noted, the establishment of an independent registry for "filing" ongoing results may also be useful. Again, the contract can do a lot here. An ethics board can also be proactive.
- Third, funding may have an ethical side. If the funding is too closely linked to performance, there might be a temptation to take short-cuts that might violate ethics with respect to how a project is run, with respect to how the publication policy is approached, even perhaps with respect to aspects of safety. This may be particularly dangerous when young, less experienced researchers, such as doctoral students, are involved. Some of the companies responding provide independent funding to doctoral projects, with less pressing performance requirements attached, and/or provide independent

donations—say from their own research foundations—to support basic doctoral research. These firms are sensitive to the fact that the funding should not lead to such pressures that ethical principles are potentially violated. Potential misunderstandings regarding funding may always exist. These should not be of an ethical nature, however. If ethical dysfunctionalities are involved, then they must be resolved—or the project should be dropped!

- The fourth and final issue deals with the fact that in both business organizations and academia there are often internal organizational kingdoms, highly compartmentalized structures, strong but isolationalist academic departments or research groups. Potentially, this can lead to unethical practices too. The potential challenge is the fact that "homemade" norms and practices might develop within such silos, which may stretch what one would normally find as ethical. It is thus important that top management—and top academic leadership as well—pay attention to the enforcement of standard ethical norms and requirements. They must not allow questionable insular ethical practices or interpretations to take hold.

A specific potential ethical conflict might stem from the fact that a university may already be carrying out cooperative research with competitors of a firm newly approaching it. Here, it seems critical that all trade secrets are indeed kept secret. To create procedures with "Chinese walls" must be key. This probably involves using entirely separate research teams on potentially competitive tasks—to mix the people might lead to working accidents. Clear human resource policies are therefore essential. The university in question should see its own reputation as a very critical asset here and it would probably not want to enter into any activities that might jeopardize such a "Chinese walls" approach. There does, in fact, seem to be a reputational safeguarding of potential ethical conflicts. Contracts typically spell out noncompetitive clauses. The potential for strategic leaks to a competitor must be minimal. However, if the sensitivity of a particular project is too high for the company, then it may be that entering into a cooperative research arrangement at all is seen as unattractive.

Finally, there seem to be diverse practice on whether to have a specific ethical board or not. Some have, but often companies do not have this. Such boards may be called for, above all, regarding the issue of ethics and judgment when it comes to safety. This is critical, perhaps particularly in pharmaceutical research. Here, concerns for the patient's safety will be absolutely paramount. Several firms have pointed out that if there are more fundamental ethical problems, then the project might actually be dropped.

Financial contributions

The general principles of the financial side of collaborative research seem to be rather straightforward: that a clear project orientation is established, and that full-fledged negotiations are being entered into when it comes to how the project is going to be financed. Competitive issues will be key here. If too costly, then other university sources might be approached to provide the service. A budget must be established. Funds must be managed on a real-time basis, only to be released when clear milestones are being met. Specifically appointed project leaders seem to be critical in all of this. The control of the financials would be part of the project leaders' follow-up. In summary, key words would be "projects," "defined budgets," "clear control," "clear negotiations of specific cost items if things get out of hand" and "clear gradual release of funds against a project's progress." There would thus be norms regarding how costs are incurred and how to handle misunderstandings. Also, the link between the financial dimension and the contractual dimension must be clear. This must also make it clear who owns the research (DeAngelis, Fontanarosa & Flanagin, 2001). In short, good project management practices must be followed (Vollmann & Whybark, 1997).

Other unforeseen conflicts

As pointed out, the contract should provide guidance on how to handle potential conflicts, how to settle, even terminate them. A good contract is therefore essential. The legal department may play an important role in the handling of contractual conflicts. There might also be some procedures for handling escalating conflict here. For instance, the *Chief Technology Officer* may end up being involved if a conflict is particularly difficult. The prestige and perceived importance of the academic institution may also play a role regarding the way conflicts are handled. There may be more tolerance towards settling conflicts in ways that are relatively more favorable to the academic institution if this is seen as a particularly prominent research team from a reputable university.

A frequently recurring potential source of conflict is intellectual property rights. Intellectual property rights typically must belong to the industry side; if this is not clearly understood, there could be potentially nasty conflicts, according to the conventional point of view of industry. This is of course related to such issues as publications, including establishing guidelines for publications that respect the intellectual property rights. We have already discussed this. Again it should be stressed, however, that on the industry side an open attitude is called for—not a dogmatic one. With the latter there would probably be little or no collaborative research at all!

In general, as long as the legal framework typically seems to work well, there might be few practical problems with the procedures for handling conflicts. The rights of the parties will then be clear and respected by all. In the case of escalation of conflicts, the more senior officers that are then involved, both from the industry side and the university side, typically seem to be able to handle this in an amicable way. The mutual will to succeed—jointly—is key! Both parties must be mature enough to live by "when in doubt—do the right thing" (Schwarzkopf & Petre, 1992) when it comes to making collaborative research happen.

CONCLUSION

The phenomenon of collaborative research between industry and academia seems to be growing rapidly. This is not surprising, given the dramatic increase in the general emphasis on relevant knowledge. The winners will be the organizations that "see" business opportunities early, before they are obvious to everyone else, i.e. those organizational entities that have the knowledge to create novel business opportunities.

Clearly, more innovative research, undertaken at an even higher speed than before, is key to this. To achieve it, the need to draw on eclectic groupings to obtain new knowledge creation will be more acute than ever. The emergence of web-based communications technology and the establishment of networks for collaboration on R & D will speed up the process. This should lead to even more collaborative research efforts.

In this chapter, I have pointed out several practical challenges when it comes to how this collaborative process might actually take place. The trends when it comes to all of this are indeed encouraging. Collaborative research can successfully take place provided that:

- there is a positive willingness—a sense of maturity—on both sides
- there is a clear commitment to quality, ethical behavior and respect for fundamental values
- there is a clear understanding of how to dismantle dysfunctional pressures and enhance ethical norms. There must be a positive view of the need to settle disputes pragmatically—one must see opportunities, not problems!
- there is a willingness to adhere to a clearly drawn legal contract, including constraints on publishing due to patents—but also to be active in the pre-competitive collaborative research area, where there would be no patents and few publication constraints.

All in all, the issues at hand relating to collaborative research seem to be manageable. One would thus expect that collaborative research will expand even more in the future, and that industry will be ready to contribute to such growth. One would similarly expect that academia will be even more prepared to deal with the industry side in the future. This may be particularly significant when it comes to attempting to develop a more open culture, with fewer silos or kingdoms, and more understanding of the need to see industry as a partner. It will be all about bringing the best brains from both sides together.

REFERENCES

Brockner, J. *et al.* (1981). "Face-Saving and Entrapment", *Journal of Experimental Social Psychology*, 17.

Brunner, J. (1986). *Actual Minds, Possible Worlds*, M.A., Harvard University Press, Cambridge.

Chakravarthy, B., Lorange, P. & Cho, H-J. (2001). "The Growth Imperative for Asian Firms", *Nanyang Business Review*, Vol. 1, No. 1.

Day, G. S. (2002). "Marketing and the CEO's Growth Imperative." Paper given at the Marketing Science Institute Conference, Boston, April 25.

DeAngelis C.D., Fontanarosa, P.B. & Flanagin, A. (2001). "Reporting financial conflicts of interest and relationships between investigators and research sponsors". *JAMA*, 1. 286-89-91.

Easterbrook, P. J., Berlin J. A., Gopalan, R. & Matthews, D.R. (1991). "Publications bias in clinical research". *The Lancet*, 337:867-72.

Financial Times (2001). "Who Accuses Drug Groups of Interference". 18 December.

Popper, K. (1963). *Conjectures and Refutations: The Growth of Scientific Knowledge*, Harper Colophon, New York.

Schwarzkopf, H. N. & Petre, P. (1992). *It Doesn't Take a Hero*. Bantam, New York.

Stern, J. M. & Simes, R. J. (1997). "Publication bias: evidence of delayed publication in a cohort study of clinical research projects". British Medical Journal, 315:640-5.

Vollmann, T. E. & Whybark, D. C. (1997). *Manufacturing Planning and Control Systems*, McGraw-Hill, New York.

Von Krogh, G. *et al.* (2001)."Making the Most of Your Company's Knowledge: A Strategic Framework", *Long Range Planning*, Vol. 34.

World Medical Association, (2002). *Declaration of Helsinki, Amended 2000*.

CHAPTER 15

The Future of University Partnerships

Frank H. T. Rhodes

INTRODUCTION

U niversities were created to nurture partnerships. Universities came into existence in the Western world in the 12th and 13th centuries to overcome the inevitable limitations of isolated scholarship. This scholarship was for centuries pursued largely in monastic seclusion and, though some individual contributions were notable—one thinks of the Venerable Bead—and a few monasteries blossomed as centers of scholarship, the limitations of secluded scholarship became increasingly evident. Those limitations remain today. The isolated scholar, sheltered from conflicting viewpoints, untouched by contemporary issues and events, unchallenged by those from other disciplines, is liable not only to limitation of viewpoint, but also to either dogmatism, on the one hand, or unalloyed skepticism on the other.

There was also another major weakness of isolated scholarship: personal knowledge frequently died with the scholar. Only in a community of younger and older scholars could knowledge itself be created, shared and perpetuated. So teaching, as well as learning, became an essential part of the new communities. By contrast to this earlier isolation, in community, knowledge itself became expansive; contested by opposing interpretations, informed by other disciplines, it gained new vigor; shared with others, this new community allowed both students and masters to enlarge their range of interests and increase their skills. Once partnership developed, both in the community of scholars, and in the community of masters and students, the circle of discussion was enlarged, the effectiveness of study was increased and the impact and usefulness of knowledge was expanded.

It was from these monastic scholarly communities that the universities emerged. Even in their earlier days, such communities became centers, not only of rote learning, but also of disputation, where one viewpoint contended with another, and where one discipline impinged upon another. It was within these communities that the earliest student guilds and faculties or colleges were formed, the prototypes of later partnerships. So canon law flourished alongside philosophy, and theology existed side-by-side with classical learning and mathematics.

The needs that led to the creation of these ancient colleges, almost a millennium ago, remain with us. Knowledge itself requires the refinement and testing that come from partnership. It is not only that existing knowledge is too vast for any solo effort, but also that it is so demanding in its assumptions, so broad in its implications and so intricate in its relationships that it becomes vital to study it in comprehensive multidisciplinary terms. Abstraction and dissection produce abstracted and dissected conclusions. Broad understanding of the implications and impact of our knowledge of the natural world, or current events or social programs or the human condition, requires this broadly integrated approach to learning.

The social benefits of the partnerships embodied in universities have been so extraordinary that all developed societies have chosen to create and support their own universities, which have, over the centuries, exercised an influence and yielded a societal benefit out of all proportion to their numbers. Educating a growing portion of the young people of their own lands and others, they have been a steady influence for good, whether in liberal education, the inculcation of civic virtue, preparation for professional careers, the advancement of knowledge, or the general leavening of the intellectual, civic and moral health of their societies. Their expanding influence has reached far beyond the ministry of the church, for which the earliest institutions were created, to such a degree that governments, communities, individual benefactors, and, more recently, industries and corporations, now continue to create and enlarge universities to serve their own social purposes. Nor is any diminution of that role yet apparent. Universities continue to expand their influence as engines of scientific discovery, as communities of technical invention and as supporters of both social analysis and economic growth. From agriculture to medicine, from architecture to international studies, from engineering to urban planning, the universities play an increasingly large role in the life and wellbeing of contemporary society.

That social contribution reflects the fact that the partnerships within the university have not been confined to those between the scholarly disciplines. From their earliest days, universities have also embraced the professions—law and medicine, for example—within their membership. And as the professions have multiplied in numbers and scope—engineering, architecture and management, for example—so each, in turn, has been incorporated within the expansive membership of the university, partners alike in both teaching and practice. Perhaps the best test of their success has been the fact that few patients would now choose to undergo major medical procedures at a facility other than an academic medical center.

It is because such professional partnerships have been so successful, that the question emerges as to whether they could, or should, be further expanded. Should we encourage still broader partnerships with industry, for example, or with professional societies, local communities, governments, or non-government organizations? If some academic walls have come down, should all be demolished? Before addressing that question, it may be worthwhile to review the existing situation.

THE PRESENT SITUATION IN INDUSTRY

- **Globalization.** When one examines the present situation in industry, there are several trends that appear characteristic across the range of particular industries. The most striking of these is the globalization of the economy and the increasingly international character of most major businesses, typified by the great multinational corporations. With this globalization, there has also emerged an increasingly multicultural membership of the corporations themselves, so that board members, senior executives and staff are now recruited and employed on a global basis.

- **Role of research.** Furthermore, with the increase in international competition has come a sharpening of focus, and—perhaps because of this—a relative de-emphasis in comprehensive corporate R & D, with the breakup of what had been integrated corporate research labs. These earlier great corporate laboratories, including those of Bell Labs, IBM, GE, and RCA, were not only centers of formidable technical expertise and development, but also of extraordinarily distinguished work in basic science. They have been replaced by three alternative means of conducting research and development: the creation of R & D centers attached to particular businesses, rather than the parent corporation; the creation of less costly R & D centers in developing countries, such as India, and, to a lesser extent, the outsourcing of R & D to universities and other research centers. With this dispersion of R & D has gone a relative decline in support for longer term research in favor of more emphasis on shorter term development.

- **Corporate education.** With these trends in industrial research has gone one other: Corporations are creating their own universities.

These range in sophistication from Hamburger University created by MacDonald's, to the John F. Welch Executive Education Center at General Electric, Crotonville, New York, and the General Motors Institute in Michigan. There are now reported to be some 2,000 corporate universities in the United States, up from 800 in 1988. In the same period, more than 100 four-year colleges have closed (Meister, 2001). The broad purpose of these various corporate universities is not only to "fill the gaps" in conventional educational programs, but also to provide employees at all levels with opportunities for lifelong learning. Admirable as those intentions are, the growing number of these institutions represents a significant competitive challenge to traditional university education and especially to university-based continuing education programs. It is a challenge that should be welcomed and accepted. In fact, it provides an opportunity for new styles of partnership.

- **Educational partnerships.** Corporate concern for continuing education has produced new partnerships. Thus, the University of Connecticut offers certificate programs in business to Hartford Financial Services Group (Meister, 2001). But, although 92 percent of U.S. corporations outsource the delivery of education and training programs and 60 percent outsource some aspect of course design, only 16 percent of all corporate education partnerships are with traditional colleges and universities, perhaps because other educational providers prove more nimble and less costly than universities. Conversely, corporate universities are now offering courses to the general public. This mixture of missions and providers seems likely to continue as demand for lifelong learning increases.

PRESENT SITUATION IN THE UNIVERSITIES

The landscape within which higher education functions is broadly similar for all universities and colleges, whatever their particular mission and goals and whatever their sources of funding and varieties of governance. In the United States, and, to some extent, beyond, several trends are now emerging.

- **Deregulation.** Universities have long had a monopoly of educational programs; self-accrediting, and self-authenticating, their monopoly of resources, whether in faculty expertise, library holdings, technical facilities or experimental equipment, has given them a unique role and a particular responsibility. That has recently changed as accrediting agencies have not only recognized, but have also credentialed and accepted a range of complementary institutions, many of them quite unlike traditional universities. These increasingly include not only the corporate universities already mentioned, but also for-profit institutions (see below). The accreditation of these emerging institutions represents for the first time a threat to the monopoly that the universities have enjoyed for almost a thousand years.

- **Privatization.** With this new accreditation, and the ability it gives for novel institutions to provide what have been traditional and limited credentials, has come a wave of privatization. For-profit providers are now an established part of the landscape and it is estimated that there are now more than 650 for-profit degree-granting colleges and universities in the U.S. Some of these are supported by for-profit companies (the University of Phoenix and Jones University, for example), and others are supported by traditional universities as free-standing for-profit ventures. Most have chosen not a direct assault upon the traditional comprehensive portfolio of universities, but a selective series of offerings, especially those in areas most likely to attract a large number of fee-paying students. The University of Phoenix, for example, has established programs aimed at the young, working adult, pursuing career-related courses on a part-time basis.

- **Competition.** The combined effect of deregulation and privatization has been a striking increase in competition. Competition has always existed for North American universities—from athletics to student admissions, faculty recruitment and federal research support—but in many other countries such competition has been regarded as unseemly, an activity unworthy of those devoted to the life of the mind.

That has now changed. Central regulation of salaries for leading faculty in the UK, for example, has been replaced by a more free market approach. New Zealand has, perhaps, experienced the most sweeping changes. Reduction in funding and lightening controls on higher education, which began in 1988, led to "skyrocketing tuition fees; the strong institutions have become stronger but a number of the weaker institutions may be forced to close and are facing bankruptcy. There has been a 20 percent decrease in higher education enrollments from the country's poorer districts." (Newman & Couturier, 2001).

Higher education is now a $740 billion a year industry and accounts for some 10 percent of the U.S. gross domestic product. And it is growing, becoming an agent of economic growth, a central player in the new knowledge economy.

It is still unclear as to how such new ventures as Barnes and Noble University's courses on Shakespeare, or those from Motorola University on continuous improvement techniques (offered at sites in 13 different countries) will compete with, rather than complement, traditional offerings. But one thing is clear: lifelong learning needs, personalization of learning opportunities, pedagogic effectiveness and institutional responsiveness are likely to be the requirements for success within this new competitive environment.

This competition is not a future prospect, but a present reality. The reported existence of more than 650 for-profit degree granting universities and colleges and an estimated 2,000 institutions of all kinds offering virtual courses to over one-and-a-half million students (Newman, 2001) are compelling evidence of the scale of existing efforts.

- **Non-traditional students.** The last two decades have seen a steady rise in what have been generally referred to as non-traditional students. These include not only students of more mature years, who have undertaken other activities before enrolling in college, but also increasingly, part-time students enrolled in urban universities, and continuing professional education students, pursuing full-time careers and incorporating such activities as specialized weekend workshops, as well as more traditional graduate and professional programs. It is estimated that 42 percent of students enrolled in U.S. colleges and universities in Fall 2000 were 25 or older (US Department of Education, 1999).

- **Research funding.** A stasis in federal research funding has become a major concern in some areas of the physical sciences, mathematics and engineering. Though funds have increased markedly in the biomedical sciences, federal funding during the nineties fell by as much as 20 percent in some fields of the physical sciences and engineering.

- **Information technology.** The precise impact of information technology on both distance learning and conventional education is still unclear. It is reported, however, that over 2,000 institutions are now offering distance learning programs, with some 1.5 million students enrolled. The extent to which distance education will replace, rather than supplement, on-site and, in some cases, residential education is still unclear. There are certain areas of learning which are demonstrably well served by distance learning. It seems equally likely, however, that other areas, including both cognitive and non-cognitive, are less easily developed in cyberspace. Nor is it clear that, while IT has improved learning in some areas, it has yet reduced teaching costs. It is particularly difficult to judge the likelihood that virtual lectures, by star scholars and "presenters," will replace traditional lectures, with faculty members acting more as coaches and facilitators than as lecturers. The range of such electronic courses is, as yet, small, but it is likely to increase rapidly [1].

- **Virtual partnerships.** While it is unclear as to just what effect IT will have upon the conventional teaching practices of the university, it is already clear that IT can provide a powerful tool for extra university partnerships, so that virtual partnerships, based on IT, may in some cases become equally effective as real communities. Among the more prominent virtual consortia are: Cardean University, which includes Chicago, Carnegie Mellon, Columbia Business School, London School of Economics and Stanford as its partners in business education; Western Governors University; Universitas 21, which includes 18 universities from 10 countries; African Virtual University; Fathom, which includes not only universities in the U.S. and U.K., but also publishers, museums and libraries; and the Jesuit Distance Education Network.

- **Unbundling of functions.** These collective trends indicate that there is a strong probability that the universities will face challenges from the unbundling of some of the many services that they now provide, together with cherry-picking of more attractive and potentially profitable areas by for-profit and other corporations. Already, such things as elementary language instruction and teaching of algebra and calculus are being offered by "knowledge providers" beyond the campus. The pattern already established in such non-academic areas as student catering, health services, books, supplies, and janitorial services, where outsourcing is already frequent, also could be pursued in the academic area.

- **Intellectual fragmentation.** In view of this, it might be supposed that the universities would exhibit a new level of internal partnership and cohesion in order to meet what are likely to be substantial external challenges. This is scarcely the case, for, while new centers constantly emerge to span the divisions between the disciplines, schools and colleges, the increasing rate of specialization within the disciplines raises the walls higher and higher, and, since appointment, tenure, promotion and salary decisions typically flow from within the traditional disciplinary departments, professors instinctively know on which side their bread is buttered and their careers develop accordingly. The barriers between the disciplines remain high and, even within the disciplines, new barriers and fences are emerging. With

---

1 The literature on this topic is substantial and the conclusions tentative. For a useful overview, see Newman, F. & Scurry, N. (2001).

many notable and praiseworthy exceptions, partnerships beyond the campus are often somewhat easier to develop than meaningful partnerships on the campus. This lack of intellectual community between undergraduate, graduate students and faculty, and between departments, schools and colleges, is one of the most glaring weaknesses of the contemporary university. And it is one of the most difficult to eliminate.

FUTURE CONDITIONS, SOCIAL AND ECONOMIC

It is increasingly clear that knowledge is the new economic capital. Though, in the past, a nation's natural resources provided the foundation of its wealth, and though these traditional resources will still be of major importance, it is knowledge that will be the most important economic driver of the new millennium. It is knowledge that provides the basis for both existing industries and for new ventures. It is knowledge that provides the means for urban renewal and social development. It is knowledge that provides improved methods of health care and public welfare. It is knowledge that allows new methods of defense and environmental protection. It is knowledge that provides the foundation for a full and meaningful life and for a just and generous civil society. Unlike other natural resources, which are depleted by their use, knowledge multiplies at the hands of its users. It expands, even as it is challenged, tested and refined. It grows, even as it is applied and incorporated. But, unlike other natural resources, which can be mined, purchased, or otherwise extracted, knowledge comes only to the prepared mind. It is available only to the informed participant.

This places a degree of responsibility on the universities, which is even greater than that of earlier times. In a period when knowledge is said to multiply every five years, and in which there is increasing mobility, not only between different "jobs", but also between different careers, there exists an increasingly heavy public obligation upon the university.

Nor is this all, for the application of knowledge to the burgeoning variety of social problems also requires the engagement of universities and a multidisciplinary approach to the issues involved. Interdisciplinary scholarship, so called, is of little help here. To be useful in interdisciplinary activity, one must first be skilled in the disciplines. What is required is the partnership of multiple disciplines, converging in addressing particular problems. For the challenges of society are no respecters of disciplinary provincialism. They sprawl across our jealous boundaries and they spread across our rising scholarly fences. If ever we are to harvest the benefits of insight, discovery and invention, we must confront the exclusivity of the disciplines and the easy adoption of reductionism as the sole approach to knowledge.

POWER OF PARTNERSHIPS

In summary, partnerships, both formal and informal, can help to restore the community that was once the university, partly by inreach and partly by outreach. Constructive partnerships can renew both the university and society; there are unlimited opportunities for new partnerships within and between institutions, departments, centers, institutes, schools and colleges, new partnerships between teaching and research, between passive learning and active engagement, between "book learning" and practical experience, between academic studies and civic engagement, between the university and industry, between the university and non-profits, professional associations and academies, museums, libraries, research centers, government—local, state, federal—and other local, statewide, international and regional bodies, as well as local communities. Each can provide direct benefit, not only to the partners engaged, but also to the activities of the partners in other fields of endeavor.

OBSTACLES TO PARTNERSHIPS

If partnerships on this scale are to be encouraged, one must ask: what are the costs and what are the obstacles? Perhaps it is useful to consider costs and obstacles as sub-headings of the same general category, since each is likely to be a deterrent to the development of effective partnerships.

- **Costs.** Perhaps the most immediate obstacle to partnerships is cost. Cost may involve both financial implications and personal commitment. Not only is the time of faculty members already under severe pressure, but the finances of universities are already painfully stressed. Even if funding can be secured and time provided for such partnerships, the dangers of dilution of individual effort and diffusion of institutional purpose are also real. The university neither can, nor should, be all things to all people. It must make a conscious decision as to how best to employ its resources, not only financial and physical, but also human.

- **Indirect costs.** One specific financial concern is that the real costs of any corporate partnership are rarely covered by the indirect support provided to the institution. Such costs as administrative, technical and faculty time, office materials, library expenses, equipment and operating costs, as well as the unremitting costs of building operation, maintenance and support, all deserve to be critically reviewed in the light of particular research programs. Though this can be dealt with effectively at the time a contract is developed, often the wishes of the department for support "at any cost" compete with the longer-term interests of the university in obtaining adequate indirect cost support, even though this will clearly increase the size of the total program proposal and cost. In any dispute of this sort, it seems clear that the institution should seek maximum recovery of indirect costs associated directly with research.

- **Time frames.** Another obstacle to such partnerships is the differing time frames on which partners typically work. What to industry is the maddeningly slow pace at which academic research proceeds is, to the faculty member, a guarantee of time for reflection and care in conclusion. Between the two, there is at present little in common and a degree of impatience on both sides tends to result. Yet there is surely ample room in this area for accommodation and compromise.

- **Intellectual property and integrity.** A more serious obstacle is the desire, on the part of some corporate sponsors, not only to protect the patent rights or corporate benefits that come from particular subsidized studies, but even, in extreme cases, to attempt to impose strictures on publication, or even modify or soften the conclusions of a sponsored study, when these are seen to be inconsistent with corporate interests. There have been accusations of such cases in some European biomedical research sponsored by pharmaceutical companies and fears in many more cases. In this area there can be no compromise. Though a delay of a month of two may be appropriate to protect patent rights, the integrity of the university will be undermined if external financial support limits the ability of faculty and researchers to publish and otherwise disseminate the results of their work.

- **Intellectual impartiality.** A comparable skepticism on the part of industry is also an obstacle to partnership, for while individual faculty members may be skeptical of industrial integrity, some corporate leaders look with skepticism upon the impartiality of members of the faculty. What is seen—rightly or wrongly—as the chilling rise of political correctness has done little to reassure institutional partners.

- **Academic turf.** Departmental protectionism and collegiate turf control, though generally secondary to the desire for financial support, remain a fact of life in most institutions. These attitudes are not likely to change quickly, though one may hope that they will be corrected over time by the positive benefits, not only to individual faculty members, but also to their students and their institutions, arising from corporate partnerships. A subsidiary aspect of this is the unspoken prejudice, even in some professional schools, that association with industrial and other external partners is in some way impure or disloyal to the institution itself, even though federal funding is seen as something to be prized. So promotion, salary increases and preferment tend sometimes to be weighted towards those who are less engaged in industrial activities.

- **Institutional concerns.** Institutional conservatism has tended to be less of an obstacle in this regard than has individual departmental inertia and suspicion. Facing growing financial pressure, institutions have tended to welcome more rewarding partnerships with industry.

- **Scholarly work.** The notion that the scholarship produced by multi-disciplinary work is not only less pure, but also less rigorous than that produced within the context of the disciplines is sometimes an obstacle to internal partnerships, including especially new intellectual coalitions between what were once independent, free-standing disciplines. But instances abound where this is not the case; the margins of the disciplines are increasingly fruitful areas of enquiry. In science over the centuries, the great discoveries have come at the margins of the disciplines by conscious pooling of the expertise derived from each. One can reflect, for example, upon the Darwin-Wallace theory of natural selection, embracing as it did so many areas—from geology to genetics, anatomy, systematics, botany, psychology and zoogeography—that are now distinct fields, or the discovery of the structure of DNA by Crick and Watson, which depended not only upon biology, but also on x-ray crystallography, exquisite structural chemical analysis, microbiology, genetics, and quantum mechanics. The same pattern was seen with the development of plate tectonics, perhaps the most significant unifying theory of the last quarter century, which involved a combination of paleogeography, geophysics, geology, oceanography, magnetism and paleontology, in order to be developed in its fullest sense. And what is true of science is no less true of other areas, whether in the professions or in the traditional humanities and social sciences. In law, for example, questions of ethics, economics, sociology and psychology are profoundly intertwined with legal aspects of many cases. In civil engineering, there is growing emphasis not only on alternative structures and materials, but also on environmental, ecological, economic and aesthetic aspects of construction, while in the humanities, the new literary criticism takes in vast areas of what had traditionally been the province of such other disciplines as sociology, psychology and anthropology.

In spite of some confusion, overlapping and jostling at the boundaries between the disciplines, these boundaries are areas of increasingly fruitful interaction. We dare not allow those issues that confront us to fall between the cracks of our ancient boundaries.

- **Academic recognition and advancement.** One practical concern for professional academics concerns less the appropriateness than the recognition, stature, support and reward of multidisciplinary studies. Because appointments, promotions and rewards still tend to come from within departments and from professional societies that are, themselves, in most cases disciplinary-based, there is a perception that multidisciplinary work tends to receive relatively less recognition and support than work within traditional fields. This concerns not only the career advancement of the individual professor, but also the financial support and publication of the work involved. This perception is, I think, a real one and it is also, for that reason, one that must be addressed. Department chairs, deans and provosts need to take this seriously if we are to provide the maximum benefits to the society that supports our universities.

- **Institutional autonomy.** A further concern is that universities will become either assimilated by, or, perhaps just as dangerously, tainted in their institutional autonomy and professional judgment by corporate partnerships, or whatever kind. In this view, it is both the integrity of the institution and the impartiality of scholarship that are seen to be at risk. It is argued, for example, that a clinical study of the effectiveness of a newly developed pharmaceutical product may be influenced if the support for clinical trials is provided by the parent company which developed the drug. This seems to be to be a legitimate concern and one that must be addressed by the creation of appropriate protocols by each institution. No protocol, of course, can cover every eventuality, but this concern is so fundamental in its implications that it must be faced squarely before any contract is finalized. A draft protocol has recently been proposed (Rhodes, 2001).

- **Student interests and concerns.** Some are concerned that, though the broad scholarly integrity of the university may be safeguarded by such arrangements, the wellbeing of students, particularly graduate students, may receive less attention than the priorities of the supporting company. The danger perceived here is that, for example, a graduate student may be assigned to a research topic, which, though it serves the direct interest of the sponsoring company, is nevertheless unsuitable for a Ph.D. thesis study. It seems to me that the only safeguard against this is openness on the part of the sponsor, professional responsibility on the part of the individual faculty member, and a clear and public understanding that neither the pursuit of the study, nor the conclusions and publication of the work will be influenced by the views or desires of the sponsoring corporation.

- **Mission creep.** A related concern involves the wider mission of the institution, with the fear that this may be diluted or deflected by too close engagement with the corporate world. What I think is needed here is careful definition and statement of what the institutional mission is. In too many cases, the institution or department has no stated mission and may drift towards any major source of funding that happens to be readily available. This is not, of course, confined to corporate funding. It may well be that a department of astronomy, for example, leading the design and advocacy of a new telescope, which may cost anything from $100 million to $1 billion, could be largely absorbed and deflected by such activities, however praiseworthy they may be in their own right.

- **The Land Grant Model.** The concern that any partnerships with industry and other non-university institutions beyond the campus is, in some way, a new and corrupting development overlooks and underestimates the success of just such a program which is now more than a century and a quarter old. The Morrill Land Grant Act of 1862 created a system of outreach by which land grant universities would cooperate, not only with county, state and federal governments, but also with individual farmers and agricultural businesses. The subsequent history of that Act has been one of the great success stories of American higher education. Indeed, it has expanded in influence to other areas of the world, with untold benefits, not only to those who work on the land, but also to the larger community which depends on agriculture for its sustenance. Furthermore, the Bayh-Dole Act of 1980 explicitly encouraged the commercial application of publicly funded research in order to promote both economic development and wider social benefit.

PROTECTING THE CORE

What must be preserved? Any partnership agreement must preserve a few essential characteristics, both of the institution and of the company and of the public which supports it both in direct and indirect ways. At the institutional level, the following qualities must be preserved:

- Institutional autonomy,

- Faculty freedom to pursue promising areas of research, subject only to the canons of the particular discipline or profession and the university's overall requirements for such things as use of human subjects,
- The integrity of the disciplines and professions involved,
- Scholarly impartiality and freedom from obligation to slant or modify conclusions,
- The best interests of both undergraduate and graduate students in relation to the projects supported,
- Freedom of expression and publication,
- The preservation of an atmosphere of openness, free discussion, wide association and mutual trust and support.

While these qualities must be preserved, it is equally important that the interests of the corporation should be recognized and encouraged. These include, but are not limited to:

- The potential reward for corporate investment, both financial and human,
- The benefits to individual discoverers of new inventions, products and procedures,
- The freedom of the company to capitalize on new discoveries and bring them to market in appropriate form and timely fashion,
- The interests of shareholders, users, employees and the public must also be given appropriate consideration and appropriation recognition. A company is entitled to see some economic promise or potential from its investment in research and development, even though occasionally it may choose to support less focused programs and proposals.

FROM PROPOSAL TO PARTNERSHIP

In order to move from theoretical support for partnerships to their practical implementation, three initiatives are needed. First, the government's role in this is to recognize the national importance of nurturing academic-industrial partnerships and to provide appropriate tax incentives and monetary policies to encourage it. This should be part of a larger program of support for corporate investment in R & D, on which the future economic health of a country substantially depends.

Second, the role of industry is critical to the success of these new partnerships. Success will require the recognition by corporate leaders of the huge research potential from university partnerships. But it will also require strategic thinking, as well as tactical thinking, on the part of directors of R & D. Any partnership will require not only respect for the autonomy of the institution, together with its mission and goals, but also the recognition of the real cost to the institution which such a partnership may involve. Industry should also recognize the unique opportunities these partnerships provide to link research, education, retraining and recruiting under a single heading, so that longer term consultancies, student internships and R & D partnerships can become part of a growing corporate program of education and research.

Third, the university also has a role to play in facilitating these partnerships. This involves not only the removal of obstacles—institutional, collegiate and departmental—but also the provision of flexible appointments, sympathetic review of shared facilities and incentives for and recognition of such cooperation. Joint appointments will involve not only joint departmental appointments, but also appointments in which part of a faculty member's time is supported by soft money contributions from industry and other sources, just as it is now in many cases by federal research funds. There are, of course, dangers inherent in such arrangements, but, with proper oversight and forethought, these can be reduced.

An issue remains as to whether or not a university professor, employed full time by the university, should be allowed to accept a position as an officer within a startup or other company. Arrangements will differ from one institution to another, but my own reaction is that such an arrangement is undesirable. While I recognize that there are potential benefits inherent in an arrangement of this kind, it seems to me that the pitfalls and conflicts are even more substantial and that this practice should not be encouraged. In contrast, I see no fundamental conflict of time or interest and much potential benefit in individual faculty members serving as directors of corporations, providing that such affiliations are a matter of public record.

THE BENEFITS OF PARTNERSHIP

When new partnerships are created, the long term benefits will be substantial. For the university, perhaps the most obvious benefit is that industrial partnerships will provide new revenue, and, perhaps, catalyze new economic activity. It is estimated that, in 1999, universities filed 7,602 patent applications, generating $641 million in university income. In financial terms alone this is a source of significant revenue. Columbia University, for example, which ranked first among American universities in earnings from patent royalties for the past two years, received more than $143 million in royalty revenue in the year 2000 (Blumenstyk, 2001). These funds were used as internal venture capital, to sponsor promising new research initiatives.

Perhaps the most striking evidence of the wider economic benefits of university research is provided by a BankBoston study of MIT which estimates that if "the companies founded by MIT graduates and faculty formed an independent nation, the revenues produced by the companies would make that nation the 24th largest economy in the world. The 4,000 MIT-related companies employ 1.1 million people and have annual world sales of $232 billion. That is roughly equal to a gross domestic product of $116 billion, which is a little less than the GDP of South Africa and more than the GDP of Thailand. Eighty percent of the jobs in MIT-related firms are in manufacturing (compared to 16 percent nationally) and a high percentage of products are exported. The MIT-related companies have more than 8,500 plants in 50 states." (Bank of Boston Economics Department, 1997).

The larger benefits for the university and the wider society, beyond the mere financial benefits, are substantial. By closer alliance with industry, teaching and research are enlivened and enriched. Students, both undergraduate and graduate, have new opportunities for identifying fruitful careers, as well as opportunities for internships and experiences that will assist them in their own career choice and preparation.

Industrial challenges pose new intellectual challenges and some of these may be of fundamental, rather than of immediate practical, significance. Furthermore, both basic research and development work have already led to breakthroughs in biomedical devices, pharmaceutical products, engineering techniques and agricultural developments, which have provided benefits for all society.

It is this wider social benefit which is the ultimate argument for encouraging closer corporate liaison. Liaison will take place only if there are clear mutual benefits for the corporate sponsor and the university, but in the interests of serving the wider public, a protocol must be clearly defined and developed.

The responsibility for developing such a protocol rests squarely with the administration of the university, but it should not and, indeed, cannot be developed by them in isolation. It will need the constant input, review and support of the university faculty involved, as well as department chairs, deans and other officers. It must be a matter of review for the board of trustees and it must, of course, commend itself as equitable to corporate sponsors. It is also important, I believe, that such partnerships should be a matter of public record.

CONCLUSION

Fears that external partnerships and outreach would create bias, distorted priorities, divided allegiance and neglect of education, have been with us since at least 1862, when the Morrill Act was signed by President Abraham Lincoln. The awareness of these concerns and the realization of these hazards should make it possible for universities to adopt protocols and encourage professional responsibility to safeguard against them. The ultimate beneficiary from new alliances and extended corporate partnerships must be the public, for it is the public that is ultimately served by both universities and corporations, and it is upon public recognition and support that both, in turn, depend for their existence and success.

REFERENCES

Bank of Boston Economics Department (1997). "MIT: The Impact of Innovation", *Department Special Report*, March.

Blumenstyk, G. (2001). "Knowledge is a Form of Venture Capital for a Top Columbia Administrator". *Chronicle of Higher Education*, Feb. 9.

Meister, J. C. (2001). "The Brave New World of Corporate Education", *Chronicle of Higher Education*, Feb. 9.

Newman, F. (2001). *The Futures Project: Policy for Higher Education in a Changing World*, Phase 1, Summary Document, August (Draft).

Newman, F. & Couturier, L. (2001). "The New Competitive Arena: Market Forces Invade the Academy," *The Futures Project: Policy for Higher Education in a Changing World*, June.

Newman, F. & Scurry, N. (2001). "Higher Education in the Digital Rapids", *The Futures Project: Policy for Higher Education in a Changing World*, June, pp. 1-40.

Rhodes, F. H. T. (2001). *The Creation of the Future*, Cornell University Press, Ithaca, New York.

U.S. Department of Education, National Center for Education Statistics (1999), *Digest of Educational Statistics*, NCES 2000-031, May.

Imprimé en France. - JOUVE 11, bd de Sébastopol, 75001 Paris
N° 311188A. Dépôt légal : Octobre 2002

Steering Committee
David P. GARDNER, *President Emeritus University of California*
Charles F. KENNEL, *Director Scripps Institution of Oceanography and Vice-Chancellor at UC San Diego*
Werner Z. HIRSCH, *Professor of Economics at UC Los Angeles*
Howard NEWBY, *Chief Executive Higher Education Founding Council for England*
Jacob NUESCH, *President Emeritus Federal Institute of Technology, Zurich*
Luc WEBER, *Vice-president LAU, Member of the Board EUA and CD-ESR*

Geneva, Autumn 2002

As head of a leading research university, this copy of AS THE WALLS OF ACADEMIA ARE TUMBLING DOWN should interest you.

The book comprises a selection of papers presented last year at the third Glion Colloquium.

We know that this issue is of profound concern to many higher education leaders and would be very interested in your comments.

Yours sincerely,

Werner HIRSCH and Luc WEBER, Editors

PS: Please use the enclosed *order form* of *Brookings Institution Press* to order additional copies

Addresses for all correspondence:
USA : Prof. Werner HIRSCH, Department of Economics, University of California, LOS ANGELES,
Phone : 001 310 476 2660, Fax : 001 310 472 7235, E-mail : whirsch@ucla.edu
Europe : Prof. Luc WEBER, Rte de Florissant 6, CH-1206 GENEVA
Phone : +41 22 347 3906, Fax : +41 22 789 3550, E-mail : luc.weber@ecopo.unige.ch